# Decline in History

# Decline in History

## The European Experience

## J. K. J. THOMSON

Polity Press

First published in 1998 by Polity Press in association with Blackwell Publishers Ltd.

*Editorial office:*
Polity Press
65 Bridge Street
Cambridge CB2 1UR, UK

*Marketing and production:*
Blackwell Publishers Ltd
108 Cowley Road
Oxford OX4 1JF, UK

*Published in the USA by*
Blackwell Publishers Inc.
Commerce Place
350 Main Street
Malden, MA 02148, USA

ISBN 0-7456-1424-8
ISBN 0-7456-1425-6 (pbk)

A catalogue record for this book is available from the British Library and has been applied for from the Library of Congress.

Typeset in 10 on 12 pt Times
by Best-set Typesetter Ltd, Hong Kong
Printed in Great Britain by T.J. International, Padstow, Cornwall

This book is printed on acid-free paper.

*For Verònica, Magali
and Anna and in memory
of my father, Patrick*

# Contents

# Preface

It was an invitation from Polity Press in summer 1993 that prompted me to write this book. I had just completed a research project on Catalan industrialization and, with time at my disposal, I was keen, after a long period spent working on local history, to try my hand at something broader. Decline appealed to me as a subject because I felt that it was relevant to contemporary Britain and Europe. Since the early 1980s there had been a growing tendency in public debate to draw on the past in shaping policy decisions. The tendency was to look at periods of national or European expansion. My own feeling was that periods of decline – like it or not – provided more relevant guides, and hence that in writing a book of this type and thereby encouraging reflection on the causes and right responses to decline, I would be doing something useful.

Having embarked on the task, I found it much more difficult to carry out than I had anticipated. In the Introduction I shall explain the method which I finally adopted. Here I shall merely carry out the pleasurable duty of recording my gratitude to a number of people and organizations that have helped me. Firstly, since my appointment, my university, Sussex, has provided a very tolerant and stimulating working environment. Olwen Hufton, Stuart Woolf and Gwynne Lewis gave me firm backing at various points when this project was under way, which was much appreciated. More specifically I was granted two periods of leave to complete the book. Numerous colleagues have been helpful. Alasdair Smith, my Dean in the School of European Studies, where I embarked on this project, has provided me with the institutional support without which I could not have undertaken work of this kind. Donald Winch and John Burrow, whose course 'Concepts, Methods and Values in the Social Sciences' I had the privilege of teaching with them, represented in different ways, inspirations to me: both communicated their enthusiasm for the materialist historical approach of the Scottish Enlightenment; Donald Winch's commitment to a social and politically 'useful' history and John Burrow's *Evolution and Society: A Study in Victorian Social Theory* (Cambridge, 1966), a masterly exercise in the historian's craft, and a demonstration of its importance, were profound influences. My subject chair during most of the period of writing this book, Rod Kedward, was consistently and generously supportive and enthusiastic, and Nigel Llewellyn, who took over as Dean of European Studies, ensured continuity in the friendliness and stability of my working environment. William Outhwaite has allowed me to experiment with my approach to decline in the form of an option, 'Success and Failure in European History', within the course on 'The Idea of Europe' which he convenes. Liz James gave me useful references on Byzantine decline, and Maxine Berg has helped with support for research grant applications and friendly interest and encouragement. Sussex students, on both 'major' and 'school' courses, and students at the Université Lumière Lyon 2, where I was *enseignant invité* during 1996/7, have participated in the development of some of the ideas in the book. I am grateful for the support of Serge Chassagne, who arranged this French visit, and of Françoise Bayard, whose teaching I was taking over for a semester, and who provided invaluable guidance in coping with teaching in a different environment. It is to Peter Burke that I owe the opportunity to write this study, and for this I am most grateful. An anonymous reader of my manuscript provided me with expert advice as well as encouragement; without this, and the helpful collaboration of Polity Press, particularly that of Annabelle Mundy and Henry Maas at the editing stage, the book would not have been completed. Finally my family, both nuclear and extended, in England and Catalonia, has been tolerant about my absorption for too long in this project: I offer them my deep gratitude for their patience.

James Thomson

# Acknowledgements

The author and publisher would like to thank the following for permission to reproduce copyright material in the book.

Academic Press, Inc. for an extract from Immanuel Wallerstein, *Modern World System*, Volume 1 (3 vols, Academic Press, New York 1974–1989).

Cambridge University Press for an extract from Robert S. Lopez, 'The Trade of Medieval Europe: The South' in M. M. Postal and E. Miller (eds), *The Cambridge Economic History of Europe*, Volume II: *Trade and Industry in the Middle Ages* (Cambridge, 1987).

HarperCollins Publishers Ltd and HarperCollins Publishers, Inc. for an extract from the author's introduction to the first edition of Fernand Braudel, *The Mediterranean and the Mediterranean World in the Age of Philip II*, Volume 1 (Collins, 1972) translated by Sian Reynolds, copyright © Librairie Armand Colin 1966, English translation copyright © 1972 by Wm Collins Sons Ltd and Harper & Row Publishers, Inc.

Oxford University Press for the table of Byzantine Dynasties from N. H. Baynes and H. St L. B. Moss, *Byzantium: An Introduction of the East Roman Civilization* (Oxford, 1961).

The University of Chicago Press for an extract from W. H. McNeill, *The Rise of the West* (Chicago, 1963).

Professor Speros Vryonis for an extract from S. Vryonis, *The Decline of Medieval Hellenism in Asia Minor and the Process of Islamization from the Eleventh through to the Fifteenth Century* (University of California Press, 1971).

Despite every effort to trace and contact copyright holders prior to publication this has not been possible in every case. If notified, the publisher will be pleased to rectify any errors or omissions at the earliest opportunity.

# Introduction

This book is focused principally on Europe's economic history. This prioritizing of the 'material' in the analysis of decline in European history is due to the need to concentrate on what has self-evidently been the primary causal agency in our past, if any sort of understanding of what is so vast an issue as decline is to be gained. In the book's writing I have adopted essentially a narrative approach. I have done this as I want above all to communicate the manner in which decline has been a constitutive part of the process of European history. It has been the reverse side of the coin to the exceptional dynamism which characterizes Europe's past, and, as is the case with its progressive counterpart, its specificity is not graspable on the basis of a static analysis.

In the first two chapters I discuss the historians whose work I have found of most use in devising my approach to decline.

Chapter 1 is devoted to Fernand Braudel's masterpiece, *The Mediterranean and the Mediterranean World in the Age of Philip II*.[1] The fate of the Mediterranean is clearly the principal issue in Europe's experience of decline: it will provide the main focus for this book. A discussion of the principal study on this topic is thus the logical starting-point. An additional aim is to contribute to making Braudel's large and complex work accessible to students. I select from the book the valuable implicit interpretation which it contains – which is in fact close to the one for which I shall be arguing in this book – and confront it with the dogmatic conclusions to which Braudel in the end subscribes. The chapter will thus, I hope, serve both as a first bid for the interpretation which this book proposes and as an exercise in historiography. I have also summarized Braudel's views on the following aspects of decline: cyclical patterns of decline, 'the social conjuncture' and links between economic fluctuations and social structure, economic decline and social instability, and the relationship between decline and cultural achievement. My intention here is both to provide a key for further use of Braudel's work – which has many of the characteristics of a challenging primary source – and also to introduce some of the main concepts and theories for the study of decline.

Having, I hope, contributed to making Braudel's *Mediterranean* a useful introduction to the subject rather than a hurdle which is difficult to clear, in the next chapter I discuss the work of historians and a historical sociologist whose methodologies I have found more constructive – including that of Braudel in a later stage of his career: Immanuel Wallerstein in his *Modern World-System*, Braudel in his second major work, *Civilization and Capitalism*, Jonathan Israel in his magisterial study, *Dutch Primacy in World Trade*, and finally Michael Mann in his *Sources of Social Power*.[2]

More particularly I describe the geographical/political/economic unit – the 'world-economy' – which Immanuel Wallerstein adopts as the framework for his trilogy on the development of European capitalism in the early modern period. It is one which I have found serves to make sense of the experiences of growth and decline in European history. Braudel found the same too. A reading of Wallerstein breathed life into the bones of his encylopaedic knowledge of the pre-industrial world. I follow my discussion of Wallerstein with a report on the fruit of this rethinking as reflected in his second major work, and I identify the slight but significant differences between the two scholars' views on the manner in which the early capitalist system functioned.

Israel's study is in part a broadside against the economic and geographical determinism, and the aversion to 'events', in Braudel's *Mediterranean*. This attack, though, is of less relevance to the post-Wallerstein Braudel. His approach, on the other hand, is of assistance in arbitrating between Wallerstein's and Braudel's different views. I use Israel, at this point, to resolve this central methodological issue.

Mann's work provided me with the macro perspective enabling me to see decline as a built-in feature of the progressive development and spatial enlargement of the Afro-Asian/European zone since the beginning of civilized history, and influenced my decision to adopt a narrative approach. I refer briefly to his work in chapter 2 in order to provide the reader with this broader perspective within which to consider European history and our problem of decline. In addition, I want to alert the reader to two of the principal mechanisms, which Mann identifies as lying behind the process of spatial, economic and cultural diffusion, and which I have found of great utility in interpreting decline. These are firstly his use of the economic theory of comparative advantage for explaining shifts in economic power (he posits that a motor for the progressive process just mentioned consists in the repeated relocation of cultures and techniques to areas in which superior factor supply situations provided advantages in their exploitation), and secondly his argument for shifts in economic and political power being occasioned by the particular advantages accruing to trading centres on the periphery of empires from their status of 'interstitiality' – Venice's rise would be a case in point but earlier progresses, e.g. those of the Mycenaeans or Phoenicians, are explained in the same way. By the status of 'interstitiality' he means that such areas, in addition to their advantage in lower factor costs, also benefited from their participation in larger trading/cultural zones to whose infrastructural costs they did not contribute. What advantaged the interstitial state clearly disadvantaged the empires which *were* bearing these costs. Mann's theory is thus useful for explaining progress and decline. It should be noted that Mann himself neither addresses the problem of decline directly, nor is principally concerned with economic development – an analysis of political power is his brief; his theories, however, are adaptable to our problem of explaining and interpreting decline, and this is what I have attempted.

As in the case of Braudel's *Mediterranean*, I have used my discussions of these historians' interpretations as a convenient point to provide some definitions and discussions of the vocabulary and concepts relating to decline of which they make use. I hope that this will be of assistance to the student in the later, narrative sections of the book.

Insofar as decline in European history has been the reverse side of success in a pluralist context, a first stage in its interpretation is an understanding of Europe's growth process. This is the cause of the local declines. In chapter 3, consequently, I have provided a compressed description, and explanation, of the geographical shifts in the centre of gravity of the European economy from the rise of Venice to that of Amsterdam. Chapter 4 is on Byzantium. Its unique bridging of the classical and medieval periods means that, like those long-lasting icebergs whose composition has been used to establish weather conditions over the long term, its history provides an opportunity to establish the character of decline both in Antiquity and in the 'European' period. If there is anything specific in decline in European history, then Byzantine history, if there was any type of connection there with what was going on in Europe, should demonstrate it, for Byzantium should have experienced elements of both types of decline. Debates among Byzantine scholars reveal that Byzantine history does fulfil this purpose. The discussions, indeed, attest to major conceptual problems occasioned by the existence of the two types of decline and considerable resulting confusion. Experience of decline of the European type (growing dependency on, and backwardness with respect to, areas at the cutting edge of European advance) has been categorized as progress in terms of Byzantine history, consequently causing the traditional interpretation of the area's history in terms of a golden age followed by decadence to be questioned. As this debate serves to illustrate so forcefully the distinction which I am keen to establish in this book concerning the specificity of the experience of decline in European history, I have reported on it in some detail, summarizing my own interpretation of the varying characteristics of the declines suffered in Byzantine history in the chapter's conclusion.

Chapters 5 and 6 on Italian and Iberian declines, and my conclusion in chapter 7 are simpler to explain. I merely document the process of economic decline, primarily in Mediterranean Europe. I should just emphasize that though I have effectively adopted conventional political divisions in these chapters, the plural for decline is intended: in Italy's case for example I consider four declines, of different parts of the peninsula in distinct periods, and in Iberia's, as well as covering Portugal and Spain separately I am at pains to show that the latter's experience of an earlier Castilian crisis and later, less severe Andalusian, Valencian and Catalan declines are accountable for in terms of Spain's place in a larger economic and political network than the nation-state. It is thus Wallerstein's and Braudel's (in his post-*Mediterranean* work) conceptualization of Europe's history in terms of a world-economy which I respect.

# 1

# Braudel's Mediterranean

Need I point out where its interest lies? It is of no small value to know what became of the Mediterranean at the threshold of modern times, when the world no longer revolved entirely around it, served it and responded to its rhythms . . . it is my belief that all the problems posed by the Mediterranean are of exceptional human richness, that they must interest all historians and non-historians. I would go so far as to say that they serve to illumine our own century.

Fernand Braudel, *The Mediterranean and the*
*Mediterranean World in the Age of Philip II*

Braudel's massive study *The Mediterranean and the Mediterranean World at the Time of Philip II*, the fruit of twenty-six years' study and reflection, is focused on the sea in which, or close to which, 92 per cent of the human experience which is relevant to our theme took place.[1] Moreover, it is focused on it during the critical turning-point in its fortunes when hegemony was in the process of being lost to the Atlantic. A principal theme of his book is thus the causes, character and results of this great reversal in European history.[2]

In what follows I shall be piecing together Braudel's description of this paradigmatic shift, and his explanation for it, collating some of his general reflections on decline and considering the utility of his approach for devising a method for this study.

## Structural Explanations for Mediterranean Decline

The leading explanation for the Mediterranean's failure which Braudel offers is its relative poverty in natural resources. Throughout the work the emphasis is placed on the contrast between the superficial splendour of Mediterranean civilization conferred by the variety in its climate and resources, and the reality of deep, underlying poverty. 'The truth is', he writes, 'that the Mediterranean has struggled against a fundamental poverty ... It affords a precarious living, in spite of its apparent or real advantages. It is easy to be deceived by its famous charm and beauty ... In fact Mediterranean man gains his daily bread by painful effort.'[3]

Climate, as well as harshness of terrain, was responsible for this penury. In the Mediterranean zone the periods of heavy rainfall in spring and early autumn do not coincide with those of greatest heat. 'The monsoon climate fruitfully combines warmth and water', he writes. 'The Mediterranean climate separates these two important factors of life, with predictable consequences': a general problem of drought.[4] Conditions, he continues, were particularly unfavourable for herbaceous vegetation. The typical agriculture of the Mediterranean zone consists in dry-farming with a particular emphasis on arboriculture. Both the techniques of irrigation and the plant types which could adapt to dry conditions – in particular the vine and the olive – spread from the east Mediterranean. 'The Mediterranean, by its climate was predestined for shrub culture. It is not only a garden, but, providentially, a land of fruit-bearing trees', writes Braudel. Ordinary trees were scarce, partly because of unfavourable conditions for forests but also because of neglect, leading to the deterioration of former woodlands into those extensive stretches of scrubland – 'debased forms of the forest' – so frequently to be found around the Mediterranean. Lack of pasture also caused deficiency in the quantity and size of livestock, with adverse consequences for diet, soil fertility (lack of manure) and traction (oxen and mules, Braudel argues, did not have the strength for the adoption of the wheeled plough which had had such favourable consequences for agricultural productivity on the plains of northern Europe).[5] Poverty of Mediterranean soil ('with its infertile limestone, the great stretches blighted with salt, the lands covered with nitre, and the precariousness of its arable land ... at the mercy of the wind and flood waters') is a further conditioning factor.

Only by constant human effort is land kept fertile and in use: 'the desert lies in wait for arable land and never lets go.' Even when the soil is well nurtured, good harvests are not assured, for 'more than elsewhere [they] are at the mercy of unstable elements'.[6]

The range of these unfavourable conditions, Braudel argues, is the cause for the frugality of the Mediterranean's inhabitants ('I dare say that a man of our country spends more on food in one day than a Turk in twelve', a Flemish visitor to Anatolia recorded in 1555).[7] Natural conditions, he concludes, have been a determining influence on Mediterranean history, the explanation for what he describes as an 'instinctive' imperialism as it was obliged to look farther afield for its 'daily bread'.[8]

## 'Conjunctural' Explanations for Decline: A Malthusian Interpretation

Shifting from what Braudel would term the 'structural' (permanent features of his geographical zone) to the 'conjunctural' (temporal circumstances), his explanation of the Mediterranean's incipient decline is that the rapid demographic growth in the sixteenth century put too great a strain on these limited natural resources, and consequently gave a decisive competitive edge to the economies of northern Europe. Population growth, which had initially been a stimulus to expansion, became a crippling handicap with 'too many people for comfort'. This factor rather than the Habsburg empire or Ottoman expansion – or the discoveries – lies behind the pattern of rapid growth followed by the 'bitter awakening of the seventeenth century'.[9]

The crisis at a later point in the book is plotted in detail. It will be useful, though, to follow Braudel's analysis of it. Portugal was the first 'Mediterranean' economy to exhibit profound weaknesses demonstrated by grain shortages and dependence on imports. From as early as the late fifteenth century grain supplies were being sought in Flanders, and throughout the sixteenth century there was a regular trade with Brittany, involving hundreds of small boats. Portugal at the time of its merging with Castile in 1580 was a 'country rotten at the core', Braudel writes. The crises were slightly later in the different regions of Spain, but they followed, one by one – Andalusia, which had been an area of surplus grain production, no longer had sufficient flour to provision the American fleet from the 1580s, and in the rest of the peninsula there are signs of a gradual deterioration from the mid-century from what had been an expansive situation. Braudel reports on a lack of consensus among

Spanish historians in explaining the difficulties, speculates whether the crisis was Malthusian ('Was the land exhausted?') but raises also the issue of a possible dialectical relationship with the forces which had underlain the period of expansion ('Perhaps even more than by the feudal yoke, which grew no lighter, the peasant was crushed by the burden of usury: it had helped him during the "first" sixteenth century, but after 1550 it was to turn against him, driving him off his land'). Declining food supplies brought with them growing vulnerability to disease. Portugal again was the first victim – in 1556 it was reported from Lisbon that 'the country is sick and in numerous regions many people are dying, it is said, from illnesses provoked by the bad food they have eaten and are still eating' – but Castile followed with demographic crises in the 1590s, 'before the recession hit any other part of Europe'. The crisis, Braudel concludes, 'disturbed a fundamental equilibrium'.[10]

Italy, Braudel continues, shared in this crisis but responded to it differently. The 1550s were again a turning-point, but for a space of some fifteen years the Italian grain deficit was made up from Mediterranean sources – surpluses drawn from the Ottoman empire. From this point, however, Turkish supplies began to dry up – there too population growth may have been straining the food supply. The crisis was resolved this time from within the Italian peninsula. This was possible firstly because urbanized, northern Italy still possessed its own surplus areas to draw on – southern Italy, Sicily, Albania and still, in certain years, the Turkish empire; secondly by the increasing use of inferior, higher-yielding grains such as millet; and finally, and above all, because home production of food was increased by a large investment of urban resources in the land, a trend which can be traced back to the mid-fifteenth century. The 'huge fortune of Venice was being withdrawn from commercial enterprise and invested . . . in the countryside and costly land improvement schemes', writes Braudel. Equilibrium, unlike in the Spanish case, was maintained by 'the widespread efforts of the Italian peasants and the ruthless determination of the landlords'.[11] From the 1590s, however, Italy came to share too in a general Mediterranean dependence on northern grains, brought in Dutch and Danish ships, especially to Leghorn, a port which flourished on the basis of this new, large-scale trade. The whole of the west Mediterranean, Braudel claims, came to depend on the new supply. The dependency, however, was not yet a permanent feature of Mediterranean life: with the new century the trade declined, relative self-sufficiency in grain supply once again being achieved. The granary of the Mediterranean, Sicily, despite experiencing repeated periods of bad harvests, continued usually to generate significant grain surpluses, its economy manifesting definite commercial vitality. 'In Sicily', Braudel comments, 'the decline of the Mediterranean cannot on any reckoning be said to have occurred prematurely.'

The geographical variations in agrarian performances clearly represent something of a problem in evaluating the issue of the decline of the Mediterranean as a whole – Braudel's concern. He resolves the difficulty by arguing that the economic fortunes of Italy, the sea's 'vital centre', can be used as a gauge of prosperity for the Mediterranean as a whole. On this basis he concludes that 'the great economic turning-point did not occur before 1620–1621 and the great biological turning-point – the wave of epidemics – not before 1630'.[12]

## Plotting the Mediterranean's Decline from the Intrusion of Atlantic Shipping

In his analysis of the Mediterranean's destiny Braudel places particular emphasis on maritime matters. He does so with good reason, as transport by sea was by far the most important form of commercial interaction, of control over shipping and shipping lanes representing the key to economic hegemony. As with his analysis of agricultural conditions, his treatment of this can be divided into structural and conjunctural categories. With respect to the former, he notes that the geographical circumstances of the Mediterranean were such that there was invariably a shortage of sailors and severe problems in obtaining timber for shipbuilding. The shortage of timber and seamen was more acute in the east and south Mediterranean than the west, he notes ('cannot the decline of the maritime activities of the Syrian coast be attributed to the exhaustion of the forests of Lebanon?'): the 'structural' explanation thus serves to explain the earlier triumph of the west over the east Mediterranean as well as that of the Atlantic.[13]

In his conjunctural analysis Braudel makes use in particular of the evidence of the 'invasion' of the Mediterranean commercial space by northern shipping. What story does this shipping invasion tell? There were two chapters in it, a first between 1450 and 1552 and a second, definitive one from 1570. The phases are separated by a period of revival in the Mediterranean's shipping fortunes.[14]

Dominant in the first wave was Iberian shipping: Portuguese, Galician and above all Biscayan, from the Basque country. The earliest involvement of such shipping may have been in the fourteenth century, but it continues to be dominant until the 1560s, extending its range to embrace the entire Mediterranean and dominating the Mediterranean–Iberia–Flanders links. The shipping of Biscay, it was claimed in the 1530s, was the jewel in the crown of Charles V. Portuguese involvement was also pan-Mediterranean and was reinforced by Portugal's early monopoly in Atlantic-grown sugar – cultivated first in Madeira, then on the West African islands of São Tomé and Principe, and finally in Brazil[15] – in demand in the Mediterranean. Portugal's participation seems to have ended sooner as this small country's shipping resources came to be focused more and more on servicing the requirements of its enormous, global empire.[16] Breton and Norman ships form a third group of northern invaders. Theirs is a slightly different case from those of the Portuguese and Basques as there is little evidence of their offering shipping services. They confined themselves rather to trading activities, generally using small ships, exchanging Breton and Norman products, and particularly linen cloth, metal goods and fish for Mediterranean ones – especially wine, raisins, coral and alum obtained either from Spain or Civitavecchia, the loading port for the mines of the Papal states. As was the case with all these northern invasions, the French traders eventually made contact with the luxury trades of the east Mediterranean.[17] The arrival of limited (at this stage) Flemish shipping in the Mediterranean is linked, principally, to the foreign-policy needs of the Flemish-born Charles V. English incursions provide a third pattern: in this case what was distinctive was the rapidity with which an autonomous trade was built up with the east Mediterranean. The obtaining of spices, oriental luxury manufactures and wines was clearly the motivation for the voyages, originating in Bristol and Southampton as well as London, which received considerable support from commercial capital in London. As in the French case, the English did not market their shipping services and had northern products to offer in return for their purchases, particularly kerseys, wools and minerals – lead and tin.[18]

All of these incursions come to a sharp halt in the 1550s, opening a last span of nearly a quarter of a century in which 'the Mediterranean [is] left to Mediterranean ships'. It should be added that there had at no stage been an interruption in the Mediterranean shipping tradition – only a dilution. But now it is Venetian, Genoese, Iberian and a newcomer, Ragusan (Dubrovnik) shipping, which dominates both in the Mediterranean and on the Mediterranean–Atlantic routes. Braudel is at a loss to explain the phenomenon. He is aware that there is a political dimension to it – the breaking of peaceful relationships between England and Spain and then the revolt of the Netherlands in the 1550s and 1560s – but his preferred explanation is in terms of the functioning of the trade cycle – the depression of the years concerned caused difficulties for weaker economic powers, relatively strengthening the position of the better-established Mediterranean commercial powers which were, however, in view of the crisis, obliged to cut costs by providing their own shipping. Only with the return to conditions of economic expansion in the last decades of the century could the luxury of employing other nations' shipping services once again be afforded.[19]

This reversal of the 'economic conjuncture' is thus the explanation offered for the initial return of northern, and particularly English, shipping on an unprecedented scale from the 1570s: 'Venice, like the other great Mediterranean cities, was ready to offer employment to "foreign" ships and mariners.' The Mediterranean economies were enjoying an Indian summer with a revival in the spice trade with the east Mediterranean, and this not only meant that Genoa, Venice and the Spanish monarchy had the resources to employ northern shipping but also that independent northern shippers were again drawn south. Additional factors account for the primacy of England in the early stages of this phase – warfare in the Mediterranean zone led to a strong demand for its minerals, particularly lead and tin, and the Habsburg–Ottoman conflict provided an opportunity for a Protestant England–Ottoman *rapprochement* which was the occasion for the granting of favourable trading capitulations in 1580. These were followed shortly by the establishment of a highly successful English Levant company. This well-funded concern represented a challenge on an unprecedented scale to the shipping and trading of the Mediterranean commercial powers. The benefits from this novel type of commercial organization, the greater honesty of English merchants, the excellence of their ships, the low price of their cloth and the ingenious convoy system which was devised to protect their trade are listed by Braudel as other factors contributing to their success.[20]

If it was demand for tin which brought the English back into the Mediterranean, it was demand for grain which was the occasion for the return of Dutch and Hanseatic shipping. Trade statistics from Leghorn show a sharp change in the home ports of visiting shipping between 1570–85, when the trade is divided between English and Iberian shipping, and the 1590s, when the Baltic powers gain an overwhelming predominance. There had been an interaction between the Malthusian crisis and the fortunes of northern shipping, with its access to Baltic grain reserves: this catalytic meeting of two causal strands is a key element in Braudel's interpretation. The trade was on a very large scale – in 1591, for example, although thirteen grain-carrying ships were stopped by a Spanish embargo, forty reached Leghorn.

From exercising this domination in the grain trade, the Dutch graduated during the 1590s and the first decade of the seventeenth century, to achieving a triumph in the Mediterranean spice trade, thereby, in

Braudel's words, 'conquering' the Mediterranean. Their double success represents, therefore, a crucial element in the sea's decline. Why the Dutch rather than their Baltic rivals, the Hanse merchants, or the British? It was the latter who had achieved the great naval victory over the Spanish in 1588: why was it not followed by commercial triumph? There were common factors in the advances of both powers, Braudel argues: their superiority in shipping. The arrival of the northerners in the Mediterranean in the sixteenth century had pitted the inner sea's oared galleys against the sailing ships of the Atlantic, and the latter had shown themselves superior in the encounter – 'the appearance of the northern sailing vessel of 100 to 200 tons, well armed and easily manoeuvred, marks a turning-point in maritime history', he writes. Common, too, was a brutality in approach: both nations practised piracy. What distinguished the two powers, he argues, was the special Dutch relationship with the Iberian peninsula: 'by her proximity to the Catholic provinces of the Netherlands', he writes, 'and by her persistence in forcing the coffers of Spain, [the Dutch] had better access than England to the Peninsula', and he coins the term 'complementary enemies' to describe Dutch–Spanish links during the eighty-year period of the Dutch revolt (1569–1648).

Let us provide a little more detail on how this intenser Dutch–Spanish relationship developed. The political events of the 1560s, Braudel argues, disturbed the triangular relationship which had formed to service the commercial needs of the Spanish empire (northern shippers assured the Iberia/north Europe trade route, Iberians providing the shipping to the Americas and East Indies and the Genoese the capital for the oceanic trades). Firstly in 1566 the Spanish crown transferred to Genoa the role of royal banker previously exercised by Antwerp. The consequence was the withdrawal of Genoese capital from the commercial ventures based in Seville. Secondly, from 1569, with the Dutch revolt, the Laredo–Antwerp trade route was cut. Dutch merchants and shippers were thus on the one hand prevented from playing their traditional role in the tripartite exchanges, and on the other provided with the opportunity of stepping into Genoese shoes in Seville. This is what they did. The Dutch economy also benefited from a further consequence of disruption – the transfer of mercantile resources from Antwerp to Amsterdam. Access to Spanish silver at Seville then served to lubricate Dutch trades with other markets (a mismatch between exports and imports in trading at this time, only resolvable by specie transfers, was a permanent problem in view of the lack of any international payments system). A further factor in the Dutch rise, Braudel speculates, was the role played by Marrano or Jewish Portuguese merchants, who emigrated in numbers to Amsterdam and preceded the Dutch in their penetration of West and East Indian markets: was there not a 'Lisbon takeover' parallel to the 'Seville takeover', he speculates. Insofar as it was the inadequacies of the finances of the Spanish state which were at the source of this whole causal process, Braudel's conclusion is that 'The balance of world history was tipped . . . by the bankruptcy of the Spanish state.'[21]

## Braudel's Reflections on Decline

Braudel includes much else in his study which is of enormous value for our subject. Rather, though, than continuing with this summary I shall be using the sample of his approach which I have already provided as a basis for identifying his interpretation and reflecting on his method, and here I shall merely direct readers to sections of his work from which they will draw benefit if they want to pursue further their interests in decline.

At several stages of the book Braudel introduces reflections concerning a quasi-mechanical staged process of rise and decline in important economic centres. The phases, he argues, take the form of (1) shipping centre, (2) commercial centre, (3) industrial centre, (4) financial centre and (5) rentier incomes/cultural centre/decadence. Thus of Venice, shifting in the sixteenth century towards a pattern of financial capitalism and investment in land, Braudel writes 'A classic pre-capitalist cycle was coming to an end.'[22] The fortunes of ports, in contrast, he argues, took the form of shorter, up-and-down cycles of success and failure ('It is as if a regular law has determined the life cycle of the population and the sea'),[23] while those of industrial towns were subject to sudden, once-and-for-all reversals (he compares these cycles to 'fitful fires scattered over a plain of grass').[24]

In the second part of his work Braudel devotes a great deal of space to the social dimension of decline. He delineates a kind of 'social conjuncture', related to political and economic change, in which economic and demographic growth increased the ease of social and horizontal (geographical) mobility, and economic depression had the reverse consequences. He writes of social change passing through 'successive phases of acceleration, slow down, revival and stagnation'. Attitudes to the poor tended to be less tolerant in a period of low social mobility.[25] Dramatizing a particular facet of the period of declining social mobility and growing social intolerance characteristic of the period from the late sixteenth century, Braudel coins the expression 'the defection of the bourgeoisie'. By this he means a change in the orientation of the 'bourgeoisie' from commercial affairs to imitating, and accepting the values of, the nobility. 'The bourgeois turned class traitor', he writes: what he means by this is that the middle class, rather than combating the aristocracy – its historic role according to Marx – was being absorbed by it.[26]

A society with less social mobility, characterized by harsher attitudes to the poor and with a 'bourgeoisie' decreasingly inclined to invest its capital productively – these characteristics brought with them rising social tension and banditry. Braudel describes some of these consequences, and his description serves to elucidate the social crisis which followed the economic one in the late sixteenth- and the seventeenth-century Mediterranean. Society came to be divided between a 'rich and vigorous nobility' and a 'growing mass of the poor and disinherited, caterpillars and grubs, human insects, alas too many', he writes. 'This crisis', he adds, 'coloured the lives of men. . . . At the heart of that society lay bitter despair.'[27]

A further dimension of decline to which Braudel gives attention is its relationship to cultural change. He argues that cultural peaks coincide with periods of decline. 'Perhaps the extravagance of a civilization is a sign of its economic failure', he writes. The 'culture' of the declining Mediterranean was the Baroque, and its achievements were such (he compares the contribution of Latin culture and, in the sixteenth century the Baroque, to 'Protestant Europe' with that of Greek culture to Rome) that he introduces a note of scepticism concerning Mediterranean decline when discussing this issue, writing of the 'decadent Mediterranean's . . . powerful capacity for diffusing a dying civilization'.[28]

## Concluding on Braudel's Interpretation

Returning to the data and views which Braudel presents on the material life of the Mediterranean, and the character of his interpretation of the decline of the Mediterranean which these imply, it can be seen that he provides a complex and fairly complete picture of a process of sharp economic and social change. He describes a fragile Mediterranean ecology, exhausted by its many centuries of servicing the material needs of a range of civilizations and no longer able to cope with the demands placed on it by a rapidly growing population. The arrival of northern shipping and its increasing dominance are a register of rising dependency. The crisis, though, is not a uniform one: the challenge from the north takes changing forms and the responses to the difficulties are varied. Thus the food shortage became apparent first in the Iberian peninsula before affecting Italy. In Iberia, Portugal is touched before

Spain. Iberia's demographic crisis comes first too. The origins of the 'northern' challengers to Mediterranean shipping hegemony become more and more distant. It is as if the economic space within which the mercantile centres of the Mediterranean economy were involved was progressively growing larger – as was indeed the case. Likewise the nature of the challenge to the Mediterranean economic centres was becoming increasingly wide-ranging: the Portuguese and Basque shippers had entered the Mediterranean as purveyors of cheap transport, principally to the orders of Genoa and Venice; the Dutch and English, we have just seen, represented a challenge in all spheres, from the start undertaking independent trades with the east Mediterranean and benefiting from a superiority in shipping and manufacturing technique. The Mediterranean was not purely having to operate within a larger economic space, it was also having to compete in a world in which industrial, shipping and commercial techniques were advancing rapidly, especially in new centres of economic power.

Responses to the crisis, we have seen, also vary. On the one hand there is a dualistic Italian pattern of adaptation with the merchants in the north shifting their investments from commerce and manufacturing to land and government securities, and the south showing signs of increasing economic dependency; on the other hand there is a relatively monolithic Iberian pattern with very little evidence of an internal entrepreneurial response to the difficulties, dependency becoming the norm.

There is little doubt that Braudel is aware of the character of this complex and differentiated crisis, with its multiple causes and manifestations. Frequent statements in the book show an acute awareness of the Mediterranean's experience of decline as a process, as Europe's economic and technical boundaries gradually grew, firstly within the Mediterranean and then beyond. An example: in the section of his work which he devotes to 'Seas' he makes a most insightful comparison between the Adriatic and Tyrrhenian Seas and their major ports, Venice and Genoa. He writes of their having been in opposition to each other, of Italy, thus, having had an east–west as well as a north–south split, and of Venice's expulsion of the Genoese from Cyprus in 1479 being 'a sixteenth-century version of the occupation ... of India by the English, ousting the French after the battle of Plassey, 1757'. He concludes that 'These swings from east to west, Adriatic to Tyrrhenian, were to determine the fate of Italy and of the whole Mediterranean on either side of the peninsula which acted as the beam of an enormous balance.'[29]

Braudel demonstrates here an awareness of the spatial stages in the Mediterranean's history as western Italy gained hegemony over east (and earlier we have noted his comment on a prior decline of the east Mediterranean), and he was well aware, we have just seen, of the further stage in this process represented by the displacement of the 'beam' to the Iberian peninsula. Oddly, however, his explanations for these changes by no means do justice to their complexity. On the one hand he favours a crude deterministic explanation in terms of overpopulation; on the other, he attributes particular importance to 'events', the Spanish monarchy's financial crisis which 'tips . . . the balance of world history'. Rather than insisting on the range of different experiences which he has documented, he is at pains to deliver a general explanation, sometimes for the whole Mediterranean – we have seen how he uses the experiences of Italy or Venice to represent the Mediterranean – and at others for the whole of Europe. For example, having vividly portrayed a 'slow, powerful and deep-seated movement [which] seems gradually to have twisted and transformed the societies of the Mediteranean between 1550 and 1660', he finishes a chapter by speculating that the crisis was a general European, rather than a local one: 'will our repeated inquiries show the true reason to be that the whole world, the Mediterranean included, was sooner or later to enter the extraordinary depression of the seventeenth century?'[30]

The reasons for Braudel's difficulties lie primarily in his methodologies and philosophy of history, and his use of his study to experiment with these. Thus the book is firstly innovatory in its adoption of a geographical and climatic space as its organizational principle. It is Braudel's argument that these features, rather than political boundaries or political events, are the dominant influences on human lives. In view of this he is on the look-out for general explanations for Mediterranean decline which will take in the experiences of the whole sea and its hinterlands – geographical and demographic factors are the only ones of sufficient breadth to serve this role.

Further insights into the methodological chaos which characterizes Braudel's work, and which undermines its value as a synthesis, are provided in the sections of the book in which he steps back from his writing of history to reflect on problems of causation. One of these is at the end of the second part of the work.[31] In this section he attempts to provide 'some tentative explanatory hypotheses'. He first makes a distinction between the types of history which he has been writing in the first two parts of his book. In the first he has been concerned with the 'near-permanent in history', in the second he has been concerned with 'change'. This is helpful: of the two interpretations of his which we have noted the first, in terms of the exhaustion of the Mediterranean's ecology over millennia, is clearly relevant to the first part of the book, the second, in terms of financial crisis in Spain and technical advances of the northern powers, to the second. He then proceeds to embroider on his interpretations for 'change'. He starts well by warning of the difficulties in linking changes in material life with fluctuations in human existence: 'For there is no single conjuncture: we must visualize a series of overlapping histories, developing simultaneously. It would be too simple, too perfect, if this complex truth could be reduced to the rhythms of one dominant pattern.' This dominant pattern itself, he argues, is complex and multifaceted: 'François Simiand[32] himself recognized at least two, when he spoke of the separate movements of the tides and the waves', he writes, but he adds that this image is too simple, 'dozens of movements' participating in the 'web of vibrations which make up the economic world'. Having delivered this dual warning, however, he throws all caution aside, adopting the established methodology of the contemporary guild of French historians, dividing European history into long-term 'A' expansive phases (characterized by rising prices, profit margins and population) and 'B' depression phases (with the reverse characteristics) to provide an explanation for his observations on the Mediterranean. In doing so all the qualifications which, we have seen, arise about the 'stages' and geographical variety of the Mediterranean's experiences during these years are discarded, and even the distinguishing of the Mediterranean from northern Europe as a valid unit for separate analysis questioned. This cyclical factor, which is referrred to as the *conjuncture* becomes the *deus ex machina* explaining changes of all kinds in the Mediterranean and elsewhere in Europe. Even cultural developments are fitted into the explanation – 'My suggestion would be that any economic recession leaves a certain amount of money lying idle in the coffers of the rich: the prodigal spending of this capital, for lack of investment openings, might produce a brilliant civilization lasting years or even decades.'[33]

The contrast between the painstaking empiricism which informs most of the work and this extreme deductivism of the conclusions is striking. It does not invalidate the book, but it does mean that it can only provide guidance insofar as the reader draws his own conclusions from the vast inventory of relevant material, and brilliant observations, which it includes. The guidance we have received concerning our subject is that it is best viewed as an intrinsic part of that gradual extension in the dimensions of the European economy over time. The character of the motors of this process, however, needs to be established – this we shall continue to explore in the next chapter – while the explanation for that variety in the experiences of decline which we have already detected will necessitate a full analysis of different declines. This will be undertaken in chapters 5–7.

# 2

# 'World-Economy' and 'World Time'

Man's ability to participate intelligently in the evolution of his own system is dependent on his ability to perceive the whole.

Immanuel Wallerstein, *The Modern World-System*

## Immanuel Wallerstein

### *An instrumentalist approach to the subject*

The strength of Wallerstein's commitment to his subject is a first source of inspiration to other practitioners in the trade. The short description of his approach with which he introduces his trilogy, *The Modern World-System*, attests to the tenacity of his attempts to establish the right methodology for the study of what he describes as 'social systems' (a term by which he means effectively 'society'). It was the establishment of the suitable unit for their study which particularly taxed him as he became aware from his fieldwork in Africa that neither the tribe nor the colony nor the nation-state were entities which enjoyed full autonomy and consequently provided a satisfactory unit within which the study of the local could be related to the full picture. He concluded that the correct unit, within which these smaller units could be satisfactorily inserted, was what he termed the 'world-economy'. As we shall see Wallerstein's alternative organizational principle for elucidating the functioning of social systems has proved a more satisfactory one than the geographical framework opted for by Braudel.

Wallerstein explains his perseverance in resolving this issue in terms of his belief that it represents an essential first step in achieving 'objectivity'. Insofar as this is an attainable goal, its premise, he declares, is the achievement of perspective over human achievement, the seeing of the whole and hence the ability to situate the local or momentary. The centrality which he attributes to achieving this goal is shown by the quotation from the introduction to his work which I have selected as an epigraph to this chapter. This desire to achieve 'objectivity' is, in turn, linked to the active role which Wallerstein attributes to the social scientist. The scholar's function, he writes, is 'to discern . . . the present reality of the phenomenon he studies, to derive from this study general principles, from which ultimately particular application may be made'. The possession of such awareness he categorizes as 'power', to be directed towards goals defined by the 'commitments' of the scholar. These in his case are the furtherance of the 'interests of the larger and more oppressed parts of the world's population' by the creation of 'a more egalitarian world and a more libertarian one'.[1]

A book such as the present one, focused on Europe rather than the Third World, cannot be so directly related to the plight of these social groups. It is, besides, written in a period in which one of the solutions advocated by Wallerstein, a transition to a 'socialist world government', appears an extremely implausible one.[2] However, Wallerstein's belief that the event can only be satisfactorily interpreted in the light of an understanding of the whole is shared. Those apparently erratic variations in the causes, manifestations and responses to crisis in the sixteenth and seventeenth centuries observed, but not made sense of, by Braudel, do become explicable and even predictable when Wallerstein's concept of a 'world-economy' (which I shall shortly be defining) is adopted.[3]

## The 'world-system'

Wallerstein's intuition that it is the 'world-economy' which provides the right unit within which to study social systems was the spark which stimulated his major historical work mentioned above. The meaning he gives to this term is clarified by contrasting 'world-economy' with what he characterizes as the other major organizational structure in history, 'world empires'. Whereas the latter attain unity by the domination of a central political unit, world economies achieve coherence via the market, which ignores the political boundaries of states and nations. The distinction is similar to that existing in current usage between a 'global economy', which can condition events within politically independent states, and a worldwide empire, such as the British was, which is territorially and politically defined: what was unusual was the application of the former concept to so early a stage of Europe's development. There is a further possible confusion with the term 'world-economy': by it Wallerstein does not mean exactly what we would mean now by global economy – he intends it to connote no more than a bigger unit that the national one, within which a range of states fitted. A 'European' 'world-economy' coexists for the medieval period from which he starts his study with an 'Indian Ocean–Red Sea complex', the Chinese region, the central Asian land mass from Mongolia to Russia and the Baltic region and is defined as the 'focus of trade where Byzantium, Italian city-states, and to some extent parts of northern Africa met'.

The relationship between 'world-economy' and 'world empire' is portrayed by Wallerstein as a competitive and conflictive one. It had generally been the experience of 'world-economies' to be absorbed by empires. That this does not occur in the European case he explains by the dynamism shown by 'the techniques of modern capitalism' and 'the technology of modern science'.[4] Wallerstein is thus showing the predominance of the 'world-economy' as a social system to be a distinctive characteristic of European history.

My study will consequently follow Wallerstein's in using a larger economic unit than the region or nation state as its organizational basis. For example, as already noted in the Introduction, chapter 5, 'Italian Declines', does not consist in a history of the decline of Italy: rather, it is an analysis of four different regional declines within the geographical space of the Italian peninsula, declines which occurred at different stages, took different forms, and can be properly understood only in terms of the general process of economic change in which a similar unit to Wallerstein's 'world-economy' was involved.

### The microeconomics of a world-economy: cores, peripheries and external arenas

Wallerstein's analysis of the microeconomics of his 'European world-economy' is also relevant to our theme. He adapts a vocabulary, which had been developed in the context of Marxist theories of economic development, to describe the various component parts of this geographical/economic unit in the pre-industrial period.[5] It is divided between 'cores' or 'core-states', 'semi-peripheries' and 'peripheries'. Other world-economies with which it traded are termed 'external arenas'. By core-areas he means those with the largest concentrations of capital, manufacturing and commercial skills, which used their leadership in these domains to dominate, to varying extents, the semi-periphery and periphery. Peripheries were in a position of colonial or quasi-colonial dependence on the core, producing 'lower-ranking goods', primarily foodstuffs and raw materials, for export to the core in return for manufactured goods and luxuries. Such areas did not possess state structures to protect their economic interests, and their labour forces worked under harsher legal conditions than those applying in the core – outright slavery, the Spanish American system of *encomienda*, serfdom in eastern Europe and sharecropping in areas of the semi-periphery.

The distinction between 'periphery' and 'external arenas' is an important one, throwing light on what Wallerstein believed the mechanics of the 'European world-system' to be and demonstrating, too, distinctions between the 'European world-economy', it would seem (there is some conceptual vagueness here), and the other world-economies which he lists. His own definitions can be used: 'the periphery of a world-economy is the geographical sector of it wherein production is primarily of lower-ranking goods . . . but which is an integral part of the overall system of the division of labour, because the commodities involved are essential for daily use' whereas 'the external arena of a world-economy consists of those other world systems with which a given world-economy has some kind of trade relationsip based primarily on the exchange of preciosities, what was sometimes called the "rich trades": within Wallerstein's scheme, the links between the core and other world-systems are clearly superficial compared to those with the peripheries, and it is the latter type of link which is the harbinger of a capitalist industrialization.[6]

Finally, with respect to all these categories, Wallerstein uses the economists' concepts of 'the slight edge' and 'tipping mechanism' to express the character of the growth process and the advance of inequalities: once specialization between zones has been established then 'the slight edge [which is the basis for specialization] is converted into a large disparity and the advantage holds even after the conjuncture has passed', cores becoming more firmly cores, peripheries experiencing a widening gap with respect to the centre. Similarly the divergence between state structures, whose relative strengths are a crucial determining factor for the conserving of economic autonomy, is progressive: 'A state machinery', Wallerstein writes, 'involves a tipping mechanism. There is a point where strength creates more strength.'[7]

## Wallerstein and decline: 'aristocratic hierarchies', 'feudal capitalism', 'debt-peonage'

Although Wallerstein's principal focus is on the emergence of a capitalist world-economy, his analysis has implications for decline and at certain points he touches on the issue directly. Firstly, it should be stressed that his slight 'edge' argument is relevant to explaining the gravity of the problem of decline in European history: the extensive industrial and commercial concentrations which resulted from exploitation of the advantages accruable to specialization within a 'world' economic space meant, when trading zones shifted, severe structural problems even in a pre-industrial economy. Secondly his reflections on the links between politics and economic life are of relevance to our theme. Although what he terms the 'basic linkage' in his world-economy is economic, this does not mean that the political is excluded. 'The state', he writes, 'becomes less the central economic enterprise than the means of assuring certain terms of trade in other economic transactions.' This latter role could, though, be a considerable one, and he identifies two archetypes. Europe's elite sought everywhere, he argues, a strong state but, depending on circumstances, the ends to which it desired that this strength should be deployed differed: for the 'emergent capitalist strata', what was sought were 'absolute monarchies' to serve as 'a prime customer, a guardian against local and international brigandage, a mode of social legitimation, a preemptive protector against the creation of strong state barriers elsewhere'. In contrast 'old aristocratic hierarchies' sought 'a brake on these same capitalist strata, an upholder of status conventions, a maintainer of order, a promoter of luxury'.[8] Braudel too, we have noted, touched on this possibility of social structures hardening to protect privilege and acquired wealth, and battening on poorer social groups. The relevance of this latter use of the state apparatus to the occurrence and persistence of decline is self-evident.

Finally Wallerstein's analysis of the exploitive relationship between core and periphery bears a direct relationship to our theme insofar as parts of Europe itself were relegated to this second category. (This too we have noted from Braudel's analysis of developments in southern Italy and the Iberian peninsula.) The principal area to experience this was eastern Europe – east and west became 'complementary parts of a more complex single system . . . in which East Europe played the role of raw-materials producer', Wallerstein writes. Our main interest, however, is not with areas whose backwardness and decline represented degeneration from situations of only modest economic autonomy, but rather with areas whose experience was one of decline from core status to that of semi-periphery or periphery: firstly the east Mediterranean which by the thirteenth and fourteenth centuries was dominated by Italy; secondly the central and western Mediterranean – Italy and Spain – which from the seventeenth century was dominated by north-western Europe. Spain, according to Wallerstein, becomes 'at best a rather passive conveyor belt between the core countries and Spain's colonies'. Southern Italy, too, becomes 'dependent' first on northern Italy and then on northern Europe. Wallerstein's analysis of the polarizing impact of the world economy is thus relevant to this particular aspect of decline in European history. Some of the mechanisms whereby dependency was imposed are described by Wallerstein and should be noted, as they will be referred to later: he writes of the introduction of a 'feudal capitalism' in the formerly core area of Lombardy in the seventeenth century, and of dependency brought about by 'debt peonage' in Italy's south – defined as a system which 'enabled a cadre of international merchants to bypass (and thus eventually to destroy) the indigenous merchant classes . . . and enter into direct links with landlord-entrepreneurs'.[9]

## Braudel's *Civilization and Capitalism*

### *Material life, market and capitalism*

The first volume of Braudel's second, major historical work was published separately in 1967. It already represented a considerable methodological advance on *The Mediterranean*. Gone was the geographical framework for ordering social and economic experience. Gone, too, was the bias towards the semi-permanent. In their place Braudel had constructed a new theory of history in terms of the existence of three layers of human existence and interaction between them: the 'material', the 'market' and 'capitalism'. Defining them, he notes that it is the market which is the most familiar. It is the category analysed by Adam Smith in *The Wealth of Nations*, constantly in progression, institutions permitting, with improvements in communications, division of labour and specialization. The first and last layers are more obscure. The former is the economic sphere below the level of the market: 'that elementary basic activity which went on everywhere ... the world of self-sufficiency and barter of goods within a very small radius'. The latter is above the market and to a degree controls the levels below: in it 'active social hierarchies ... manipulate exchange to their advantage and disturb the established order ... they create anomalies ... a few wealthy merchants in ... sixteenth-century Genoa could throw whole sectors of the world economy into confusion.' This second, 'obscure' zone is to a certain extent an 'upper limit' of the market level of human existence and the 'favoured domain of capitalism'. Its dominance is largely attributable to privileged access to commercial techniques and information: 'privileged actors were engaged in circuits and calculations that ordinary people knew nothing of.'

The other two volumes in the work, and a revised version of the first volume, appeared in 1979. The titles of the three volumes are *The Structures of Everyday Life*, *The Wheels of Commerce* and *The Perspectives of the World*. As in *The Mediterranean*, it can be seen that Braudel is proposing a tripartite division to human experience, but this time his approach is more materialist – all three levels fall within the economic field. He is cautiously resorting to a form of economic determinism: 'this volume will give most prominence to one sector of history – the material and economic', he writes in his preface to the third volume, and, justifying this approach, he continues: 'Of all the ways of apprehending space, the economic is the easiest to locate and the widest-ranging ... its significance is not confined to the material aspects of world time: all other social realities, whether favourable to it or not, are concerned ... constantly intervening or being in turn influenced by it.'


## A history of events in 'world time'

As in *The Mediterranean*, it is with the base in this tripartite division that he begins the work, but in this case the ordering does not represent the attribution of a causal predominance. This is apparent from a distinction which Braudel makes between the approach which he has adopted in the different volumes – that in the first two takes the form of what he describes as 'thematic research', meaning by this an examination of structures and continuities, whereas that of the third consists in 'a chronological study of the forms and successive preponderant tendencies of the international economy. In a word ... a history'. His approach to history has thus experienced a total about-turn – rather than showing a faith in the semi-permanent, he has taken the 'gamble' of 'drawing as widely as possible on history, which is now seen as unfolding in chronological order, with its different time scales': in other words the history of *events*, or at least *economic events*.[10]

Between the publication of the first volume and that of the last two, Braudel had been able to read the first volume of Wallerstein's work. Wallerstein's influence is demonstrated in the character of the 'social system' whose 'chronological order' Braudel describes – it is Wallerstein's 'world-economy'. This term is not actually introduced into the title of Braudel's third volume, we have seen, but the phrase 'world-time' shows his dependence on the concept: what he means by it is the phases of growth in the 'world-economy' which, he goes on to argue, have a specific rhythm of their own. The spatial organizational principle is thus the same as Wallerstein's, but here Braudel is defining it according to its diachronic functioning.[11] He defines the concept further in his introduction: 'world time', he writes, 'might be said to concentrate above all on a kind of superstructure of world history; it represents a crowning achievement, created and supported by forces at work underneath it, although in turn its weight has an effect on its base.'[12]

## Rules of the 'world-economy'

When Braudel comes to define 'world-economy', it is more or less precisely Wallerstein's definition which he reproduces: 'a world-economy is a sum of individual areas, economic and non-economic, which it brings together ... it usually crosses the boundaries of other great historical divisions.'[13]

It is going to be helpful, however, to run through what Braudel describes as the 'rules' of the 'world-economy'. A first relates to the division of the globe between different world-economies and the relative lack of communication between these different spheres. The point is similar to that made by Wallerstein concerning the relative insignificance of the links between a European world-economy and 'the external arena'. All that needs noting here are two comments made by Braudel in this context. Firstly he emphasizes the exceptional expansiveness of the European world-economy *vis-à-vis* others: 'Europe miraculously extended her frontiers at a stroke, or very nearly so, with the great discoveries at the end of the fifteenth century', he writes. The 'European' world-economy was clearly already one with dynamic qualities which were lacking in the others. Secondly, he emphasizes, the effort which was required to keep open these links with other world-economies: such as to exhaust 'the pioneer of the route, Portugal'. It is an oversimplification but, as so much in Braudel, represents a brilliant historical insight concerning a decline with which we shall be concerned in chapter 6.[14]

Braudel's second rule is that a world-economy is always dominated by a large, powerful urban centre: 'A world economy has an urban centre of gravity, a city, as the logistic heart of its activity. News, merchandise, capital, credit, people, instructions, correspondence all flow into and out of the city.' Such centres stood out in their contemporary societies by the freedoms which are enjoyed within them and by their cosmopolitanism: of Venice it was written 'If you are curious to see men from every part of the earth, each dressed in his own different way, go to St Mark's Square or the Rialto', and Descartes wrote of Amsterdam in the seventeenth century as 'a sort of inventory of the possible'. Around the 'urban centre of gravity' there grew up a string of secondary towns which contributed to its domination – Braudel uses the metaphor of an 'archipelago' to portray these groups of towns which 'stand guard around it [the centre], direct the flow of business toward it, redistribute or pass on the goods it sends them, live off its credit or suffer its rule' (see map 1).

A sub-clause to Braudel's second rule is that 'cities take it in turns to lead': '*world-cities*' are in perpetual rivalry with one another and may take each other's place', Braudel notes. Although the statement implies that economic competition is the principal cause of such reversals, Braudel raises the issue of the part sometimes played by political decisions, drawing a comparison between the epochal-changing switches of the capital of China from Nanking to Peking in 1421, and of Spain from Lisbon to Madrid in 1582. In both cases the consequences of the changes were that continental ambitions were prioritized over maritime ones: of the latter switch, Braudel writes, 'The only thing of which we can be sure is that if Lisbon, encouraged by the king of Spain, had triumphed, there would have been no Amsterdam.' Whatever the causes, transfers were highly disruptive: 'they interrupt the calm flow of history and open up perspectives that are the more precious for being so rare. When Amsterdam replaced Antwerp, when London took over from Amsterdam, or when in about 1929, New York overtook London, it always meant a massive historical shift of forces, revealing the precariousness of the previous equilibrium and the strengths of the one which was replacing it.' The disruption is all the greater in view of the build-up of imperial territories by economic centres: 'If the capital city of a world-economy fell, it sent ripples throughout the system to the periphery. . . . When Venice began her decline, she lost her empire: Negroponte in 1540, Cyprus . . . in 1572, Candia (Crete) in 1669.'[15]

Finally Braudel qualifies what he means by the term 'dominating centre' by noting that it does not imply uniformity in the character of the succession of towns in Europe which exercised hegemony – his list is Venice, Antwerp, Genoa, Amsterdam and London. These cities' economic specializations varied: Venice had no banking, Antwerp neither shipping nor political autonomy, Genoa by the time it was an economic centre was politically subordinate to Spain and exercised its domination purely in the financial sphere – its period of primacy is identified by Braudel as a 'between-acts' period in European history when 'no one was quite sure where the centre of gravity really lay.' Finally Amsterdam and London stand out in having possessed the whole 'arsenal' of economic power: 'they controlled everything, from shipping to commercial and industrial expansion, as well as the whole range of credit.'[16]

## The 'motor' of the world-economy: differences from Wallerstein

In a third rule Braudel exposes the character of the vertical links which connect the economic centre with the large hinterlands which it dominates – effectively it is the links between 'capitalism' and 'markets' with which he is here concerned. What struck him during his long years working on the Mediterranean, he notes, were the continuities in the character of life at the market level despite the change in the localization of the areas dominating the Mediterranean during the sixteenth and seventeenth centuries. This leads him to argue for the relative autonomy of the two top tiers of his tripartite division of the material world. The nature of the economy was such that there was always a dominating centre, but the localization of this centre is accountable in terms of an autonomous causal process within the 'capitalist' stratum, and the impact of changes on this level on that below is minor – there is 'a dialectic between a market economy developing almost unaided and an over-arching economy which seizes these humble activities from above, redirects them and holds them at its mercy'.[17] At other points in the work Braudel concedes that there is some interaction between the different strata – for example he writes in the introduction to the third volume of a 'two-way exchange from the bottom upwards and from the top down', the relative strength of the respective flows in which has depended on 'place and time'. We are close here to the idea used in his *Mediterranean* of *conjuncture*. Overall, however, it is the autonomy argument to which he attaches greatest weight. He writes, for example, of isolated regions such as those described in his first volume as being 'on the margin of official history', that is, on the margin of 'world time'.

In this respect, then, there is a sharp division with the viewpoint of Wallerstein. In his case, too, there are three spheres of economic activity – core, semi-periphery and periphery – but he argues, we have seen, for far more systematic links between them, and, in particular, for a process of exploitation of the periphery by the core. This is a different sort of process from the means by which Braudel sees profit accruing to the capitalist sphere (the mystique of 'foreign exchange').[18]

## 'World time' and decline

I shall adjudicate this difference in approach between Wallerstein and Braudel by reference to Jonathan Israel's work in the next section. Otherwise, Braudel's work serves to reinforce the commitment already made on the basis of Wallerstein views to adopt the 'world-economy' as the unit within which to interpret European declines. I shall be following Braudel too in focusing principally on the economy in my analysis in the belief that this is the determining sector in the history with which we are concerned. This history, like Braudel's volume III, will be a narrative one, charting like his 'world time', but focusing on the areas which this world time leaves behind. As such, it will effectively be a selective history of decline – it will not be all declines that are covered, but above all those of areas which had previously been at the centre. Our faith in the relevance of such a focus comes from Braudel's and Wallerstein's insights into the influence that such 'centres' already exercised in the pre-industrial economy.

## Jonathan Israel's *Dutch Primacy in World Trade*[19]

### Israel's world economy and its centre

Israel follows Wallerstein and Braudel in writing in terms of a world economy. His world economy is not quite the same as theirs, however: its creation follows the vast expansion in European trading networks of the fifteenth and sixteenth centuries. It *really* is, thus, a world economy, rather than being simply a notional unit exceeding the nation-state in size and owing its cohesion to economic forces. He differs, too, from Braudel in terms of the idea of this world economy being dominated by a single centre, arguing that, 'given the relatively limited geographical frame of the Venetian trade empire of the later Middle Ages, and subsequently those of Antwerp and Genoa', western Europe was still in the 'late-medieval poly-nuclear' phase of expansion rather than being dominated by a single centre, as was to be the case with Amsterdam. Braudel, on the other hand, as we have just seen, admits the existence of ambiguity about a centre for the world economy during the sixteenth century: possibly he should have been more cautious in his use of vocabulary. There may be a better case, however, for regarding Venice as centre to a European world economy for the period before the sixteenth century. Less of the world had been discovered, but over that area of the world which was integrated within a European trading system Venice exercised a high degree of control.[20]

In further analysis, designed in part to demonstrate this discontinuity between medieval and modern commercial centres, Israel throws useful light on the extreme character of that geographical shift in the centre of gravity of the European economy between 1500 and 1700 with which we were concerned in our discussion of Braudel's *Mediterranean*. It was not just a shift from south to north, of Catholic to Protestant, he argues, but from a wide range of commercial centres distributed throughout Europe in favour of a small strip of the north-west of the continent:

> There was no such thing as a general shift to northern or 'Atlantic' Europe. After 1590 Lübeck and the Hanseatic League were in full decline. The great emporia of south Germany and France were on the wane. After 1572 the economy of the South Netherlands was heavily disrupted. What happened in fact was that economic vitality in Europe was transferred not to a large part of northern Europe but to a mere tiny fringe, the extreme north-western corner of the continent.

This is Israel's transition to a 'mono-nuclear' system of economic centres.[21]

## Israel and the motor of the pre-industrial economy

Israel is right to emphasize the extent of discontinuity represented by the Dutch success, and I shall be making considerable use of his analysis in the following chapters. What is of more central concern at this point is the light which his interpretation of this shift throws on the character of the 'motor' of the pre-industrial world-economy, for it permits us to arbitrate between the divergent views of Wallerstein and Braudel on this question, and hence settle finally our own method in this study.

Israel notes that there are two schools of thought concerning the causes of this change: one which attributes Dutch success to dominance in the bulk trades, and principally shipping, and another which attaches greater importance to success in the so-called 'rich trades', in spices, high-quality manufactures and colonial foodstuffs. Braudel's interpretation in *The Mediterranean* he attributes, reasonably fairly, to the first type of explanation (reasonably: we have seen in fact that Braudel introduces different types of explanations for the decline of the Mediterranean as a whole as a long-term process and for the reversal in conjuncture, and that in the case of the latter he places the emphasis on Dutch success in penetrating the Spanish rich trades). Israel himself, however, demonstrates convincingly that the key element in the rise of the Dutch to world primacy was not their long tradition in the bulk trades and the provision of shipping services, but their comparatively sudden success in the rich trades at the end of the sixteenth century. An analysis for the period 1647–72 shows that Dutch participation in the four rich trades, with the Levant, the East Indies, Cádiz and Archangel, while only employing some 100 ships (against up to 4,000 used in the Baltic trades), accounted for the bulk of the value of Dutch trade, some 50 million guilders. These trades 'nourished each other' and the monopolies which the Dutch obtained in these markets were crucial in providing them with scarce luxuries, including bullion, for their successes in the others. Israel concludes that the evolution of Dutch world commercial hegemony is linked 'in some respects' with the 'ebb and flow of Dutch bulk carrying but is primarily defined by shifts in the Dutch share of the high-value trades, both those in Europe and those in the non-European world'.[22]

Israel's views are thus consistent with a view of the European economy being driven, until well into the eighteenth century, by success in the rich trades. Exploitation there was in such trades. The most dynamic rich trades in the late seventeenth and early eighteenth centuries were sugar and tobacco, in whose production slavery was being extended; but as they were trades in luxuries, they were not such as to involve more than a minority of the space included in the European world-economy. The links of such trades with the market or material strata of economic life, or with periphery or semi-periphery, were thus not of the systematic kind consequent upon the exhaustion of possibilities of profit within Europe implied by Wallerstein. Connections of this sort were to develop at a later stage in the rise of capitalism. Israel's work thus effectively supports Braudel's decision to confine his narrative to the 'capitalist' stratum of Europe's economic life. I shall be operating the same principle of selection and focusing in particular on the experience of decline in former 'centres' of the European 'world economy'.

# Michael Mann's *Sources of Social Power*[23]

## *'World time'*

Michael Mann's work takes the form of an analysis of the nature of power in human civilizations from their very beginnings in the third millennium BC. He is a 'sociologist', but his approach is historical. This choice he explains firstly by his concern with 'processes of social change'; secondly because 'Societies are not self-contained units to be simply compared across time and space . . . [but] exist in particular settings of regional interaction that are unique even in some of their central characteristics' and are thus not comprehensible in terms of comparative sociology; and thirdly because in focusing on 'power' he is dealing with a force which was transformed over time. Using a vocabulary akin to Wallerstein's and Braudel's, he writes that 'It is more important to capture this history than to make comparisons across the globe. This is a study of "world time" . . . in which each process of power development affects the world around it'.[24] There are other similarities with Wallerstein and Braudel: his is not a general study of power in all states, but rather he analyses it, as Wallerstein and Braudel analyse economic change, in the most advanced sectors of the world, at the cutting edge – firstly in the Near East, where civilization started, then, progressively further west, in Europe.[25]

## *The 'macrohistory' of the Afro-Asian/European zone*

Mann's approach breaks new ground. In the first place, he attributes qualities to the early stages of Near Eastern and eastern Mediterranean civilization which very often are held to belong purely to a European tradition. From its very commencement, he argues, the civilization which developed around the Rivers Tigris and Euphrates in Mesopotamia – to a great extent because of the wide variety of geographical and climatic conditions adjacent to it – was outward-looking, involving itself in trading with, and consequently giving rise to cultural diffusion to, neighbouring geographical zones in the 'fertile crescent'. 'The alluvium is situated amid great ecological *contrasts*', he writes. 'That was decisive, producing both boundedness [a stimulus to social stratification] and interaction distinct from, say, that of the relatively even terrain of Europe. Such contrasts seem the recipe for the emergence of civilization.' Such openness was a contributory factor, he argues, in the development of a uniquely pluralistic political and economic culture in the area. Concluding on these qualities he writes:

> The first major peculiarity of the civilization to which the modern West is heir was that it was geopolitically multicentred, cosmopolitan, and non-hegemonic. It had three ecological roots: irrigated river valleys and confined plowlands, the core of the land empires of the Near East; more open, extensive plowlands in Europe: and the inland seas that connected with them. The juxtaposition of such ecologies was unique in the world: therefore, in world historical terms, so was the civilization to which it gave rise.[26]

It was the zones of irrigated agriculture which represented the 'cores' initially of this space – he uses the Wallersteinian vocabulary of core and periphery – a status which they enjoyed on the one hand as a consequence of their technical superiority, which enabled them to gain benefits from 'unequal exchange',[27] and on the other, at a later stage of development, when they became military-dominated, relatively centralized regimes ('empires of domination' is how he describes this stage of their development) as a consequence of some of the economic advantages accruing from empire, for example law and order, investment in infrastructure, monetarization and accelerated cultural and technical diffusion.[28] The existence of empires of domination with these dynamic characteristics, and surrounding peripheries with a different set of natural resources, gave a unique economic and social dynamism to the zone.

His study then goes in some detail into how economic and political power was diffused from the centre. He makes two particular points, one primarily relating to economic costs and resource allocation, and the other to social and political structures. With regard to the former, an argument running through the study is that there was a tendency for civilization to be diffused from its Near Eastern area of origin to the north and, above all, to the west, as these areas possessed more abundant material resources which enabled them, once techniques had been transferred, to produce at lower cost than the initial centres of civilization. The shifts became more rapid with the iron age since iron ore existed in far greater abundance in these northerly and westerly zones, and the revolution in the extent of availability of tools and weapons consequent upon the use of iron favoured in particular the more diffused and democratic settlement characteristics of the western and northern 'rainfall-agriculture' communities over the concentrated and more regimented empires of domination.[29] The second point relates to the social and political dimension of this process of diffusion. Mann's argument is that areas on the periphery of the empires of domination, while benefiting from some of the trading advantages to which their political dominance gave rise, did not themselves have to bear the cost of this political policing and themselves enjoyed looser political structures. This was a further contribution to their being able to produce and trade at lower cost than areas within the empires, and thus a further stimulus to economic and commercial diffusion. Adopting here a different vocabulary, Mann refers to these zones of contact on the edges of the empires as 'the marches', these outsider participants in trading and cultural interaction with the empires as 'marcher lords' and the character of their situation in relation to the empires of domination as 'interstitial': they were involved to some extent within the cultural zone of the empire but without being in any way controlled by it.[30]

The cultural and economic diffusion contributed to political challenges by these 'marcher lords' to the empires of domination. Empires were invaded. The incursions of the Hittites towards the end of the second millennium BC are an example of one such incursion. Such intrusion was not necessarily retrogressive with respect to the dialectic of change ('macrohistorical process') with which Mann is concerned: the incorporation of rival marcher lords within the empires of domination, or the taking over of empires of domination by marcher lords, could represent a catalyst for institutional change and a basis for general reinvigoration. Otherwise the political challenge took the form of the development of new power blocs outside the areas of the empires of domination, and principally in the Balkan peninsula, which then proceeded to challenge their hegemony. It should not require too much imagination to pinpoint the historical developments to which Mann is making reference – in the process of economic diffusion it is the achievement of the Phoenicians, and their practice of establishing trading colonies along the length of the Mediterranean, which he emphasizes and in that of political power (combined with, but of greater significance than economic progress in this case, he argues) it is the Greeks. Of the Greek achievement he writes: 'Nothing like this had been seen before: It required the historical conjunction of Iron Age innovations plus a unique ecological and geopolitical location astride maritime trading routes between semi-barbarian plowland and civilized empires of domination.'[31] The reverse side of the coin to these emerging, dynamic, 'interstitial', 'marcher' states was growing institutional rigidity within the 'empires of domination', which had a negative impact on their efficiency as societies. The military challenge from the marcher lords exacerbated this tendency. 'The organization to defeat them', writes Mann, 'weakened the social base of the initial success and potentially led to an excess of coercion over cooperation.' The same fate would be met by these marcher areas in their turn: 'After a long, successful process of power development . . . their own organizations became institution-alized and rigid.'[32] Recapitulating on the whole process, Mann writes: 'decentralized multi-power actor civilizations lying on the marches of established empires of domination exploited the success plus the institu-tional rigidity of these empires to "emerge interstitially" and establish their own autonomous power organization.'[33]

Developments in the Italian peninsula, it is Mann's argument, mirrored those which had occurred a half a millennium or so earlier in the Balkans: marcher lords, benefiting from lower costs and cultural transfer, develop politically to emerge slowly from a position of depend-ency. However the Roman empire he regards as causing a qualititative change in the dialectical process of economic, cultural and political diffusion with which he is concerned. He categorizes it as a 'territorial empire' rather than an 'empire of domination' in that it achieves a genuine cohesion not via a pure exercise of military power but by the spread of an ideology which comes to be accepted everywhere by the empire's elite – a notion of Roman citizenship and its duties. Cultural and technical diffusion continues to occur, but the mechanism is now more military than commercial. This accelerates diffusion, and Mann writes of a 'Keynesian legionary economy' in which the legionaries are the instruments of technical transfer and the introduction to northern Europe of the civilization of the Mediterranean. In practice again, however, though the agencies of cultural and technical transfer are different, the essence of the process, and some of its consequences, reflect the same macrohistorical process: the economic techniques which originated in the Near East are being put to uses in areas in which the factor situation for their exploitation is more favourable, resulting in a gradual displacement of economic activity to the north and to the west. In this case it is more than just technical and cultural transfer – east Mediterranean resources via taxation, and technicians in the form of Greek slaves, serve to accelerate the process of diffusion. Consequences are parallel too: one of the reasons for the collapse of the empire is held to be the damaging consequences for the centre of Roman power, the Italian peninsula, of this centrifugal process. However, from another point of view the empire is different: its territorial principles and creation of frontiers led to a cessation of that dialectic between empire and marcher lords which had characterized empires of domination, and a resultant loss of creativity and failure to integrate barbarian groups.[34]

Mann believes that the institution of a territorial empire might have succeeded.[35] It did not, and the entity of Europe which later develops came to share with the eastern civilization which he has portrayed that characteristic of creative political pluralism – a set-up which he accounts for in terms of the Christian Church providing the sort of collective infrastructure provided in other societies by empires ('ideological extensive power'). In his analysis of European development he is at pains once more to emphasize that the cutting edge of economic changes is in small states, interstitial areas, not in the larger political entities ('there is a correlation of economic wealth and dynamism with weak states').[36] His concern, though, at this point of his work is not with regional variation in economic experience so much as the macro explanations for Europe as a whole developing in the way it did: he describes this period of domination by small political entities and then, from the second half of the twelfth century, the growth in the influence of nation-states.[37]

## Adapting Mann's theory to European decline

Mann to a certain extent is giving a spatial and international dimension to a statement by the Italian political theorist Mosca concerning power shifts within states. Mosca stated:

> One might say . . . that the whole history of civilized mankind comes down to a conflict between the tendency of dominant elements to monopolize political power and transmit possession of it by inheritance and the tendency toward a dislocation of old forces and insurgence of new forces; and this conflict produces an unending ferment of endosmosis and exosmosis between the upper classes and certain portions of the lower.'[38]

The spatial opening up of the Afro-Asian and European geographical zone by the techniques developed originially in the Near East occasioned a continuous shifting in economic frontiers and thus a repeated cycle of progress and decline as centres graduated from marcher status to that of centre, and finally were challenged in turn by areas to their west or north. His work thus provides a strong reinforcement to the insights obtainable from Braudel's *Mediterranean* referred to above – the seeing of decline as an intrinsic part of, the reverse side of the coin to, Europe's unique expansiveness – with the added advantage of demonstrating that this pattern, rather than being unique to European history, characterizes the whole history of civilization in the Near East/North African/European zones since its inception. Mann's analysis, we have noted, does not pursue the European experience of economic growth at the regional level, but I shall be using the insights drawn from his macro analysis – particularly with respect to the geographical extension of the European 'world-economy', interstitiality and institutional rigidities – on a micro level in accounting for success and failure within different European regions.

# 3

# The 'Rise' of Europe

It is not any particular set of institutions, ideas or technologies that mark out the West but its inability to come to a rest. No other civilized society has ever approached such restless instability. . . . In this . . . lies the true uniqueness of Western civilization.

W. H. NcNeill, *The Rise of the West*

I have established in the previous chapters that a distinctive characteristic of the civilization of the Afro-Asian/European zone was a steady process of cultural diffusion over a growing geographical area and that 'European history' inherits these characteristics, but with some modifications: the political unit within which such changes made their impact became smaller, and the pace of technical and commercial progress quickened. Proceeding from this, it has been my argument that decline forms a structural feature of such a civilization: the process of geographical diffusion involved repeated shifts in the economic centre of gravity of the area, resulting in repeated experiences of decline and linked structural problems. It follows that a first step in interpreting decline in European history is an understanding of the stages whereby the 'frontier' of the 'world economy' shifted from its Mediterranean origins to the west and to the north. This is what I hope to communicate in this chapter.

## Venice

We are principally concerned in this book with the 1,000 years between
the expansion of Islam in the seventh century, which split the
Mediterranean, converting it into a frontier rather than the centre and
focus which it had been during the classical era and thus bringing the
period known as late antiquity to an end, and the rise of the Atlantic
economies during the seventeenth century. Venice played a significant,
dominating or prominent role for almost nine tenths of this period, and
it existed as a powerful state beyond it – until its absorption into the
Napoleonic empire in 1797. Venice's history thus encapsulates a great
deal of what is of concern to us.

As a preliminary to summarizing aspects of this history, however, note
must be taken of what was to become effectively a structural feature of
the medieval European economy, one which distinguished it from the
Roman economy which preceded it, and which was to be a principal basis
for its enrichment. This is the growth in Europe of two economic poles of
development, with different comparative advantages, which interacted
with each other, that of Flanders and that of North Italy. Braudel
describes this relationship as 'one of the major features of European
history – possibly the most important of all', and it is the case that
European growth through the Middle Ages was concentrated along
the axis between these two areas. In accordance with our policy of
focusing on the 'centres' of the European economy we shall be concentrating on the Italian end of this exchange initially, as Italy was the
dominant partner. *En passant*, I would register, though, that the Flemish
zone is an area specially suitable for decline studies, for its geographical
position ensured that, unlike Italy and Spain for example, it was never
fully relegated to the margins of history.[1]

Venice was not a Roman town. Its formation was due to the Lombard
invasions of the sixth century. The Lombards were a tribe of some
200,000, one which, unlike earlier Germanic invaders, had had no prior
contact with civilization. From an area north of the Balkans, just south
of the Carpathian mountains (approximately where Hungary is now
situated) they entered northern Italy in 568 from the east, crossing the
Julian Alps, and advanced along the Po valley, wreaking destruction
wherever they passed. The inhabitants of the towns of the narrow plain
between the Alps and what is now the Gulf of Venice, directly in the
Lombards' path, were forced to take refuge in small settlements along
the coastline between the town of Grado and the River Adige, south of
Chioggia, which then formed one long chain of marshes, lagoons and

islands. Some sixty small islands, providing refuge from the land and, on account of the shallowness of the water, from the sea, formed the site of what became Venice.

The quality of Venice's site, and the advantages of its geographical position for trading with the plain of Lombardy, or, through the Alps via the Brenner pass, with central Europe, were clearly contributory elements to its success as a commercial centre, but they were not determining ones. Such advantages were not unique to Venice. For example the position of the port of Comacchio, on the mouth of the Po and the sea lake of Comacchio, was from some points of view even more favourable. The city's emergence to prominence has to be seen firstly as a part of a general, peninsula-wide process occurring between the seventh and tenth centuries, in which trading activities were transferred from foreign merchants – Jews, Syrians and Greeks – to Italians. Crucial in this was the survival of the Byzantine empire's presence as a coastal enclave round most of Italy through to the late eighth century – over three hundred years after the fall of Rome. Areas situated in this enclave were forced by their frontiers to draw much of their subsistence from sea trading. A commercial vocation was forced upon them. In addition, their status as Byzantine possessions entitled them to serve as border markets for the tightly controlled Byzantine trades. Trade was also developed with the interior – the Lombards needed outlets to the Adriatic and granted trading concessions to Venice and its neighbouring ports on the Adriatic. Political factors were thus catalysts to the process of commercial emancipation.

While drawing advantages from this continued link with Byzantium, these Italo-Byzantine commercial centres on the other hand suffered from few of the disadvantages which handicapped traders within the empire – there were not the same institutional controls exercised, and in addition Byzantine political control over them was too frail to stop them trading with the dynamic Islamic empire from the seventh century onwards. Their position was effectively 'interstitial' in the sense defined by Mann (see chapter 2). In southern Italy, and in ports facing the Tyrrhenian sea, trade with Islam became the main basis for expansion. In this area, too, as in the north Adriatic, small specialized shipping/trading towns, with no agricultural hinterlands, grew up, supplanting the Roman ports of Naples and Rome – in particular the towns of Gaeta and Amalfi, of which more will be said in chapter 5. Venice, however, principally because of its geographical position far closer to the Byzantine empire, played the Byzantine card, lending ships to the emperors for war, transportation and state mail. It was rewarded from an early stage for its fidelity with lower tariffs on the Dardanelles.

**Map 1** The central and eastern Mediterranean

CRETE

CRETE

Candia

RHODES

CYPRUS

ANATOLIA

BLACK SEA

Caffa

Trebizond

Adrianople

Galata

Constantinople

Nicomedia

Nicaea

Cyzicus

Thessalonica

Athos

Pergamum

Sardis

Phocaea

Demetrias

NEGROPONTE

CHIOS

Philadelphia

Priene

Corinth

Athens

Argos

Nauplion

Modon

Mistra

Coron

Antioch

Seleuceia

Jaffa

The turning-point for the town came, though, with the renewed political turbulence of the eighth and early ninth centuries. This led to the loss by the Byzantines of the majority of their remaining Italian possessions – including Comacchio and Ravenna, two of Venice's principal rivals – to the Franks and Lombards. In addition, rival commercial ports in Istria fell to Slav invaders. Venice became the strongest surviving coastal city in the area, and its position was fortified yet further by both Istrian and Dalmatian cities accepting its sovereignty in order to preserve their independence. The growth in Carolingian power could have been detrimental – Charlemagne signed a treaty with the Byzantine emperors in 813 to set up direct commercial relations between the two empires, and this could have ended Venice's entrepôt role. The treaty however remained a dead letter, and it was with Venice, finally, that the Carolingian emperor Lothar signed a treaty providing mutually favourable trading conditions. This treaty marked Venice's final achievement of primacy among the Italo-Byzantine ports. As Lopez writes, 'with the Dalmatian raw silk coming in as tribute and with state-controlled xenodochia where foreigners were admitted on the same terms as they were in the lodging-houses of the Byzantine capital, Venice was a little Constantinople in the West.'

From the ninth century then, though evidence is sparse, progress would appear to have been steady. Venice would have benefited from a recovery and expansion in the Byzantine empire during the ninth and tenth centuries. Its close connection with the empire was increasingly a privileged one with respect to the rest of Italy, bringing advantages in technical and cultural transfer. The closeness of the connection is revealed, of course, in the city's architecture, and also by the matriculations at the University of Padua which included large numbers of Greek students. The strength of the links is also illustrated by the continued use of Byzantine currency until 1284, the lack of need for a personal monetary system causing Venice to be a latecomer with respect to some financial developments. From the eleventh century the economic recovery in Europe, and the consequent expansion in international trade, stimulated growth yet further, and the balance in the relationship with Byzantium began to shift in Venice's direction. The Crusades were a further fillip, but they did not represent a turning-point for Venice as we shall see them doing for Genoa. On the contrary the favourable situation which Venice had acquired for itself in the Byzantine trade initially caused it to have some reservations about an enterprise likely to contribute to increasing European competition in the east Mediterranean.

From the twelfth century Venice emerges as one of the most powerful players in the politics of the central and eastern Mediterranean.

While this success had at its core the economic functions which the city fulfilled in terms of a well-placed international trading centre, it is evident that the extent of the city's increase in power – a graduation from a position of subservience to one of domination of the Byzantine world by 1204 – has, again, a political side. Venice was the most successful of contemporary 'interstitial powers'. Situated on the periphery of four power blocs stronger than itself – the Byzantine, Islamic and German empires and the papacy – it was able to profit from all of them, promoting persistently its principally economic interests. Diplomatic skills and political unity were basic to this success – one power was played off against another. The increasing interaction between Europe and Byzantium in the eleventh and twelfth centuries with the joint experience of the threat from Turkish expansion, the expansive commercial situation, the establishment of the Norman kingdom in south Italy and Sicily and, finally, the Crusades provided unprecedented opportunities for the use of these skills by Venice – which by now, to use W. H. McNeill's phrase, was acting as the 'hinge of Europe'. It was as a substantial power in its own right that it allied itself to Byzantium in 1080 and countered the Norman threat to Durazzo by sinking its fleet, and it is this which explains the extraordinarily generous trading terms which it was granted – it was not absent-mindedness on the Byzantine emperors' part. Further evidence of Venetian strength is provided by its participation with a fleet and 15,000 soldiers in the capture of Tyre in 1122.

A further contributory element was Venice's political stability. The city was influenced here again by the Byzantine link. Its Doge (Duke) was originally a Byzantine appointee as military governor. Strong, centralized rule was to characterize Venice both under the Doges and, later, when it became an aristocratic republic. 'The central fact', writes McNeill, 'was that Venetian military, political and economic institutions functioned better than those of any of their immediate neighbours and rivals.' One area to which this interventionist state paid particular attention was shipbuilding – it was by provision of shipping that Venice obtained its entrée into the Byzantine world, and its prominence in the Crusades, and shipping remained the key to its success. A state-run shipbuilding yard, the Arsenal, was created and became the largest manufacturing concern in Europe.

Setting the achievement of Venice in the longer-term process of economic change with which we are concerned, then, it was firstly significant in that it represented a successful transfer of the existing economic inheritance, in terms of commercial and technical skills, and a good slice of accumulated capital, to Europe from the Near East. Shipping and navigational skills were the most fundamental of these transfers, and Venice set a pattern, which was to be followed by succeeding maritime powers, in first achieving dominance in this sphere. More was involved than a pure transfer. The economic legacy which had been introduced had been blended with some of the individualistic and dynamic qualities inherent in the nascent European civilization, imparting to them an expansive quality which they had lacked in the Byzantine world. This may of course be merely a restoration of some of the qualities for commerce which characterized early Phoenician, Mycenaean and Greek traders. However, what was new was the relative solitude of Venice and the extent of the accumulation of skills and capital in a single town. This concentration, politically induced, as we have seen, does distinguish Venice from anything which had preceded it. Larger cities had existed, but not cities purely concentrating on trade, the concentration was characteristic of a commercial recovery in an environment which was predominantly hostile to commercial values.[2]

## The Broadening of the Commercial Expansion

From the twelfth century there is less justification for focusing solely on the experiences of Venice. Not only were there other participators in the east Mediterranean trades from this point – particularly Pisa and Genoa – but also commercial expansion in other parts of the Italian peninsula was gathering momentum. The core to this extension in commercial prosperity was in Lombardy. This province is unique for the Mediterranean zone in its possession of a wide strip of fertile land, with good communications and well irrigated by the River Po, in proximity to the principal trade arteries. The towns of the area benefited from this. It was principally towns on the main arteries of communication, the Po and the former Roman roads, and at the foot of the great passes through the Alps, which expanded, the beginnings of this process of urbanization being traceable to the eighth and ninth centuries. The same international politics which caused trade to be funnelled through Venice – control of the Tyrrhenian Sea by Islam and difficulties of navigation in the Adriatic – also caused a focusing of communications in the north of the Italian peninsula – the Tyrrhenian sea, for example, being barred.

By the thirteenth and fourteenth centuries a dense urban network had come into existence. The growth of the city of Milan to nearly as great a size as Venice by the end of the thirteenth century – with a population of some 75,000 against 90,000 – unusual for a commmercial centre in an interior area, is representative of the force of this growth in interior trading. The urbanization of this area reached a first peak in the second half of the twelfth century, with some thirteen cities extending their fortified perimeters to contain larger populations. The existence of such large urban centres was in itself a stimulus to secondary urban growth – the provision of the food required for these cities necessitated extensive market development. Lopez has plotted this second stage in the urban revolution, demonstrating how cities like Parma developed on the basis of local fairs, servicing the requirements of the Milan area. The whole of the area around Milan, indeed, became urbanized, linked as it was by a most advanced canal and navigable river system created in the twelfth and thirteenth centuries:[3] it possessed a complex cycle of annual fairs which served as the essential mechanism for trade. As well as providing for the requirements of travellers and pilgrims, supplying the market needs of the major cities and acting as centres for carters and carriers involved in the transalpine trades, some of these secondary centres became involved in international trade themselves. Initially it was other towns in Lombardy which graduated to this stage of development, in particular Pavia, Asti, Piacenza, Milan and Cremona. From the thirteenth century, however, the current moved across the Apennines to involve Tuscan centres including Florence, Siena, Lucca, Pistoia and even a village like San Gimignano. Florence, in particular, was in the ascendant, having inherited Pisa's maritime tradition, playing a major role in papal finance (itself a major stimulus to economic development, the Papacy being the principal contemporary multinational enterprise in Europe) and developing into Italy's principal cloth production centre in the thirteenth century. Its population was about the same as Venice's – some 90,000 – on the eve of the Black Death.

In addition to these favourable geographical and natural conditions, another factor which gave a particular dynamism to north Italian growth was the lack of open space, such as that existing in northern Europe, in which to expand. The consequence of this, as Lopez points out, was that commerce became the Italian frontier. The coincidence between a period of intense urban expansion, with towns extending their fortified perimeters, and a change in mercantile practices, consisting in Italian merchants travelling to achieve sales rather than remaining *in situ* to receive their customers, is a sign of the force of this demographic stimulus. Italian capitalism thus acquired an expansive force and served as an important instrument for technical and commercial diffusion. The diffusion was geographically very widespread and also socially mixed, involving the whole range of professions, from the distinguished wholesaler to the humblest artisans. Sailors, cobblers, shipwrights, mercenaries and pedlars travelled throughout Europe to market their products or skills.[4]

Genoa, with a population of some 80,000, was the other centre in this north Italian quadrilateral of commercial dynamism. Its trade was less focused than Venice's on the east Mediterranean, and less dependent too on privilege, politics and monopoly. The city played the principal part in the radiation of Italian dynamism to the west Mediterranean as the commercial revolution of the Middle Ages attained its peak in the thirteenth century. It had first whetted its appetite for involvement in oriental trading by military incursions in North Africa. This interest it was to sustain, attempting from the eleventh century to develop direct routes across the Sahara to obtain African gold and ivory, and trading with north Morocco and the Islamic kingdom of Granada for a range of products. Expeditions were also mounted for beyond the straits of Gibraltar and down the west coast of Africa from 1250 which reached as far as Senegal, where a colony was established, and to the Canaries. Two Genoese, the Vivaldi brothers, even set out to find a route round Africa to the east in 1291, anticipating the Portuguese voyages of discovery by over two hundred years and giving further evidence of the extraordinary expansiveness of European society at this moment.

It was the Crusades, however, which represented the turning-point in the city's destiny. Genoa, in conjunction with Pisa, had been involved in the gradual expulsion of Islam from the west Mediterranean. In 1015 and 1016 the Genoese drove the last Muslim forces from Corsica and Sardinia, and in 1088, in conjunction with the Amalfitans, they stormed and captured the town of al Maddiyah, the Arab capital in North Africa. The Crusades permitted Genoa (as well as Pisa, but Pisa's commercial career was to be cut short by Genoese and Florentine aggression in the twelfth century) to carve out a stake for itself in the east Mediterranean. Genoa's geographical position favoured it, as its westerly situation meant that it was better placed than Venice for transporting the predominantly French and English knights who set out for the Holy Land. Military and shipping support was exchanged with the military authorities for commercial advantages – for example for their support at the siege and conquest of Antioch the Genoese were rewarded with thirty houses, a bazaar and a well, and in return for a relief force of 120 ships which they sent for the besieged crusaders at Jerusalem they and the Pisans were granted an entire quarter in the port of Jaffa. Involvement in the eastern Mediterranean trades brought the profits and the status of a major international trading city to Genoa and later caused it to clash with Venice in that hundred-year war to which reference was made in chapter 1.

Genoa's mother trades were salt and grain. Built on the side of a mountain range, with minimal agricultural resources, the process of feeding its population gave rise to a network of trading links extending from Provence to Naples, Sicily, Sardinia and Aragon. Even more than for the people of the plain of Lombardy, trade was thus a frontier for the Genoese, and overwhelmingly an overseas frontier. 'So many are the Genoese – so scattered world wide – that they form other Genoas – wherever they reside', recorded a vernacular poet of the thirteenth century.[5] As the Spanish Reconquista progressed, trade along the Spanish littoral built up, especially with Valencia, Cartagena, Murcia and Alicante. The capture of Seville in 1246 was a turning-point. This city rapidly grew into a major trading centre. It and the surrounding country-side had benefited, as had much of the Spanish littoral, from the impact of centuries of Islamic advanced intensive agricultural techniques. It was thus a source for the types of luxury agricultural products in heavy demand – rice, oranges, nuts, wine, olive oil. It was like having a bit of the east Mediterranean incorporated into a west European nation. The conquest of Spain also facilitated links with Atlantic traders. Basque and Portuguese shippers grew rich in Genoese service. Traders from Bilbao, Bayonne, Bordeaux, Nantes, Southampton and Flanders met Genoese merchants at Seville or at the fairs of Medina del Campo or Zamora. Expansion also occurred beyond the straits of Gibraltar. The develop-ment of northerly trades in the Atlantic were more successful than ventures to the south. The gradual elimination of the Islamic wedge between north Europe and the Mediterranean, and the participation of areas of northern Europe in the reconquest, must have occasioned the psychological shift necessary for the development of these new sea routes. The first sea voyage was undertaken in 1277, and by the early fourteenth century there were regular annual trading convoys from both Genoa and Venice exchanging Mediterranean products – especially wine and colouring agents, alum and pastel – for, above all, wool and woollen cloth. Genoa dominated in these northern trades. Again the extent to which the city's development consisted on the one hand in filling the commercial vacuum left by the retreat of Islam, and on the other in providing new channels for interaction between northern and southern Europe is well documented.[6]

## Checks to Growth and Adaptation to Them: The 'Crisis of the Middle Ages'

This century of expansion before the Black Death represented, as Robert Lopez writes, the 'high tide of four centuries of accelerated commercial growth', as long a period of unchecked expansion as the

European economy has yet to experience. The Black Death was to hit Italy as harshly as anywhere else. More harshly in fact, because it affected urbanized areas such as north Italy most. Population levels slumped – that of Florence was more than halved – from the figure of 110,000 in 1338 to between 45,000 and 50,000 in 1351. Rural areas lost people to the plague, and then more people to the towns. The population of the region round Pistoia fell to a mere third of its pre-plague levels. Historians, though, now debate whether the turning-point in Europe's destinies can be attributed merely to the plague – the dynamism had gone before the plague occurred, population ceilings had been reached[7] and that expansiveness which had characterized Europe had already been lost – with setbacks in the east Mediterranean (the restoration of the Byzantine emperors), an end to the extension of frontiers in eastern Europe as well as in the west (the colonization of Ireland for example being put on hold) and in the south – a full two hundred years separates the capture of Seville from that of Granada.[8]

Knock-on effects from events in the neighbouring Islamic civilization were a major cause of difficulties. The thirteenth-century Mongol invasions, which were devestating to Muslim civilization, had brought unprecedented benefits to western traders. The range of the Mongol empire, from China to Hungary, had created easier communications for spices and valuable textiles by a more northerly route, straight across central Asia to the Caspian and Black Seas. Italian traders, and particularly the Genoese who had gained trading privileges from the restored Byzantine Palaeologi dynasty in 1261, had benefited most from this displacement of the Muslim intermediary and the resultant more regular flow of products. The Black Sea had become effectively a Genoese lake, with the foundation of new trading centres, and Italian traders also established themselves in the Mongol capital of Tarbuz. In these circumstances the break-up of the Mongol empire had adverse effects on Italian trade, cutting off these exceptional trade routes and giving rise to a less hospitable attitude on the part of Mongols – for instance in 1339 European traders were massacred in Almaligh, the capital of Turkestan. To these Mongol threats were added those from the Ottoman Turks with the expansion of their empire: the spice trade once again became irregular, and prices rose as its principal axis shifted back to the Red Sea/Egypt route. Political events within Europe also deflated business confidence – the Hundred Years War damaged cross-European trades, the fairs of Champagne declining – and the similarly prolonged war between Venice and Genoa caused major destruction to European shipping, capital and human resources in the Mediterranean.

There is no question that the Italian economy suffered from these various checks. Lopez puts it best: 'The truth of the matter is that while reacting vigorously against continuing adversity the commercial Revolution wore its impetus out ... the buoyancy of the age of open opportunities fell flat, social mobility waned, and conservation became a more desirable and attainable goal than growth.'[9] However, Italy fared better than northern Europe, and consequently the Italian dominance of the European economy was conserved, even though it was no longer a dominance capable of exercising the spread effects that had been characteristic of the twelfth and thirteenth centuries. The reasons for this greater resilience were various. Firstly, the impact of population collapse on the ratio of land to people had resulted in rising real incomes and hence a growing demand for luxury goods. This shift favoured the greatest provider of luxury goods in Europe – Italy. As H. A. Miskimin shows, the scarce bullion supplies of northern Europe were channelled south regularly to pay for luxury imports, rising demand for which may also have been contributed to by other factors, such as the omnipresence of death giving rise to a 'consume-now' mentality. Secondly, the very factor which had stimulated the commercial diffusion from Italy, the highly urbanized nature of Lombardy and Tuscany and the need to export in order to finance food imports, meant that, despite the population decline following the Black Death, there was sufficient local demand for food to prevent any disconnection developing between urban and rural areas. There were also creative responses to the new situation. A trend towards extending manufacturing in the peninsula, which had begun during the period of expansion – Florence, we noted, had emerged as a cloth-manufacturing centre and developed into one of the largest in Europe, with a production of 80,000 pieces in 1380 – was sustained for the woollen industry, but decisively improved upon with respect to two previously imported products from the south and the east: silk production, which had entered Italy via Sicily, expanded, first at Lucca and then at Genoa and Milan, and that of cottons and fustians developed first at Genoa and then over the Ligurian highlands at Cremona.[10] In addition, in the eastern Mediterranean the drying-up of possibilities in the spice trades was met by the development of new commercial routes – in particular via the town of Caffa on the Crimea in the Black Sea to south-east Europe, making possible trade with the Tatars, Russians, Poles, Romanians, Bulgarians, Armenians, Greeks and Turks. Caffa grew to become larger than its Italian mother cities with a population of 100,000. Areas of the Black Sea and Aegean were increasingly used as a source for industrial raw materials and foodstuffs as much as for exotic products. In Greece, the Venetians developed exports in wine, raisins and cotton, and in

Cyprus and Crete sugar plantations and wine production, but it was the Genoese above all, less committed as they were to the spice trade, who made most progress in this area – they traded with the new Turkish empire, developed a big import trade in grain, silk and other commodities from the Black Sea and, in particular, made the isle of Chios a commercial and industrial centre of vast importance – a source above all for alum, but also for a range of other products. Concluding on these various developments, Jacques Heers writes of 'Caffa and its trading posts' as 'the first solution for the easy supplying, by the shipload, of towns of the inland sea, with products from the north' and of Chios representing 'The archetype of the Mediterranean island exploited for international trade'.[11]

These last developments show that the Italian city-states were still able to take advantage of their position as interstitial powers to profit from the empires on their doorsteps. The crumbling Byzantine empire retained resources for exploitation, and Venice between 1388 and 1423 added Argos, Nauplion, Corinth and Thessalonica to its territorial possessions in the area – and benefits could be drawn from both Mongols and Turks. The logistics of warfare and statecraft were still favourable, it seemed, to the city-state, and indeed during these years Venice, Milan, Florence and Genoa added territorial ambitions to their trading priorities, Venice between 1405 and 1427 becoming for the first time a mainland state, occupying Padua, Verona, Brescia and Bergamo. The position of Venice, in particular, was consolidated following its final defeat of Genoa in the War of Chioggia in 1381: it used its now considerable political power to impose its commercial dominance in the east Mediterranean, making use of the fleet system to protect its cargoes and establishing a chain of fortified colonies all along the route to the east. As Luzzatto points out, however, these political changes implied a major shift in the relationship between the major commercial centres of the peninsula and their hinterlands. From being animating centres for market development, and diffusers of economic growth, a process was starting which was to be characterized by their exploiting, and living off, their neighbourhoods. Secondary commercial centres, such as Verona and Padua in the Venetian region, came to lose population to the metropolis. In southern Italy, Luzzatto writes, 'Naples and Palermo absorbed the life of two entire regions.'[12]

## The First Shift to an Atlantic-Dominated Europe

In 1453 the Turks conquered Constantinople. This was also the year in which the Hundred Years War came to an end. The Turkish conquest of

Constantinople was to close the east Mediterranean to Italian shipping. Towns like Caffa had to adapt to trading in a Turkish-dominated world, the growing Turkish capital of Istanbul (as Constantinople was later renamed) absorbing its food surpluses. There was a steady recession of the Italian position in the Aegean and east Mediterranean generally. For Genoa, the fall of Phocaea to the Turks – its principal source of alum – was a particularly heavy blow, depriving the island of Chios of its principal trade: 'The crisis of alum shattered the rhythm and structure of Genoese trade in the East Mediterranean', Heers writes; '1460 [the date when Chian alum supplies dried up] is a key date in the commercial history of the Levant.' Once again the Mediterranean was broken in two (the first division being that occasioned by the expansion of Islam in the seventh century), though the division now was east/west as well as south/north, Italy itself becoming a frontier. With the Ottoman advance, Europe found itself confined to almost as small a place as it had occupied at the height of the original Arab expansion.

The coincidence of the Ottoman conquest and end of the Hundred Years War adds a second dimension to the shifts that were occurring. The balance of power was now to shift decisively towards larger political units – the Ottoman empire, England and France. In addition, via a succession of dynastic marriages between the 1450s and the end of the century, the Habsburg family was assembling the basis of an empire including the Low Countries, Burgundy, Austria, Spain, Naples, Hungary, Moravia, Silesia and parts of north Italy. Imperial expansion, assisted by technological progress in the arts of war – the development of gunpowder – was to leave little space for 'interstitial' powers in the sixteenth century.

The rupture accelerated those developments which had been taking shape in the western Mediterranean since the late thirteenth century. The changing distribution of Genoa's investments and trading patterns provides the best register of the shift. Genoa, throughout a follower commercial centre with respect to Venice, and never so dependent on privilege for its situation, as we have noted, had been forced by its need to survive to be flexible – 'Genoa, exclusively mercantile, had to give higher priority to resolving these difficulties very quickly, had to be more audacious', Heers writes. Now excluded from the east Mediterranean, the efforts which had previously been applied throughout the sea were concentrated purely on its western half. New supplies of alum were discovered in Rome. Majorca, ideally situated half way between Spain and Africa and directly on the Genoese route to the straits of Gibraltar, became a trade emporium to rival Chios, and alternative sites to those of the east Mediterranean for cotton, sugar and wine were discovered, first in Andalusia and later in the Atlantic islands. Sugar cultivation thus continued the itinerary which had taken it across the Mediterranean, from Palestine, through Cyprus, Crete, Sicily, Morocco and southern Spain into the Atlantic, first to the Algarve and then to the islands of the east Atlantic.[13]

This shift westwards in the centre of gravity of the European economy, however, cannot be understood purely in terms of problems (the fall of Constantinople), and stimuli (Genoese investment) from the east. These factors met with expansive pressures being generated in the Iberian peninsula and the Atlantic. It was Catalonia and the crown of Aragon, with the early completion of their reconquests, which had been the most dynamic states in this area. Now it was the turn of Portugal and Castile. Castile, as we have noted, had been a site of Genoese investment since the thirteenth century and earlier, and had developed a substantial and valuable wool trade. However it was the contribution of Portugal which was to be the more innovative of the two. Its reconquest had been completed earlier, in 1253, and, in the period of demographic recovery after the Black Death, it had followed this with the conquest of Ceuta in North Africa, and then made steady progress following exploration down the west coast of Africa. Essential to the progress was the strength of the Portuguese monarchy, which provided leadership and resources (Henry the Navigator, the fifth son of King John I, who set up his home in Sagres near Cape St Vincent, surrounded by cartographers and navigators, to direct the efforts at exploration is the outstanding example of this royal involvement). Additional contributors to the expansion were the continued crusading drive of the Reconquista – Christianity was to be a principal export to the east – and exceptional navigational and shipbuilding skills, to the formation of which the challenge to mariners posed by Portugal's long Atlantic seaboard and large river estuaries had contributed. Finally Portugal's poverty ensured, despite its small population, a constant stream of migrants to man its ships and populate its settlements. The isle of Madeira was occupied in 1420, the Azores rediscovered in 1430, the Cape Verde islands in 1455, the islands of Fernando Po and São Tomé in 1471, and the River Congo reached by 1482. The pattern was for initial royal reconnoitring in solitary ships, to be followed by large-scale exploitation of the trades by merchants as the possibility of leapfrogging what had previously been trans-Saharan trades emerged – those in ivory, gold, pepper and slaves were the most important. Finally in 1488 Bartholomew Diaz returned to Lisbon to announce the discovery of the Cape of Good Hope. The route to India was open. A decade later Vasco da Gama sailed with a fleet of four ships to exploit the new opportunity. Continents had now been leapfrogged, undoing an economic geography of the Euro/Asian/African zone which had prevailed since history began.[14]

Columbus's discovery of America had of course come five years earlier, but its economic impact on the European economy as a whole was initially small – the years immediately following it were occupied in the establishment of settlements and conquest, and it was not until the 1550s that silver began to flow in abundance. It was not a trade-induced empire like Portugal's, even though its existence did give rise to far greater demand on shipping and labour than the small-scale, value-intensive Portuguese trades.[15] In contrast, the Portuguese development of the sea route to the east made an immediate impact. Within two years of his departure Vasco da Gama's small fleet returned to Lisbon loaded with spices. What had been a slow shift in the centre of gravity of the European economy in the direction of the Atlantic now threatened to become a revolution. The changes involved, it should be added, were by no means purely geographic. The fact that it was Portugal which had discovered the route, and the extensive property rights which consequently it was granted in 1493 by the Papacy over a large share of the non-European world (confirmed by the Treaty of Tordesillas with Spain a year later), meant that the exploitation of the resources of the east would be carried out on its terms. Genoese capital had participated in the commercial expansion, and would continue to, but it had to do so within a commercial framework in considerable part modelled by Portugal. We thus encounter what was to be a distinctive feature of capitalist development during the next century and a half or so – a partnership, a very uncomfortable one as it was to turn out, between established commercial powers and strong but firmly traditional political regimes.

The 'framework' into which the new Lisbon/East Indies trades were fitted was that which Portugal had been developing over the course of the previous hundred years and more as it pushed its commercial interests to the south, down the African coast. If Genoese capital had been involved in this, so too had Flemish, and in particular strong links had been established with Bruges and Antwerp, which were markets and distribution centres for African products and also suppliers of cloth and of other needed industrial products. It was also a meeting point with important currents of trade from England – the English 'Merchant Adventurers' commercialized their cloth in Flanders – and also from southern Germany, which was an important mining area, providing a range of metals – iron, copper and silver required for trading in Africa and, later, in the east. From 1488 the trade had been principally with Antwerp rather than Bruges, the principal entrepôt in the area. The change was a consequence of politics. The inheritance of Flanders by the Duke of Burgundy had been followed by the resistance of Flemish commercial centres and, consequent upon this, Brabantine Antwerp was given particularly advantageous trading privileges in this year, drawing to it the bulk of the English and German trades. It was this which caused Portugal to grant the town the spices staple in 1499, and this finally made the fortune of the town.

The strength of the south German participation in the Portuguese 'framework' requires some added comment for little has been said up to this point of what were in fact very important developments in this area. A range of commercial centres in these regions – Ulm, Basle, Augsburg, Zürich, St Gallen, Geneva and, above all, Nuremberg – emerged during the late fourteenth century and even more during the fifteenth, to play a central role both in commerce and manufacturing. The explanation for this lies on the one hand in the warfare which was afflicting competing industrial and commercial centres south of the Alps and west of the Rhine – the best trade route between the Mediterranean and north Europe shifted to the east side of the Alps – and on the other hand the spread of Europe's commercial revolution to the east, to include Poland, Hungary and Bohemia – this placed southern Germany on the edge of an expanding frontier. The extensive mineral resources – silver and iron – of the area were a further strength, particularly in view of the exclusion of Europe from the mineral resources of the east Mediterranean. Closeness to Italian sources of technology and know-how, and to Italian commercial outlets, was a further advantage. By the mid-fifteenth century, as Lopez notes, 'Nuremberg had become the central hub of a network of overland communications between eastern Central Europe and the Rhineland and between the Mediterranean and the northern seas.' The development of the area was thus a sign of the broadening of the process of economic change in Europe during the fifteenth and sixteenth centuries, and of a northern technical diffusion from Italy, as well as the western one on which we have been commenting. It was to give rise, as we have just seen, to important, lateral, east–west trade movements in Europe complementing the previously dominant north–south ones.

The first cargoes of spices reached Antwerp in 1501. The link was then institutionalized, a Feitoria de Flandres being founded in 1508 as a subsidiary to the Lisbon Casa de India. The town's star rose all the more rapidly with the accession of Charles V to the throne of Burgundy in 1515, which was followed a year later by his inheritance of the throne of Spain. The Low Countries and Spain found themselves consequently within the same empire, and Charles's policy was to maximize their commercial and financial integration. As Charles's needs for commercial and financial services were even greater than those of Portugal – with the undertaking of the vast enterprise of colonizing the New World and his heavy involvement in Europe-wide political conflicts (Charles, further to his inheritance of the Spanish and Burgundian crowns, was elected Holy Roman Emperor in 1519) – the business attracted to Antwerp was to convert it soon into a boom town, and it doubled in size between 1500 and 1550 to attain a population of 100,000, something unprecedented in northern Europe. Bruges had been an important centre, but had served only local North Sea and inland Flemish commercial and industrial needs. Antwerp was a new Venice on the North Sea, a bigger Venice in that for a while it serviced the transaction requirements of the Mediterranean as well as the burgeoning Atlantic economy.

Antwerp's experiences thus serve as one of the best registers for charting the increasingly complex process of economic change during much of the sixteenth century. There were three phases in the city's growth, as Braudel has demonstrated. The first was the expansion engendered by the stimulated Portuguese link. The arrival of the Portuguese spices, in addition to the troubles in the Mediterranean, caused the rich traders of south Germany to switch the bulk of their mineral sales from Venice to Antwerp. Similarly Antwerp's links with the Baltic and with English cloth exporters were stimulated. In 1502–3 only 24 per cent of Hungarian copper exported by the Fuggers went to Antwerp; by 1508–9 the figure was up to 49 per cent, and Venice's reduced to 13. In addition, the Germans channelled their silver to Antwerp – essential for payment for the spices in the Far East – and it has been estimated that in 1508 60,000 marks of silver were in transit for Lisbon. German merchants – the Imhofs, the Welsers, the Fuggers of Augsburg, the Schetz of Aachen – were thus at the heart of Antwerp's boom, participating in the capital-intensive redistribution of spices to European markets as well as providing silver. High rates of capital accumulation were achieved. From 1523 there was a check in the rate of expansion. Various factors explained this. The Valois/Habsburg wars paralysed international trade, and this had a major impact on southern Germany; there had been a gradual revival in Venice's spice trade, and Lisbon itself had assumed responsibility for distributing some of its spices, sending quantitities to Seville, whence, too, it began to draw part of its silver requirements. The Portuguese links and profits were, however, by no means cut off completely – 328 Portuguese ships anchored at Antwerp in 1539 and 1540 – and, in view of this, the increasing impact on the city of Spain's growing needs for its services caused it to enter its golden age from the mid-1530s to the 1550s.

What precisely did the Spaniards require from Antwerp? An important item was manufactured products for the internal market and for export – more than 50,000 pieces of cloth were purchased in Antwerp in 1553 – and in addition bulk products, including grain. They also needed agents for the commercializing of their own exports – wool, in great quantity, iron from the Basque country, dyestuffs, above all cochineal and indigo from the Americas, and also other Mediterranean and Atlantic island products such as sugar, wine and currants. Where else should they take products other than to the Low Countries, now part of their empire? Finally and crucially, Spain's rulers required finance: vast military expenditure was to make indebtedness a permanent condition for the Spanish Habsburgs, and it was this which provided most stimulus to the city, attracting Europe's major financiers to it. They needed regular and very large advances on their tax returns and in anticipation of their silver imports from the New World. The very fact of the ending of the pepper boom facilitated the growing dependence on Antwerp as the German speculators in pepper switched to lending money to both competing parties in the wars of northern Italy, Antwerp remaining a centre for their enterprises. It was thus in Antwerp that Charles V found financial houses with the stature both to provide him with credit and to act as intermediaries for moving funds throughout Europe.The crisis which brought this boom to an end is also instructive. In 1557 the Spanish crown went bankrupt. This bankruptcy affected the whole space of the Habsburg monarchy and destroyed the fortunes of the German bankers on whom Spain had been depending. It was followed by the bankruptcy of the banks of Lyon, on which the Valois had been depending. From this point to the early seventeenth century, it was on Genoese finance that the Habsburgs were forced to rely. There was thus a shift back to the Mediterranean in this respect.

The trade of Antwerp was not destroyed by this episode. After the Treaty of Cateau Cambrésis, which brought the Habsburg–Valois conflict to an end, although there was no return to the role of financial capital, Antwerp resumed its position as entrepôt for the Spanish, Italian, Baltic, French and American trades. Its position, though, was increasingly insecure. From 1568 the English moved their cloth business to Hamburg following the outbreak of war with Spain, and during the 1560s the growing religious tensions in the region led to insecurity on the sea routes to Spain. This situation was only to grow worse in the years to come as the religious conflicts became more severe: in 1568 the Netherlands revolt against Spain began and this, the sacking of Antwerp by Spanish troops in 1576, and finally the blockading of the Scheldt, Antwerp's outlet to the North Sea, by the Dutch from 1585, occasioned the wilting and then the final demise of Antwerp as a centre for international trade. The triumph of the Atlantic in the European economy, which had appeared assured, was placed in doubt as Philip II prioritized the southern half of his empire in his plans.[16]

## Dutch World-Economy versus Habsburg World Empire

The combination of the interruptions to the strong links between Flanders and Iberia which had characterized the first three-quarters of the sixteenth century, with the stimuli now given to the Mediterranean zone by Philip II's making Genoa his principal financial centre, contributed to an Indian summer for the Mediterranean economy. Further stimuli were the rapid progress in the Seville trade, the channelling of all Habsburg military endeavours through Barcelona, Lombardy and, from there, over the Alps via the St Bernard pass – the so-called Spanish Road – and finally the merging of the Portuguese and Spanish crowns in 1580, permitting a greater interaction between the Iberian East Indian and American trades and the Spanish and Portuguese economies. Our story has been marked by the impact of Europe's major cities. The new, and dominating cities of these years, and thus effectively Europe's frontiers for the moment, were Seville, Lisbon, Madrid and the silver-mining centre in Peru, Potosí, all of which grew rapidly to close to, or above, 100,000 inhabitants. Rather than rivalry between the new trade routes and the old, there was now a politically based collaboration, with Philip II using Venice for a while as the main distribution centre for the spices arriving via Lisbon and looking to Italy for the servicing of his loans. The Spanish crown's need for finance was complementary to the search by Italian investors for safe and prestigious (in that they involved no labour) placements for the capital accumulated over centuries. Italy buzzed with prosperity. 'What shall we say of the State of Milan?' it was asked. 'Is there a duchy more abundant in victuals, grain, rice, livestock, cheeses, wines, and flax, more replete with artificers and traffic, more densely populated, or more conveniently located?' Similarly Venice abounded 'in all things which the fertility of the land, the industry of man, and a suitable location usually bestow on a well-regulated commonwealth . . . Trade flowed into the city from all parts, so much so in fact . . . that she was deemed possibly greater at that time than she had ever been in days past'; for Genoa, it was the city's moment of international leadership: Braudel, quoting the Spanish historian Ruiz Martín, writes of the years 1557–1627 as the 'century of the Genoese'.[17]

It was a sharp reversal for all the trends had been flowing in the opposite direction – it was north-western Europe which had been making the running in the new oceanic trades, the Dutch, English and Baltic trades which had been in expansion, trans-European links had been gaining at the expense of south–north transactions, Atlantic shipping profiting at the expense of Mediterranean, and north European cloth gaining at the expense of Mediterranean producers. The change had been brought about principally by political factors – Spanish power, Spanish silver, Spanish military expenditure, Spain's European empire. Effectively what was occurring was a conflict between those opposing principles for economic, social and political organization discussed in the last chapter – a 'world empire' was confronting a 'world-economy' whose centres had been shifting towards north-western Europe. Empires of the Habsburg type were, we have argued, strangers to a European tradition characterized by political pluralism and the operation of a powerful 'world-economy'. It was in this period, however, that one came closest to being established. The defeat of this effort thus represents a crucial event in European history, confirming that tradition of world-economy and political pluralism. It was the Dutch who emerged as the champions of the latter principle, and it is to their success that we must now turn.[18]

The Dutch Republic consisted in what is now the Netherlands, a minority slice of the Spanish Low Countries (seven out of seventeen provinces) which, in 1576, eight years after the beginning of the general revolt of the area against Spain, seceded from the Spanish empire to form the 'United Provinces', later also known as the Dutch Republic. During the war which followed the revolt, the area was to achieve an economic predominance not only over Europe but over the world-economy which was quite unprecedented and possibly has not been repeated since. More than a repetition of the previous successes of great trading entrepôts was involved. Jonathan Israel, the principal historian of these developments, has argued, we have seen, that with the Dutch success the 'poly-nuclear' economy of medieval Europe gave way to a 'mono-nuclear' one in which the province of Holland achieved an 'astounding ascendancy . . . over world commerce, shipping and finance', one which lasted from the 1590s to the first decades of the eighteenth century.[19]

In fact, though, the parallels with Venice are almost eerily close. Amsterdam and Venice, two ports, face each other over what is virtually the closest point between the Atlantic and Mediterranean. In both cases they are artificial cities, created in swampy areas and dependent on canals – situations from which they drew both commercial and defensive advantages. In both cases their 'mother trade' was the refining and commercialization of salt – a condiment as crucial to Europe's development as its more exotic companion, pepper. In both cases they were 'interstitial' powers whose progressions were dependent on a relationship with an imperial power – Byzantium and Spain.

It is this interstitiality which represents the key to the Dutch success. Braudel in fact suspected this, we have seen.[20] Firstly, the whole area of the Low Countries benefited from the dynastic accidents which led to its becoming part of the Habsburg empire during the sixteenth century. A strong complementarity resulted with Spain from which it stood to benefit – manufacturing, banking and wholesale trading in and around Antwerp and the Dutch bulk trades, and particularly salt and shipping, all progressed. Secondly, as a consequence of the rebellion all these dynamic sectors came to be concentrated in the narrow space of the Dutch Republic. The story is a familiar one. With the Netherlands uprising against Spain, the warfare, and religious intolerance in the region led to a gradual migration of humans and capital away from Flanders and Brabant, where they were chiefly concentrated, principally to the northern provinces. With the Spanish campaign of 1584, which saw the fall of Flanders and Brabant and then that of Antwerp, the trickle became a flood. Antwerp's fall was followed by the blockading of the Scheldt and, as important, that of the entire Flemish coastline as far south as Dunkirk, by the Dutch. Some 100,000 skilled workers moved north to the Dutch Republic. Merchants were initially more hesitant, their resources enabling them to be more selective, and the future of the Republic initially looked no more promising than that of the southern provinces. By the late 1580s, however, it had emerged that the Dutch Republic had a resilience and political strength which had not been anticipated. It was showing itself capable of surviving as a tough, cohesive, independent state – and this, and a political event, Philip II's switching in 1590 of his armies from the Low Countries to France because of the accession of the Protestant Henri IV, caused the commercial elite of Antwerp and its surrounding area to opt for the Dutch Republic too. There was a massive transfer to Amsterdam – a city which during these years (1567–1622) mushroomed from containing 30,000 to over 100,000 inhabitants.[21]

The distinctiveness of Israel's interpretation, we have seen, lies in the importance which he attaches to the transfer of the 'rich trades' – that is the spice trade and those in luxury manufactures, colonial commodities and expensive raw materials – to the northern provinces. In contrast to previous interpretations which have stressed the centrality of the Baltic bulk trades to the Dutch achievement, he argues that it was the acquisition of these which provided the key to the Dutch global success as well as contributing most to capital accumulation. Both types of success, however, can be related to the interstitial Dutch relationship to the Iberian peninsula and Habsburg empire.

The achievement has two principal causes: the degree of destruction which the wars of the period wreaked on other commercial centres, and the intrinsic characteristics of Dutch internal development which gave a particular dynamism to its expansion. The first point is emphasized by Wallerstein: 'Nor had Spain declined alone', he writes, 'She had brought down in her wake all those parts of Europe that had been linked to her ascension: northern Italy, southern Germany, Antwerp, Cracow, Portugal.'[22] The near-success of Habsburg political ambitions had led to the destruction of centuries of commercial accumulation, and accentuated thereby the degree of economic concentration in the Dutch Republic.

The internal developments which complemented the international trends favouring the Dutch were various. Firstly, and crucially, as we have just seen, the Dutch Republic showed a political drive which enabled it to resist the Spanish and also to provide the type of backing which a global trading empire required. The importance of such political power was shown in the Portuguese and Spanish cases. As in theirs, the forcing-ground for Dutch nationalism lay in the initial struggle to achieve political independence. The strength had deep roots, in that the Dutch political system represented not only the cities but outlying suburban and rural areas as well. The Dutch Republic had a popular base, which gave it a particular resilience: power had been transferred to the state, but not to the extent that the autonomy of locality and region were threatened. 'The bourgeoisie of Holland', writes J. W. Smit, 'had carried through exactly the degree of reform it needed to promote economic expansion and yet feel free from over-centralization.' Secondly, these qualities of co-operation also came to characterize Dutch business organization. The original Dutch capitalism in the Baltic bulk trades was characterized by small investments by exceptionally large numbers of investors. The result was a collaborative, risk-sharing approach. Similar qualities went into the later joint stock companies which were set up to operate Dutch overseas trade – for example the Dutch East India Company of 1602. There were many investors, and in addition the democratic nature of Dutch society facilitated the collaboration between such organizations and the government.[23]

The cohesion of the Dutch nation was increased in that there was no sharp barrier between agriculture and industry. On the contrary, the drawing of most of its grain requirements from Baltic surpluses made it possible for Dutch farmers to specialize to an exceptional degree in the production of livestock, vegetables and industrial raw materials.

This increased economic interaction, and the possibility of drawing their subsistence from elsewhere, released labour for the industrial and commercial sectors. Labour shortage was a problem, however. Wages were higher than in Flanders, for example. This, and fuel shortage – there was peat but no coal and little prospect for hydraulic power – led to another distinctive characteristic of the Dutch economy, its innovativeness. From the development of the *fluitschip* (large, serial-production cargo ships requiring only small crews) to the massive use of windmills to provide industrial power, and of canals for transport, the Dutch mastered and elaborated on the European technological inheritance which had been passed to them with the immigration of Flemish skilled workers. It was perhaps the extent of economic concentration in the area which was a principal cause for these achievements. Similar explanations would apply for another area of creativity – in the financial and commercial spheres. The Dutch perfected the skills – in terms of maintaining stocks, providing information services, establishing credit institutions, insurance, futures markets – which lay behind the operation of a successful entrepôt. A result of this efficiency was that interest rates in the Republic were a half or less than anywhere else in Europe, giving Dutch traders an enormous advantage.[24]

It was a curious 'interstitial' relation which the Dutch sustained with the Spanish empire during these years, and the parallels with the Venetian/Byzantine experience in part break down. Theirs was not a case of a primitive trading centre single-mindedly preying on a civilized but decadent empire. On the contrary, it was one of a trading centre containing a concentration of all that was progressive in the European economy, and increasingly in European culture – the Dutch Republic became an area of refuge for the persecuted throughout Europe – fighting for survival against, but also continuing to gain economic advantages from, a dynastic empire which showed an unhappy characteristic of wreaking destruction wherever it operated. For the eighty years of the conflict Spain played a cat-and-mouse game with the rebellious state. Warfare was interspersed with periods of peace, notably the long truce between 1609 and 1621. These switches were themselves catalytic to Dutch development. They occasioned disruption, but they also enforced experiment in new trades, the opening of new markets. It was thus Philip II's trade embargo of 1598, which restricted the principal trade with Spain, which gave rise to the first, major Dutch East Indian voyages. Similarly it was the renewed warfare between 1621 and 1647 which, by increasing the difficulty the Dutch had in financing their East Indian trade (lack, for example, of Spanish bullion), stimulated the innovatory Dutch development of a trading network between Asian areas. It was also the preliminary for the foundation of a Dutch West Indian company which proceeded to occupy part of Brazil, taking from the Portuguese the major portion of their slave and sugar trades. A further political measure also had important consequences for the Dutch: intolerance in the Iberian peninsula, combined with the embargoes on Dutch trade, caused a crucial emigration of New Christian merchants to Amsterdam, bringing with them the resources, know-how and trading networks necessary for their trades to be run from there.[25]

## A Spatial Interpretation of European History

The study of Europe's 'rise' thus serves firstly to confirm the points made in the previous chapters about the 'continuity' in the history of the European zone of a gradual process of expansion, as techniques and commercial values were extended from places of origin in the east Mediterranean to the west and north. Such a process was bound to give rise to shifts in the location of Europe's economic centres and consequent structural problems.

The description just provided, though, will also have served to demonstrate that, although such a 'dialectic of diffusion' underpins European history, the process of economic change can by no means purely be depicted in such economic terms. In particular, it has emerged that privilege and political decisions and actions underlay the gains of successive economic centres, and that, with the shift of the core of the European economy from the Mediterranean to the Atlantic, economic life, which had been the affair of small, fairly autonomous interstitial states, became allied to larger and more powerful political units. The link was to prove a virtually incompatible one in the case of the Iberian powers, but was more successfully managed by the Dutch Republic, and was to be managed best of all in Britain. The implications of these differering politico-economic interactions for the character of economic development has now been touched upon; their implications for the character of decline in different parts of Europe should emerge in later chapters.

# 4

# Byzantium: Declines in the Transition from Antiquity to the Middle Ages

A revolution which will ever be remembered, and is still felt by nations of the earth.

The fate of the Greek empire has been compared to that of the Rhine, which loses itself in the sands, before its waters can mingle with the ocean.

Edward Gibbon, *The History of the Decline and Fall of the Roman Empire*,
on the declines of Rome and Byzantium

The source of what was to be a long-enduring entity, the Byzantine empire – it was to outlive the Roman empire by over a 1,000 years,[1] thus enlarging the Roman imperial span to some two millennia – was a decision taken by emperor Diocletian in AD 285 to split the empire into western and eastern sections in order to ease administration and defence. A further measure of Emperor Constantine in 330 made the small city of Byzantium, later known as Constantinople, into the eastern empire's capital. By this decision it was raised to equal status with Rome and consequently, with the deposition of the last emperor in the west in 476, it was to it that sovereignty passed.

This long life of the Byzantine empire, and its consequent participation in all phases of Mediterranean history from the decline of Rome to the late Middle Ages, in combination with the succession of political events which altered at various points the empire's extent and geographical situation, have resulted in considerable difficulty in conceptualizing its history in terms of progress and decline. The consequence has been a sustained controversy among Byzantinists about the question which concerns us. In this chapter, after a brief introduction concerning the various shifts in the dimensions of the 'world-economy' of which Byzantium formed part, I shall be summarizing the different viewpoints expressed in this controversy as a preliminary to an assessment of the character of Byzantine decline. This approach will involve a certain amount of repetition as we shall be reviewing different historians' interpretations of the same process. I make a plea for patience on the reader's part: the repetition will assist in communicating and consolidating a sense of the shape of Byzantine history, and the variety of conceptual approaches which I shall document should contribute ultimately to clarifying definitions of decline. However if the reader is already informed about Byzantine history, or finds the report on the controversy too heavy going, he can proceed straight to my conclusions on p. 88.

## Changes in the Shape of the Medieval European World-Economy

Following the fall of Rome, the attempts by 'barbarian' states to adhere to Roman policies, and the successes of Justinian in the first half of the sixth century in reconquering much of Italy, North Africa, parts of Spain, Corsica, Sardinia and the Balearic islands, as well as attaining recognition of his sovereignty from the kings of Gaul, resulted in a considerable degree of continuity with respect to the space with which we are concerned. The eastern empire succeeded in regaining control of the Mediterranean, which could thus continue to operate as a single unit, albeit at a less than optimal level. However, with the extraordinary expansion of Islam from the 630s, this continuity with the Roman period, and thus in the shape of our world economy, was interrupted. 'In those years', writes R. I. Moore, 'the ancient world gave way to the modern' and 'the Mediterranean basin, upon whose commercial and cultural unity classical civilization had been built, was divided for ever.'[2]

A further major development altering the political and economic geography of the Mediterranean was the Slav–Avar invasions which swept through the whole of the Balkan peninsula between 580 and 600. As Perry Anderson writes, 'the loss of Illyricum to Slav migration and settlement cut the historic overland linkage of the Roman imperial world; no single event was to be so decisive for the rupture of unity between Eastern and Western Europe in the Dark Ages.'[3] In the face of these seismic fractures, the eastern Roman empire, from being the core of a Mediterranean-wide trading system, became an isolated Christian outpost, surrounded by Islam and with its communications to the west, south and east severely restricted. Isolation intensified in the centuries which followed, Crete, the key to the Aegean, being captured by the Arabs in 826 and remaining in Islamic hands until 961. This situation was not to be markedly changed until the eleventh century, when the repulse of Islam, in the west Mediterranean, Sicily and southern Italy and the Holy Land with the Crusades began a new phase in history characterized by an enlarging 'European' world-economy, embracing, true, only the northern half of the Mediterranean initially but incorporating, for the first time, areas to the east and north of the Rivers Rhine and Danube, and benefiting from a far intenser trans-European interaction with the Atlantic. Byzantium was thus involved again in a large trading area. The empire itself, it should be added, experienced territorial changes which brought its centre of gravity closer to Europe: while it lost the central plateau of Anatolia to the Seljuk Turks, it gained the inner Balkans in 1018, Crete in 961 and Cyprus in 965.

This reshaped 'European' world economy provided, with minor changes, the context within which the Byzantine empire operated during the last 400 years of its existence. The changes consisted firstly in an extension of the economy's frontiers to the east as a consequence of the Mongol expansion in the thirteenth century, which opened a direct continental route to China via the Black Sea, and secondly in a reverse contraction of these frontiers with the beginning of the disintegration of the Mongol empire from the 1330s, and consequent restrictions on western trading in the Black Sea on the one hand, and on the other the concurrent expansion of the Osmanli Turks through Anatolia, which was to culminate with the fall of Constantinople in 1453.

## Traditional and Revisionist Views on Byzantine Decline

Turning now to the differing interpretations of Byzantinists with respect to the categorizing of the stages of Byzantine history in terms of progress and decline, I shall first summarize the traditional viewpoint and then confront this with revisionist views which have been developed over the last thirty years or so. For this traditional interpretation I shall start with the classic work of Charles Diehl, *Byzantium: Greatness and Decline*, which tells the story in terms of personalities, and follow with more recent literature which puts more emphasis on economic and social matters.

Diehl's account is marked by a strong identification with the autonomous Byzantine state which emerged following the decline of Rome and the expansion of Islam. He traces the origins of such a distinct entity back to the period before the fall of Rome – already then, it is his argument, the eastern empire was distinct in terms of language, religion and greater centralization of authority. Justinian's sixth-century attempt to revive the Roman empire he judges to have been heroic but imprudent, an interruption in the 'seemingly natural and necessary process' of an 'eastward evolution' of Byzantium. It caused severe overstretch, making the core of the empire vulnerable first to the Persians and then to Islam. It precipitated, he argues, the empire's 'darkest period', between 610 and 717, when its very survival was at stake. The crisis, though, served as a catalyst for that Byzantinization of the empire which he felt to be necessary and desirable: 'one important, indeed essential, fact emerges at the end of this perturbed and fateful period', he writes, 'The Byzantine Empire had come into existence, diminished indeed, but more compact, relieved of the dead weight of the West and of the danger of rifts in the East, an Empire capable of being strongly organized and, given firm guidance, of enduring.'

This firm guidance, it is Diehl's argument, was provided by the Isaurian dynasty (717–867), whose strong leadership and generalship resulted in thwarting threats from Islam and the Bulgars, and which created a strong Byzantine state, characterized by religious unity and a reviving culture in Constantinople. Losses in the west are judged of minor significance – indeed Diehl posits that they were virtually beneficial, turning 'Byzantium fully and finally towards the East'. Thus from the beginning of the ninth century, 'there existed a distinct Byzantine nationality . . . and the now truly oriental Empire moved toward its zenith.' This zenith he places between the beginning of the tenth and middle of the eleventh centuries, which he describes as 'a hundred and fifty years of splendour, prosperity and renown'.[4]

The heroes in Diehl's account of these some 200 years during which Byzantium moved towards its peak of greatness were a succession of great emperors, members of the Macedonian dynasty (867–1081), Basil I, Nicephorus Phocas, John Tzimisces and Basil II, great statesmen as well as military leaders. Their military successes caused the empire's frontiers to be extended almost as far as they had been under Justinian – from Syria to the Danube, from Armenia to southern Italy. The achievement was not, though, purely military: like the Roman empire before it, the Byzantine had become an agent of civilization, spreading the Orthodox religion, its culture, art, language and science of government to surrounding 'barbarian' races – Croats, Serbs, Bulgars and Russians. The vast capital of Constantinople became a metropolitan centre for the whole east Mediterranean zone, 'the Paris of the Middle Ages'.

## Byzantine dynasties and emperors from Justinian

**Justinianean dynasty**
Justin I, 518–27
Justinian I, 527–65
Justin II, 565–78
Tiberius II, 578–82
Maurice, 582–602
Phocas, 602–10

**Heraclian dynasty**
Heraclius, 610–41
Constans II, 641–68
Constantine IV, 665–85
Justinian II, 685–95
Leontius, 695–8
Tiberius III, 698–705
Justinian II (restored), 705–11

**Decline of imperial power**
Bardanes, 711–13
Anastasius II, 713–16
Theodosius III, 716–17

**Isaurian dynasty**
Leo III, 717–41
Constantine V, 741–75
Leo IV, 775–80
Constantine VI, 780–97
Irene, 797–802
NIcephorus, 802–11
Stauracius, 811
Michael I, 811–13
Leo V, 813–20

**Phrygian dynasty**
Michael II, 820–9
Theophilus, 829–42
Michael III, 842–67

**Macedonian dynasty**
Basil I, 867–86
{ Leo VI, 886–912
{ Alexander, 886–913
Constantine Porphyrogenitus, 912–59
Romanus I, 919–44
Romanus II, 959–63
{ Basil II, 963–1025
{ Constantine VIII, 963–1025;
{ sole ruler 1025–8
Nicephorus II, 963–9
John I Tzimisces, 969–76
Romanus III, 1028–34
Michael IV, 1034–41
Michael V, 1041–2
Zoe and Theodora, 1042
Constantine IX Monomachus, 1042–55
Theodora, 1055–6
Michael Stratioticus, 1056–7

**End of the Macedonian dynasty**
Isaac I Comnenus, 1057–9
Constantine X Ducas, 1059–67
Romanus IV Diogenes, 1067–71
Michael VII Ducas, 1071–8
Nicephorus III, 1078–81

**Comnenian dynasty**
Alexius I Comnenus, 1081–1118
John II, 1118–43
Manuel, 1143–80
Alexius II, 1180–3
Andronicus, 1183–5

**Dynasty of the Angeli**
Isaac II, 1185–95
Alexius III, 1195–1203
Isaac II, restored with Alexius II,
    1203–4
Alexius V, 1204
(Fourth Crusade, capture of
    Constantinople)

**East Roman emperors in Nicaea**
Theodore I Lascaris, 1204–22
John III Ducas Vatatzes, 1222–54
Theodore II Lascaris, 1254–8
John IV Lascaris, 1258–61
Michael VIII Palaeologus, 1259–
    82
(1261 Recapture of
    Constantinople)

**Dynasty of the Palaeologi**
Michael VIII, 1261–82
Andronicus II, 1282–1328
Michael IX, 1293–1320
Andronicus III, 1328–41
John V, 1341–76
John VI, 1341–54
Andronicus IV, 1376–9
John V (restored), 1379–91
John VII, 1390
Manuel II, 1391–1425
John VIII, 1425–48
Constantine XI Dragases,
    1449–53
(1453 Capture of Constantinople
    by the Turks)

*Source*: N. H. Baynes and H. St L. B. Moss, *Byzantium:
An Introduction to East Roman Civilization* (Oxford, 1961), pp. 422–3

Decline from this position of hegemony is also attributed by Diehl to
Byzantium's rulers: 'the reins of government', he writes, 'fell . . . into the
hands either of women or of inferior, negligent men' – which two categories he apparently equates. Weak leadership resulted in an inability to
cope with renewed military threats, from the Seljuk Turks in the east and
the Normans in the west. A key defeat was the battle of Manzikert in
1071, following which the Turks advanced to the very walls of Constantinople. These disasters amounted to 'crisis' rather than decline, however
(Diehl categorizes Byzantine history not as 'a straight line running steadily downhill, but a series of rising and falling curves'): Byzantium was
saved again by another dynasty of great emperors, that of the Comneni
(1081–1204). The Normans were repulsed in Italy, successes were
achieved against the Serbs and Hungarians and in Sicily. Constantinople
remained a major cultural centre: 'Byzantine society was unrivalled in its
elegance, its interest in the things of the mind, and its love of the arts.'
However these achievements are categorized as a process of recovery
and consolidation rather than a return to the peaks achieved at the end
of the tenth century. The Turks remained in Iconium and in the Balkans,
and the Slavic people were founding independent states; 'It was perhaps
too late for the Comneni to restore the empire to its past glory.'

The decline, definitive this time, which took place from the late twelfth century, is attributed by Diehl on the one hand, again, to debilities of leadership – Manuel Comnenus is judged, like Justinian, to have overstretched Byzantine resources by his campaigns in Italy, and also to have antagonized potential Latin allies against the Turks, and the dynasty which succeeded to the Comneni, the Angeli, was 'weak' – and on the other to the greed of the Latin states: their participation in the Crusades had been a mistake (it caused 'two worlds that were incapable of understanding one another' to meet) and had, in revealing to the west the wealth of the east, incited the west's covetousness. Weak leadership on the Byzantine side and this new western ambition were the factors which then interacted to result in the disastrous (for the Byzantines) diversion of the Fourth Crusade against Constantinople, its capture in 1204 and, following that, fifty seven years of Latin rule over the Byzantine capital. From 1204 the decline *is* continuous. There was to be a return to Greek rule in Constantinople with the restoration of the last great Byzantine dynasty the Palaeologi in 1261, but now the situation was beyond remedy by individuals: the small Latin states which continued to exist in what had been parts of the empire, the Balkan Christian states of Bulgaria and Serbia, and the presence of the Turks, whose capital was first situated in Brusa, just the far side of the straits from Constantinople, and then, from the middle of the fourteenth century, in Adrianople, made a mockery of any continued Byzantine claims to hegemony in the area. Finally there was a growing loss of internal cohesion in the remnants of the empire, with class conflict and religious struggles. Only Byzantine culture continued to flourish, with the provincial centres of Trebizond, Mistra and Athos joining Constantinople in an Indian summer of Hellenistic intellectual and artistic life. Fittingly, in this history told largely in terms of the prowess of its leaders, Byzantium's last emperor, Constantine XI, died sword in hand in the breached ramparts of his city.[5]

The more recent work on the ups and downs in Byzantine history, in which greater emphasis is placed on social and economic factors, is brilliantly synthesized by Perry Anderson. The greater resilience of the eastern over the western empire in resisting barbarian invasion, Anderson notes, was occasioned not by geography – the area was just as exposed, the first Hun and Visigoth incursions occurring in Moesia, not Gaul, the first serious defeat of imperial cavalry taking place in Thrace – but by social structure. In contrast to the western empire, where the novelty of Roman power meant that there was little in the way of alternative socio-economic traditions to resist the imposition of *latifundia* and slave labour, the east, before its absorption by Rome, was characterized by a well-developed urban civilization and a predominance of small property. Hence the type of decadence experienced by Rome – as its agricultural system fell apart, a collapse in the very foundations of its society – was avoided: 'It was this internal configuration that gave the East the political compactness and resilience to resist the barbarian invasions that felled the West.'[6]

A 'galvanization' of these social features, one whose exact configuration is the subject of much debate among Byzantine scholars, was then responsible for the empire's capacity to resist the triple threat of the seventh century from the Slav–Avar invasions in the Balkans, Persia and Islam. A process of social equalization appears to have occurred as the dominating pattern of large- and medium-sized property was disrupted by the invasions, and peasants, benefiting from the confusion, freed themselves from their adscription to the soil. The process may have been promoted by imperial reforms which created a class of 'soldier-smallholders', holding land in exchange for military service within a 'thema system': territorial divisions, held to have been introduced by Emperor Heraclius (610–41) for the purposes of defence. The consequence of these changes, and the decline in the empire's towns apart from Constantinople, was to create an unusual social structure of small-scale farmers with direct fiscal responsibilities to a strong, centralized state, and little in between. This social structure provided a strong fiscal and recruitment base for the Byzantine state.

Byzantine stagnation and decline – or to put it in Anderson's words its 'remain[ing] transfixed between slave and feudal modes of production, unable either to to return to the one or advance to the other in a social deadlock that could only eventually lead to its extinction' – has also been explained in social terms. The egalitarian social structure which had provided the social basis for the robust military achievements of the Heraclian and Isaurian dynasties (610–711 and 717–820) proved vulnerable to the predatory actions of the provincial ruling class. Peasant land was engrossed, and attempts by the Byzantine state to prevent this process were thwarted because of connivance between local bureaucracies and the provincial nobility. The state thus gradually lost control of the themata to local magnates and found that a powerful intermediary social group had inserted itself between it and the peasantry. The implications for Byzantine military and political power were clear – 'a para-seigneurial system in the countryside meant the end of a metropolitan military and fiscal apparatus capable of enforcing imperial authority throughout the realm.' Hence the civil wars and the defeats of the eleventh century.

Anderson's optic is Byzantium's failure to develop a dynamic synthesis, as he argues was being achieved in western Europe, between the mode of production of classical antiquity and that of the invading barbarian (Slav and Turanian in the Byzantine case) tribes, and the empire's consequent failure to develop a full-blown feudal system and thus to engender that dialectic which led to the rise of capitalism. This clearly is a slightly different one from this book's but, insofar as a principal element in the Byzantine failure is not so much a steady downward slide but a failure to progress, which made it increasingly vulnerable to more dynamic societies, and in particular to western Europe from the eleventh century, it is not irrelevant to our theme. Gibbon, himself, Anderson notes, categorized Byzantium's decline in this manner, describing it as 'A tedious and uniform tale of weakness and misery ... passively connected' with 'revolutions which have changed the state of the world'. We have noted Gibbon's contrasting judgements on the two declines in the epigraph.

Anderson accounts for the stagnation primarily in terms of the survival of a strong central authority in Byzantium, with no break in this respect from Roman times. This, and the continued existence of slave labour, particularly in the industrial sector, inhibited the growth of seigneurial authority, he argues – a sign of the survival of central power was the continued existence of the principle of universal taxation – as well as circumscribing the freedom of towns, preventing any 'communal revolution'. The ruling class thus, Anderson argues, 'itself remained halfway between the clarissimate of Late Antiquity and the baronage of the early Middle Ages. In its own body was inscribed the frustrated tension of the State.' The 'impasse', he continues, contributed to the immobile character of the state, particularly apparent in its poor record with respect to technological change. The one area of restlessness, he argues, was in the state's combat record, and in this respect he delineates a repetitive pattern of expansion and contraction, which goes a long way to account for the specific shape of Byzantine destinies, characterized by a zigzag pattern (we have seen) rather than a steady cycle of rise followed by decline. Byzantium's inheritance of Roman claims to universal empire, he claims, led to repeated periods of expansionary policy – Justinian's, those of the Macedonian emperors in the eleventh and twelfth centuries, that of Manuel Comnenus in the twelfth century, even the fruitless recovery of Constantinople by the Nicaean-based Paleologus dynasty in the thirteenth – which inevitably gave rise to retaliatory ripostes from neighbouring powers, and eventual humiliating withdrawals. 'Each phase of expansion', Anderson concludes, 'was thus succeeded by a more drastic contraction, the unfailing penalty for it.

It is this jagged rhythm which makes the course of Byzantine history so different from that of Rome, with its comparatively smooth curve of ascent, stabilization and decline'.[7] Diehl's categorization of the pattern of Byzantine history is thus confirmed by Anderson.

Like Diehl, and reflecting what had been up to his time of writing a consensus among Byzantine scholars, Anderson, however, grants that one crisis was greater than all others – the defeat of Manzikert and the resultant loss of much of Anatolia. This débâcle has been explained in terms of a power struggle following the death of the last Macedonian emperor between members of the state civil service in Byzantium and the increasingly powerful regional nobility or 'dunatoi'. In order to decrease this nobility's influence the civil service had reduced the role of the themata in the supplying of provincial armies, relying instead on mercenaries to a greater extent. Civil wars had resulted, and the Turkish victory was more a consequence of lack of any opposition because of disunity among the Byzantine elite than of military superiority. The split, and its consequences, Anderson notes, bears striking similarities to that between the civilian and military branches of the imperial order in the Roman empire. 'Anatolia was left an undefended vacuum, into which Turcoman nomads steadily drifted over the next decades.'[8]

An immediate collapse of the Byzantine empire, however, was averted by the 'informal' character of the nomadic, Turkish occupation of Anatolia – Byzantium was able to counter-attack and regain control of the coastal areas and river valleys of the zone. The fortunes of the empire were now, however, Anderson argues, on a persistent downward slope. The accession of the Comnenian dynasty (1081–1185) represented the passing of imperial power to one of the principal military dynasties which had occasioned the debacle of Manzikert. Under their rule the barriers to the feudalization process were broken – benefices (or *pronoiai*) being granted to gentry landowners, and the peasantry losing their independence to become *paroikoi*, close to the status of the European serf. A similar dissolution occurred in the formerly state-controlled commercial and industrial sectors, but to the benefit here of Italians: a chrysobull of 1082 granted the merchants of Venice exemption from the imperial sales tax, enabling them to gain a monopoly over the internal and external trades of the empire. A relationship which for over half a millennium had taken the form of Italian dependency and technical inferiority *vis-à-vis* Byzantium was reversed, the Byzantines now becoming the importers of luxury manufactures. Independent enclaves of Italian merchants were established in Constantinople, benefiting from imperial franchises. The capture of Constantinople in 1204, and following it the full-scale implantation in the western Mediterranean of a predatory variant of west European feudalism, were thus the climax (Anderson argues, following the traditional interpretation of Byzantine fortunes) of a steady process of deterioration. The Byzantine reversion to feudalism had not had the dynamic consequences which the genesis of this system, according to Anderson, had had for western Europe: 'its institutions were a simulacrum of Western forms entirely lacking the historical dynamic that had produced the latter.' The cause for this was that whereas in the western case their development had represented the fruit of a dynamic interaction between previously distinct social systems, in the Byzantine case it came as 'the end-result of a secular *decomposition* of a unitary imperial policy that had lasted largely unaltered for seven centuries.' The only 'progress' took the form of spin-offs from this process of disintegration – a cultural effervescence and a diffusion of commerce to other centres of the empire as 'the cultural traffic with the west diluted the grip of Orthodox obscurantism.'[9]

What Anderson categorizes as the 'last significant episode of Byzantine history' was a major municipal revolt which took place in Thessalonica between 1342 and 1349, giving rise to the establishment of an independent republic in the empire's second city. The revolt, Anderson argues, represented an interaction between the stimulus on the area from Latin influences and some of the consequences of the downward spiral in the empire's fortunes: it 'combined', he writes, 'the manifestation of new ferments generated by the incipient feudalism of the Greek East, with the influence of processes derived from the crisis of descendant feudalism in the Latin West.' It demonstrated Byzantium's participation in western European trends – the 'crisis of the Middle Ages' and the extensive communal protest movements which characterized it, the closest parallel to the Thessalonica uprising being the Genoese communal revolution of 1339. However, the inferior nature of Byzantium's social development *vis-à-vis* western Europe made its suppression inevitable: 'the dwindling Byzantine social formation was incapable of sustaining any such advanced urban form, which presupposed an altogether different economic and social tonus.' Decline was thus not reversed or delayed by this event, and Byzantium, for the last 100 years of its existence, had become a shadow of its former self – 'a forlorn tributary of Turkish power in the Balkans.'[10]

Revisionism in the field of this traditional and well-established interpretation of the shape of Byzantine history was initiated by M. F. Hendy in a provocative article entitled 'Byzantium, 1081–1204: An Economic Reappraisal' which was published in 1970. Although focused in particular on the twelfth century the article in fact challenged all aspects of the traditional interpretation – arguing that during its supposedly decadent period following Manzikert the empire was successful and prosperous, and that during its supposed 'golden age' it was in decline.

The faulty, traditional interpretation is attributed by Hendy to the lack of quantitative source materials – 'the economic history of the Empire is throughout heavily based on what can be gleaned from the occasional reference in chronicles, hagiographies, legal codes, and a few monastic archives and descriptions by foreign travellers', he writes. To set the issue right Hendy on the one hand reviews interpretations made on the basis of this traditional type of evidence and on the other makes use of two forms of evidence which do permit 'comparative estimation', those drawn from archaeology and from details of imperial coinage. These latter types of evidence, it should be added, were becoming increasingly available at the time Hendy was writing and have become yet more abundant since. The existence of better sources has thus been a principal basis for the new approach.

With respect to traditional types of evidence, Hendy firstly questions the significance attached, for the future of the empire, to the loss of its Anatolian provinces following Manzikert. The grounds for doing so, he notes, was, following earlier research by Ostrogorsky and Vryonis,[11] their supposed dense urbanization and hence crucial contribution to the economic viability of the empire. Hendy questions this position, arguing that as early as the beginnings of the Christian era there had been a deterioration in the area's landscape – rather as in that of Rome's in Italy – consequent upon the 'reckless spread of large-scale commercial farming'. The result of this was that the Anatolian peninsula experienced an economic polarization between its highland interior, lightly populated and with limited agricultural resources, and an urbanized and intensely farmed periphery, limited to the coastline and its river valley hinterlands. The view that the whole area had been highly urbanized he attributes to probably confusing sources relating to episcopal sees. He emphasizes, too, that the view that the area was prosperous and highly urbanized flies in the face of 'all that is known of the general facts of the contemporary situation' which seemed to have required 'a drastic reduction of both rural and urban life': two devastating plagues, under Justinian I (527–65) and Constantine V (741–75), the Persian invasions under Phocas (602–10) and Heraclius (610–41) and the then constant incursions by Arabs from the mid-sixth to the mid-ninth century. The area had thus experienced a discontinuity – a process of deurbanization – from the pre-Graecian and Roman periods, and surviving cities of the interior served principally defensive roles. He quotes Arab sources to support his argument – one from the ninth century recorded that 'In the days of old cities were numerous in Rum [Anatolia] but now they have become few. Most of the districts are prosperous and pleasant and have each an extremely strong fortress on account of the frequency of the raids . . . To each village appertains a castle where in times of flight they may take shelter.'

It was these interior, less prosperous areas that the Byzantines lost to the Turks after Manzikert: Hendy's argument is thus that, influenced by this mistaken view of the Anatolian area, both Byzantine prosperity during the ninth and tenth centuries and the consequences of the area's loss following Manzikert have been exaggerated. Aggravating the misinterpretation, he emphasizes, has been the additional failure of Byzantinists to take note of the fact that these losses were compensated by territorial gains in the west – the inner Balkans (Byzantine from 1018 to the late 1180s), Crete (from 961) and Cyprus (from 965 to 1191). The actual size of the empire consequently actually remained virtually constant, though the 'overall territorial concentration had . . . tended to shift away from Asia in favour of Europe.'

With respect to some other arguments supporting the traditional interpretation of the chronology of Byzantine history, Hendy's position is trenchant. He is sceptical about arguments for or against different forms of providing for the empire's defence – use of mercenaries or reliance on a form of feudal system – the *pronoia* grant of land against military service. Equally he shows an awareness of the dangers of Comnenian centralization of authority in that it created hostages to fortune with respect to the quality of imperial leadership and ran against the central tendency of the period – 'the growth of the great territorial interests'. However, on the issue of the increasing Italian penetration of the empire's commercial networks he is more clear-cut. He argues firstly that it did not occasion any shift in trade routes thus depriving the empire of revenue. 'By its very geographical situation Constantinople straddled a main north–south trade axis', he argues, and would dominate the east–west one as long as it maintained most of the strategic points in Asia Minor, Crete, Cyprus and the southern Peloponnese. It may have been the case, he concedes, that Byzantine shipping had declined in relative importance since the ninth and tenth centuries 'when the Empire had been further advanced economically than most of its neighbours, and all of its western northern ones', but he denies that this failure necessarily represented an impoverishment in view of the continued importance of its manufactures and raw-material production. The evidence of Byzantine mercantile decline he counters by indicating a Byzantine commercial diaspora, from Alexandria to Barcelona and Béziers. Finally the key issue of the supposedly fatal consequences for Byzantine commercial life of the granting of customs rates concessions to Italian merchants is countered by Hendy with a range of arguments: the concessions were restricted to parts of the empire only, trade with the Black Sea and Cyprus being excluded from them; the overall increase in trade over the eleventh and twelfth centuries would have meant that, despite the smaller duties enforced, the gross fiscal yield to the empire would have increased; that the presence of Italian merchants in the empire would have resulted in considerable investment, and that the growth in the trade with the west would have stimulated Byzantine production.[12]

Hendy's justification for crediting evidence concerning imperial coinage with the quality of providing 'absolute or even comparative information', in contrast with the patchy picture emerging from the documentary sources just discussed, is based on the assumption that the credit facilities available to government at the time were limited: coinage and its minting thus bore a direct relation to economic reality. What the study of this evidence shows is firstly that 'the denominational pattern of the monetary system of the middle Byzantine period . . . compares unfavourably with those of the periods preceding and following it': to be specific, whereas for the middle period there were only three coin denominations, a gold unit (nomisma), a silver one (miliaresion) and a copper one (follis), in the preceding period each of these metal categories had subdivisions, and such a 'pluralist' system was resumed with the monetary reforms of the first Comnenian emperor, Alexius I, in 1092. The history of minting practices is parallel to this pattern affecting denominations – an initial system of provincial mints, in Thessalonica, Nicomedia, Cyzicus and Antioch as well as Constantinople, shrank to one in which all minting was concentrated in the empire's capital; and again it was only from the eleventh century that provincial mints reappeared – in Thessalonica under Constantine X (1059–67) and in central Greece from 1092. Data on volume of coinage produced is more sparse, but Hendy judges the evidence to reveal a rise in the production during the first half of the twelfth century. The 'coinage of the twelfth century', he concludes, 'represents a level equalled only by that of the sixth. It is certainly to be regarded as a more flexible and efficient instrument of exchange than the stable but rigid, sparse and in a word primitive system prevailing between the eighth and eleventh centuries.'

Details of coin finds from archaeological digs in Corinth and Athens in Europe, and Sardis, Pergamum, Priene and Antioch in Asia, support this evidence concerning denominational patterns, minting and production – large finds for the sixth and seventh centuries, virtually none from the second half of the seventh century to the first half of the ninth, and then an accelerating increase into the eleventh century. For the twelfth century the yields in the European cities are described by Hendy as 'overwhelming', in the Asian sites they are 'less strong' but pick up in the second half of the century and continue into the thirteenth. Details on construction and likely population trends can also be garnered from the archaeological sites, and these too support Hendy's revised periodization of Byzantium's fortunes. The Corinth and Athens sites show urban stagnation through the seventh and eighth centuries of 'depressed remnants' of the Roman and early Byzantine cities, and then accelerating recovery from the ninth century, which reached a climax in the twelfth. 'The developed form of the medieval community at Corinth', it has been noted, 'was that of the twelfth century.' Athens's excavation has revealed the same pattern, and digs at Condurachi, Brnea and Diaconu in the Lower Danube area have also shown rising densities of population from the reign of Alexius I onwards. As a final element in his argument, Hendy cites a letter from a Jewish emigrant in Seleuceia Isauria in 1137 to a relative in Cairo urging him to follow his example, and that of eleven other Jews known to them, and to emigrate to the empire. 'This', the historian of the Cairo Jewish community has written, 'reflects the state of relative security and prosperity enjoyed by the Byzantine Empire at that time, over sixty years after the Seljuk invasion.'[13]

Hendy concludes his attack on the traditional interpretation by presenting a selection of collateral evidence in support of his argument. The internal poverty of the empire was such – he cites the case of a revolt in the recently conquered territory of Bulgaria in the first half of the tenth century against an attempt to switch from taxation in kind to taxation in coin – and that of Byzantium's potential customers to the north and west too (he emphasizes that prospects to the south were poor as 'the main trade axis of the Arab world would seem . . . to have been aligned on an east–west . . . basis') – that there clearly were not the markets available for the extent of commercial development implied in older views of Byzantium. In contrast, the multiple evidence for commercial expansion in western Europe from the eleventh century and the fact of the Crusades which increased the commercial penetration of Syria and Palestine are consistent with his revised views on the twelfth century.[14]

Since the publication of Hendy's article the focus of the debate concerning the stages in Byzantine development has been the eleventh century. Hendy, we noted, was less emphatic in his interpretation of the political trends of this century. By contrast, the Soviet historian, A. P. Kazhdan, strongly criticized the traditional view, originally developed by G. Ostrogorsky, of the negative consequences of the splintering in the power of Byzantine central government consequent upon the rise of provincially based territorial magnates. Such a move towards a western-style 'feudalism' he judges as 'progressive' (we have seen that Anderson's optic was similar). It was rather the existence of a strong central authority, which was reactionary and destabilizing and, in counterpart, the accession of Alexius I, himself from a territorial magnate background, which served to resolve the tension by incorporating the 'feudal' stream within the imperial system.[15] The French Byzantinist P. Lemerle, in contrast, while revisionist, approached the debate from a different angle. There was no crisis, he argued, the effects of Manzikert having been exaggerated and difficulties only *began* with the accession of Alexius I: his feudal inclinations undermined the imperial tradition of strong central power, he neglected Asia Minor and fatally opened up the imperial trading system to Venetian traders. He consequently created a 'société bloquée' by his neutralization of the progressive elements in the Byzantine world – progressive elements which for him were the 'bourgeoisie' who ran the administration.[16]

As Michael Angold, on whose summary of recent views on Byzantine history in the eleventh and twelfth centuries I have drawn in the previous paragraph (and shall do in this and the next three paragraphs), emphasizes Lemerle's position is effectively a new version of Ostrogorsky's, and the debate between him and Kazhdan can essentially 'be boiled down to the question of whether Alexius I Comnenus was working with or against the grain of history'. Angold himself favours the latter interpretation: the type of political system operated by Basil II (976–1025), he argues, with its tight controls over the economy and society, was no longer practicable in the eleventh century in view of the economic growth occurring. Alexius's development, thus, of a revised form of rule on the basis of quasi-feudal structures was the only course that could have been taken. A study by A. Harvey, *Economic Expansion in the Byzantine Empire, 900–1200* (Cambridge, 1989), provides further support for this process of economic expansion in the empire through the eleventh and twelfth centuries: the apparent inconsistency between this growth and the political weakness of the Byzantine state he attributes to the tendency of economic change in the medieval period to be destructive of centralized authority.[17]

Further studies have provided additional emphasis on the achievements of Alexius I in a trend which is reminiscent of Diehl's interpretation of Byzantine history in terms of the quality of its emperors. In addition, analysis has been focused on the key issue of the Byzantine relationship to Venetian and other Italian traders. There are conflicting views on this question. Against Lemerle's argument of the damaging consequences of the trading concessions to the Venetians and others, Hendy, as we have already seen, and also R. J. Lilie, have argued that the Italian impact on the empire was not significant. The Venetians, Lilie holds, made little difference to the Byzantine economy overall, which remained predominantly a subsistence society. The relationships between the two powers were, of course, as much political as economic. D. Nicol, indeed, in a study of Byzantine/Venetian diplomacy, has shown that for the Byzantines it was only political and military considerations that determined their agreements with Venice, though economic considerations were paramount for the Venetians. He argues that the 1082 chrysobull altered the balance of power in the Venetians' favour. Angold's view in this case aligns with those of Lemerle and Nicol: he argues that Byzantium's penetration by western business interests was to its disadvantage, and that to dispute 'the importance of the commercial sector or the significance of western influence amounts to a refusal to acknowledge that any significant change occurred in Byzantium over the eleventh and twelfth centuries'. The *significant changes* which he pinpoints are firstly the greater penetration of government by private interests and secondly the greater openness of Byzantium to external influences. Both these changes could work both ways which may be one of the reasons for the difficulty in establishing a definite identity for these centuries. The greater involvement of private interests in government could work for the best when such interests were given clear direction, as they were by the Comneni and 'Byzantium had much to gain from foreign penetration, but possibly more to lose.'[18]

The effective majority granting of a bill of good health with respect to Byzantine destinies in the eleventh century, at least for the short to medium term, inevitably results in a greater emphasis on interpretations of the twelfth century, whose conclusion was so soon followed by the disastrous, this time undisputed, turning-point of the capture of Constantinople by the Latins. Again the focus of the debate is on a single individual, the last great Comnenian emperor Manuel I (1143–80), a powerful and ambitious man, as we saw from Diehl's summary above, but one whose reign witnessed both a most serious military defeat at the hands of the Turks, rivalling Manzikert in significance, at Myriokephalon in Asia Minor, as well as diplomatic reverses and humiliations at the hands of the Venetians and Crusaders. A new study by Paul Magdalino vindicates the emperor from blame, arguing that all was still well at the end of his reign and that in a society like the Byzantine, institutions rather than individuals are the source of difficulties. Angold's view is different. Manuel's foreign policy was on a scale which was disproportionate to Byzantine resources. Often forgotten is that the involvement of western Europe in the east Mediterranean was balanced by a reinvolvement of the Byzantine emperors in European affairs – there it soon became apparent that they were boxing above their weight. The greater links with the the west also had the unfortunate by-product of an anti-Latin backlash in the empire. Following Magdalino, Angold admires Manuel's lucidity in his difficulties, a sign of a great ruler, but argues that having lucidity does not spirit away problems, and that some of Manuel's solutions, such as that involving getting foreign powers to underwrite the succession of his son to the throne, were later to prove liabilities – an excuse for foreign intervention. Angold's view is effectively that the empire was most certainly crumbling politically well before 1204: it was in a situation reminiscent of those of the closing years of the reigns of Justinian or Basil II. 'It needed to readjust.'

On this occasion the readjustment was not achieved. Anderson's 'jagged rhythm' this time reflected disaster culminating in the events of 1204. Who or what was to blame?: Manuel's successor Andronicus (1182–5), the succeeding Angeli dynasty (1185–1204) or social and economic changes beyond the power of any emperor to control? J.-C. Cheynet clears Andronicus of blame to confer it on the Angeli, devoid of 'charisma', who thus lost the power to rally members of the Byzantine elite. He draws a contrast between the eleventh century, when provincial Byzantine aristorcrats were committed to imperial power, even in outlying provinces in Italy, and the twelfth century, when the consorting to Constantinople by members of the provincial nobility led to their cutting their links with their localities and no longer acting to transmit the pulse between capital and province. Angold gives qualified support to this viewpoint but his analysis shows a sensitivity to more powerful forces for change than those of imperial capacities or aristocratic behaviour. He stresses the significance of a major change in the urban configuration of the empire with the continued growth of provincial centres such as Philadelphia in Asia Minor, Adrianople in Thrace or Thessalonica in Macedonia. The political impact of this development was not so much occasioned by the absence of the local elite but by the fact that these centres had now major interests to defend. Besides, they possessed local caciques, known as *archontes*, who provided them with leadership. The major difference from the previous century was that it was now independence, rather than a better deal with the political centre, which they sought. 'The fragmentation of the Byzantine empire', Angold concludes, '. . . was already being prepared.' The crisis was also contributed to by more purely political difficulties – a growing schism in the Church – damaging insofar as an innovation of the Comnenian dynasty had been the increasing use of the Church in a political role – and new fractures in the elite consequent in particular on the Angeli promotion of bureaucrats.[19]

Hendy, too, has summarized recent research relating to the phases of Byzantine development in an article entitled 'Byzantium, 1081–1204: The Economy Revisited Twenty Years On'.[20] I shall summarize briefly points which he raises which serve to elaborate on his original intrepretation. A first development on which he reports provides a social complement to the geographical points made in the earlier article concerning Anatolia. Recent work has established that those internal *meseta* (tableland) areas whose loss to the Turks, it was his argument, was not of such great significance to Byzantium's future, were generally owned by members of the nobility and devoted to ranching activities. The implications of this point are that their loss may have actually been of direct benefit to the Comneni dynasty, for among the principal landowners in the area were the *dunatoi* whose plotting had been making imperial rule so difficult. Such noble families, in the face of the loss of their Anatolian estates, had three possible courses of action, Hendy emphasizes: they could try to adjust to Turkish domination, they could play off Turks against Byzantines in an attempt to retain the autonomy of their territorial holdings, or they could attempt to use the good services of the emperor to attain substitute estates in the newly acquired territories in the Balkans. All three were opted for. Whatever the course taken, however, the political effectiveness of this noble class was reduced.[21]

In the article Hendy also returns to the attack on the traditional views of a golden Byzantine age between the eighth and tenth centuries by reporting on recent archaeological work in the Balkans and Asia Minor related to the period between the seventh and tenth centuries. All the research, he notes, tells the same story 'of physical diminution and fragmentation; demographic recession; the loss of planning, public monumentality and services; not uncommonly a degree of geographi- cal displacement; and above all militarization'. This evidence of deurbanization in provincial Byzantium makes all the more apparent the extent of dominance of Constantinople, with its population of some 200,000, in the empire. It was demand from its population, for example, which provided the principal prospect for developing a commercialized agriculture. In this connection Hendy makes a further geographical point which serves further to reinforce his arguments concerning Anatolia. It was estates in the Balkans, he claims, which were best placed for meeting this demand in view of the prevailing north-west winds in the Aegean, which slowed down shipping from south Anatolia. Hendy's argument, thus, is for an increasing commercialization of the Byzantine Balkans from the tenth and eleventh centuries, which left Anatolia way behind, with commercial modernization there only starting in the twelfth and thirteenth centuries. As well as making this regional point, however, Hendy also makes a general one about the empire as a whole: this evidence of commercial change shows that it was not as inert economically as once thought – 'the course of development of the Byzantine economy over the crucial period *c.*800–1200 was not as different from that of its western equivalent as has traditonally been supposed', he writes.[22]

Insofar as this Byzantine development clearly did not achieve the momentum of its western equivalent, Hendy raises the issue of whether it was not the overcentralization of urban life in Contantinople which was to blame for this. Had not Constantinople become 'simply too big for the reduced territorial base of the empire . . . its basically parasitical nature . . . becoming too obvious and so causing severe economic and social strains?' he asks. Successive emperors tried to check the city's powers but the imperial position *vis-à-vis* this dominating bureaucracy tended to slip in the case of a mediocre succession. Hendy's position, it can be seen, is effectively close to Kazhdan's, with feudalization characterized as a 'progressive' trend and the political and social domination of the capital diagnosed as the problem:

> This, then, may have been Lemerle's 'société bloquée' [he writes] and indeed the blockage – above all social and political – at this stage, which seems to have been critical in the west [what does he mean by this? That the franchising of the blockage was critical in the west? Or that social and political developments were crucial for the west's different experience?], may well have been one of the decisive factors in the ultimate failure of the Byzantine mercantile classes to develop beyond a certain point.[23]

Certainly the response of the inhabitants of the city's hinterland to the plight of its patrician class following the city's fall in 1204 suggests a total lack of sympathy between city and hinterland: 'The peasants and common riff-raff jeered at those of us from Byzantium', a chronicler recorded, 'and were thick-headed enough to call our miserable poverty and nakedness equality.'[24]

Concluding his article, Hendy persists with his initial revisionists aim of 1970 – to defend the credentials of the twelfth century as a period, still, of economic and, until a late stage, political success. Thus he argues that, although 'the maintenance of a large and centralized bureaucracy . . . and of a powerful standing army and navy; and of a huge and essentially parasitical city; upon the base of a technologically primitive and geographically inhibiting agricultural economy, was ever – and at the best of times – a problem of immense difficulty and precariousness, involving economic and social strains of a continuing high order', a period of 'of relative order and peace internally at least, with few of the constant usurpations that had marked the late eleventh century, with the great majority of major imperial campaigns . . . being mounted against external enemies' was sustained for a full century following the Comnenian accession. Hendy's approach is effectively a liberal one, a modernized version of Diehl's, in which no problem is insurmountable provided leadership is at hand. It is only following the 1204 débâcle that a note of determinism enters his analysis: 'the shattering disaster ...', he writes, marks 'the end of the empire as a recognizable survivor from the ancient world and the beginning of its reduced existence as an eclectic and amorphous entity possessing neither the basic structure of the late antique empire nor the superstructural possibilities of an emergent "nation" state along contemporary western lines'.[25]

I shall conclude this survey of the literature relating to the pattern of Byzantine history by referring to an article by A. P. Kazhdan and A. Cutler entitled 'Continuity and Discontinuity in Byzantine History' which has the virtue for our purposes of operating at a very high level of generalization. The article consists in an attack on an interpretation of Byzantine history by a German Byzantinist, Gunter Weiss. Weiss had made the case for 'continuity' being the defining feature of Byzantine history. In doing so, of course, he was following one of the strongest traditions in Byzantine scholarship, the achievement of continuity with the Roman empire being the very *raison d'être* of the Byzantine state, and the apparent success in this aim representing the principal contrast between Byzantine and 'European' history.[26]

In making his case, Weiss had distinguished between three types of social development: firstly development within a context of 'preservation of structure', secondly changes involving 'alterations that have no qualitative significance and affect only certain external events while the substantial structure remains the same', and finally shifts representing a 'change in structure'. It is the third type of change which Kazhdan and Cutler were concerned to demonstrate as having occurred in Byzantium. A preliminary to doing this was to establish what would amount to 'structural change', as Weiss's definition they judged too nebulous. For this purpose they used the western Mediterranean as a model: there structural change, they claimed, consisted in the 'established fact' of 'the transition from Antiquity to the middle Ages'. Establishing 'structural change' in the Byzantine empire thus required the proving of a similar change there. What social phenomena, though, required monitoring in order to establish the occurrence of such a change? What was the 'structure' of 'Antiquity'? Kazhdan and Cutler's answer to this question was that

> the most appropriate definition would understand it as an urban social structure, that is based on the polis or municipium, in which structure the existence of the city as the prime social unit determined both the forms of ownership, the relationship of social groups or classes, the nature of microstructures (microgroups) and the ideological, socio-psychological, religious and esthetic self-consciousness of society.

In view of this whether structural change occurred appears 'prima facie to be a question about the fate of the late antique city at the time of the transition to the Byzantine era'.

In answering this question Kazhdan and Cutler, making use of the same new sources as Hendy, argue for a 'hiatus' in the development between Antiquity and the medieval period in Byzantium in the seventh century, one of a similar kind to that experienced in the west Mediterranean: they note that the antique polis had virtually ceased to exist in Greece and Asia Minor by the eighth century, and that it was only from the ninth century that the medieval town revived in Byzantium. The evidence can brook no other conclusion, they maintain, referring to Hellas and Thessaly, where most Roman poleis do not survive the sixth century and there is no evidence for building activity before the ninth century, and pointing out that it is only in the second half of the ninth and in the tenth century that several antique poleis are again recorded in the sources. As for Asia Minor, Kazhdan and Cutler follow Foss rather than Vryonis and his evidence for three stages in the urban history of the area – the fourth to sixth centuries during which 'the cities of Asia Minor retained their ancient shape', a century of crisis, the seventh, when the 'majority of them was ruined, abandoned or sharply reduced' and finally a third period of 'revival from the tenth century' leading to their 'restructuring on medieval principles'.

The establishment of the causes for this deurbanization might on the one hand appear too simple to require analysis – it is evident that the seventh century was that of the triple threat from Persians, Islam and the Slav–Avar invasions – or on the other seem to be of only indirect relevance – it being the fact of the hiatus that required clarification. Such a response, however, would be incorrect on both scores, if we accept Kazhdan and Cutler's interpretation – the collapse of the former eastern Roman empire's urban system was caused by a social crisis within it which preceded the invasions – 'the catastrophe of the Late Antique urban system' only occurred 'because the preconditions for the "urban catastrophe" already existed' – and the fact that the collapse occurred primarily on account of social developments reveals it to be a change of significance, one qualifying for acceptance as a change of 'structure'.

What was the character of social life following this hiatus? Here Kazhdan and Cutler provide us with further details to complement those given by Anderson concerning the character of Byzantine society from the seventh to ninth centuries, in the ascendant phase according to traditional interpretations. With the decline in the polis, the extent of urban ownership of land and dominance of the countryside evidently decreased. There were changes with respect to the concept of private property – more limitations to which were accepted than in the Roman period (for instance the introduction of the principle of supreme state ownership of land). Social structure adapted from a system in which status depended on a range of variables, including wealth, power, inherited position and also varying degrees of 'freedom', to a simpler structure described by Kazhdan and Cutler as follows: 'On the one hand, there was formed a relatively uniform mass of agrarian populace obliged to carry out state duties or services, including military service, and on the other a vertically mobile ruling class that replaced the senatorial aristocracy.' It should be added, as was noted by Anderson above, that the transition was less violent than in the west Mediterrean insofar as 'senatorial landownership', *latifundia* and the use of slavery had been less developed in the eastern half of the empire.[27]

The changes at the level of what Kazhdan and Cutler describe as 'microstructures' took the form of a decline in a system of social solidarity provided by the polis – one which included the provision of mutual help and a 'clan system' (units characterized by extended parental relationships) – in favour of a far tighter and more stable nuclear family which became by far the most powerful subgroup.[28] A further shift was towards what Kazhdan and Cutler refer to as a system of 'non-economic coercion and non-economic exchange': by this they mean that, with the breakdown to a barter economy, and also with the extension of Christian and arbitrary state and military considerations into economic transactions, the precision which governed ancient fiscal systems and economic exchange was lost. In intellectual life the shift in structures is most visible of all because of the existence of more extensive evidence. With the disappearance of the polis went that of ancient learning – the higher schools go in the seventh century, elementary schools decrease in

number, books become rarities, authors very few and restricted principally, as in the west, to monastic milieux. A falling off in creativity affects
other areas too – for example building and painting. It is the character
as much as the quantity of the new culture, however, which reveals best
the metamorphosis which had occurred, as Kazhdan and Cutler argue.
They formulate the change as follows: 'we might assert that the general
pattern of Byzantine literary activity is as dissimilar to that of Antiquity
as the immobile image of the icon intent on grasping the Supreme being
is dissimilar to dynamic Greco-Roman sculpture rooted in the sensuous
world.' It is for the visual arts that evidence is most abundant. In interpreting it Kazhdan and Cutler favour a contextual approach, relating art
objects to the social circumstances of the time in which they were
produced. The chief changes which they note are from 'openness', which
characterized the empire in its proto-Byzantine, pre-Dark Ages period,
typified by the scores of mosaics found in Cyrenaica which show similarities to pavements from all round the east Mediterranean, including
Greece, Cyprus, Palestine, Syria and Asia Minor, through isolation,
during the Dark Ages, to a style (when cultural recovery began) characterized by some renewed openness (the models being successively
Muslim from the eighth and ninth centuries and Latin from the twelfth)
but greater standardization, partly of course due to the intensified grip of
Christianity. In addition, a system of plenty gives place to one of scarcity
– they cite the example of a fifth-century monk possessing 300 books and
insist that no monk for the remaining history of Byzantium would have
possessed so many. Other contrasts were that art for private enjoyment
became more important than art for public display – consistent with the
changes in microstructure already described.[29]

I have reported Kazhdan's and Cutler's views on a major discontinuity
in Byzantine history, a decline from the seventh century, in some detail,
partly because it is an imaginative reconstruction of the micro and macro
processes of change at all levels, from the material base to high culture,
but partly too as it provides an approximation to the characteristics
of decline in Antiquity (including that of Rome), characteristics which
I shall be arguing were different from those of 'decline' in European
history.

Kahzdan and Cutler complete their broad brush-stroke characterization of 1,000 years of Byzantine history by a discussion of those (minority) elements in the empire characterized by continuity. These include
ethnos and language, which remain Greek and Hellenized, and a tradi-
tionalism with respect to technical equipment which had the result that
'although Byzantium, during the earlier centuries, was ahead of the West
in economic development, owing in part to the Mediterranean climate

and ancient traditions, in part to a shorter duration of the caesura', from the eleventh century on it gradually fell behind.

Two other linked elements, the unique role of the capital and the character of the state apparatus, as will already have emerged, are bigger issues. The former invites reflection. Constantinople's situation was impoverished following the seventh-century invasions, but it benefited from a transfer of resources and manpower from the destroyed cities of the rest of the empire, and also from Christians in Syria and Egypt. It had never had a commercial and industrial tradition – Syria and Palestine had possessed the greatest commercial centres of the Roman world, the largest shipyards were in Beirut and Egypt, and it was Egypt which had emerged as the greatest Roman manufacturing centre:[30] the trans- fers were thus qualitatively as well as quantitatively significant, and Constantinople was to provide a model which was relevant throughout medieval and early modern European economic and social history, and which contrasted with the classical period, of a commercial and industrial centre swollen in size because of the generally unfavourable conditions for commercial and industrial activity elsewhere (similar characteristics for medieval commercial centres were noted in the previous chapter). Kazhdan and Cutler emphasize too, however, the role of the imperial tradition in Constantinople's extent of urban predominance. Only from the twelfth century, as already noted, does Constantinople's near urban monopoly come to be seriously challenged – a sign, we have noted, of that broadening of social and economic change in the empire as western influences increased. Kazhdan and Cutler speculate on the causes of this inability of the city to profit from a 'conjuncture' which was theoretically favourable to urban growth. 'Would it not be plausible', they ask, 'to connect the economic decline . . . with similar processes which had ousted older Mediterranean centres like Montpellier or Amalfi, in their turn replaced by new powers? Was the traditional economy paralyzed or powerless against the onslaught waged by the Venetians or Genoese?'

Conditions were not, of course, identical between west and east. It is in continuity in the 'state apparatus' that they judge the most striking contrasts to lie and, like Hendy, they argue that this unique character of Byzantine autocracy provides the key to both the failure and the success of Byzantium. They highlight three phases in its role. Firstly, up to the fourth and fifth centuries, and even till Justinian's reign in the sixth, it organized the defence of the empire and underwrote the polis. 'For a while', they argue, 'the polis sensed the unity between its fate and the fate of the Empire.' This unit collapsed in Justinian's day, and a more isolated imperial power, though supported by its Constantinople bureaucracy, created the demand and protection for guilds, which guaranteed commercial and industrial continuity: 'Although it was not the only cause, it was this activity of the centralized state that helped Byzantium to cross the caesura of the Dark Ages earlier than the West did.' In a final phase, however, the impact of imperial power became negative, the state preventing or slowing down the adjustments which were necessary to enable Byzantine society to cope militarily and economically with the challenge from the Latins. With 1204 'The Empire ceased to exist as an autocracy.'

Concluding their article Kazhdan and Cutler emphasize how pervasive the commitment to continuity in the Byzantine empire was, a continuity with respect to both Rome and the Christian heritage. This obsession with the past they judge to be in itself something separating Byzantium from the ancient period in which there was a preference for the making of contrasts with other civilizations to introspection about roots. Similar distinctions were made long ago by Toynbee, who categorized such a posture as 'the nemesis of creativity: Idolization of an ephemeral institution' and blamed it for the failure for the empire to develop (a lack of 'progress towards self-determination' is his expression).[31] The strength of the commitment to the principle is attributed by Kazhdan and Cutler to psychological factors – the search for an 'illusory stability' in an unsettled world. However, they argue that the shadow must not be confused with the substance: 'Sometimes', they write, 'it is the Byzantine yearning for continuity which prevents us from seeing discontinuity.'[32]

## Conclusion

Byzantium, in its bridging the antique and medieval periods, was a unique civilization. This specificity should cause its decline to manifest 'traditional' and 'European' characteristics. This indeed, I shall argue, is the case, complicating the interpretation of Byzantine decline, causing it to differ, in the manner implied by the comments from Gibbon which provide the epigraph to this chapter, from the more clear-cut Roman story.

From the contradictory views of the Byzantinist historians which have just been discussed, three distinct declines can be identified, three major shifts in the direction of the fortunes of the empire which override the zigzags referred to by Diehl and Anderson. The first of these is the crisis of the seventh century. This, it has emerged from recent, largely archaeological research, caused nearly as great a hiatus as the fall of Rome in the west. The arguments of Kazhdan and Cutler appear convincing.

*Table 4.1*   Percentage shares of total population in three zones of
Middle East, 400 BC to AD 1000

| | | | BC | AD | | | | |
|---|---|---|---|---|---|---|---|---|
| | *400* | *200* | *1* | *200* | *400* | *600* | *800* | *1000* |
| 1 Anatolia, Syria, Lebanon, Palestine, Jordan | 39 | 43 | 45 | 45 | 34 | 26 | 30 | 33 |
| 2 Arabia and Gulf states | 18 | 18 | 20 | 22 | 32 | 41 | 37 | 34 |
| 3 Iraq, Iran, Afghanistan | 43 | 39 | 35 | 33 | 33 | 33 | 33 | 33 |
| Total in millions | 15.2 | 17.8 | 20.2 | 21.8 | 23.7 | 26 | 27.7 | 26.8 |

*Source*: C. M. McEvedy and R. Jones, *Atlas of World Population History* (London, 1978),
pp. 133–56. Figures are approximate.

There was a break in the urban tradition of the classical epoch.
Byzantium was distinct from the west not so much in its material
development but in the survival of Constantinople which provided a
political rallying-point. From a cosmopolitan, urban civilization Byzantium became a backwater, the major trade currents and the human
capital of millennia of development in the east Mediterranean shifting
south to form the mushroom cities of Baghdad and Basra. 'The urbanization of the Islamic world thus reflects the rapid destruction of the
economic base in the former Byzantine provinces', writes David
Abulafia.[33] Demographic details give an approximate idea of the dimensions of the shift, and of the human resources which lay at the basis of
Arab expansion: as the table shows while the populations of Anatolia,
Syria, Lebanon, Palestine and Jordan stood at a mere 58 per cent of their
AD 200 level in AD 600, that of Arabia and the Gulf states had nearly
doubled. The clash of the giants, Byzantium and Persia, had favoured a
peripheral, 'marcher' area.

The second turning-point is that traditionally pinpointed by
Byzantinists, in the eleventh century, following its 'golden age'. As
a political entity, compared with its neighbouring civilizations, Byzantium indubitably reaches a relative peak of achievement during the tenth
and early eleventh centuries. Success should be rated in terms of the
standards operating at the time of the calculation: Byzantium then had
no rivals in Europe, where the micro city-state was the most effective

political unit, the two powers with wider ambitions, the Papacy and German empire, being ineffective and checking each other's expansions; nor were there rivals to the east and south. There, the shift of the Islamic capital from Damascus to Baghdad in AD 750 had served as a first cause of diminution in the pressure on Byzantium's frontiers, and the disintegration of the power of the caliphs from the ninth century into four dynasties, Spanish, North African, Egyptian and Eastern, made Byzantium into the largest and most powerful state in the Mediterranean/Near East zone. This was an even more decisive change. Byzantium's period of glory is explicable above all by these political developments in the Arab world. It was a political success above all, but economically too the Byzantine empire could be said to have been in a powerful position in relation to its neighbours during this period. The eighth and ninth centuries, which had been characterized by the exceptional economic performance of the Islamic world – Abulafia writes of a 'breakdown of localism, or incorporation into a vast oikoumene unrivalled since the urban expansion of Hellenistic times' – had given way in the tenth to one in which economic recovery in Europe was beginning to be the principal stimulant to trade in the fractured Arab caliphates of the Mediterranean – 'the history of trade *through* the lands of Islam, towards Europe, becomes a dominant theme in the development of Muslim trade', writes Abulafia – as well as causing a more intense Europe–Byzantium interaction.[34] If it was European recovery which was the principal stimulus to growth, however, it was the older civilizations which were still the core areas in this world-economy, particularly the Jewish and Syrian traders of Egypt and the Greek traders of Byzantium. Hendy himself, though reluctant to attribute prosperity to the empire in this period, concedes that in the ninth and tenth centuries it was 'further advanced economically than most of its neighbours, and all of its western and northern ones'.[35] From this position of political and economic hegemony there is, without question, a sharp decline from the eleventh century – the treble consequence of the empire's internal crisis, diagnosed by Ostrogorsky and a succession of Byzantinists, the emergence close to, and then within, the Byzantine empire of a strong disruptive force with the appearance of the nomadic Seljuk Turks from central Asia and the reversal of the balance of power in the economic and increasingly political relationship between Byzantium and Europe, which was symbolized and reinforced by the Crusades from 1089. Byzantium lost its primacy and, as Diehl emphasizes, though experiencing some political recovery under the Comnenian dynasty, was not in a position to regain its past glory.

Thus there was a second decline, though not as clear-cut as the first, one indeed concerning which some of the data are contradictory. As the revisionist literature has shown, urbanization was increasing, agriculture was becoming more commercial, population densities were growing, trading links with the west were intensifying, monetary circulation expanding and the Comnenian dynasty succeeded in asserting imperial political authority once again. Similarly the social developments judged damaging to the Byzantine state, the growth in the power of the territorial magnates, are seen as 'progressive' by Marxist historians such as Kazhdan and Anderson, insofar as they were steps towards the emergence of a form of social organization, feudalism, that was compatible with economic and social change. Who is right? Diehl, Ostrogorsky and supporters of the traditional view of an eleventh-century turning-point, or the revisionists who would place the decisive moment in 1204. It would seem that it is conceptual and linguistic problems which are the principal causes of the difficulties. Firstly there is a need to define what it is that is declining. The focus of the traditional interpretation is on the Byzantine state. There does not seem to be much doubt that this experienced some absolute decline in its effectiveness from its period of greatest success in the tenth century. Its *relative* decline seems quite certain. Angold is surely being excessively circumspect in suggesting that Byzantium had 'much to gain from foreign penetration, but possibly more to lose': can there be any question that the Latin penetration reflected and sharpened a political weakening? Similarly defeat at the hands of the Seljuk Turks and the loss of territory on the Anatolian frontier reflected a growing relative inferiority in this sphere too.

The focus of the revisionists is (a) on the level of economic development of the empire, and (b) among Marxist revisionists on the catalytic role of the political dissolution of Byzantine autocracy to a dialectic of economic development involving 'stages' of history: feudalism as a first step, and the rise of a bourgeoisie as a second. The evidence on both scores appears convincing: there was increased prosperity, a revival in provincial cities, an aristocratization of Byzantine culture, and population growth. Does this evidence, however, mean that the traditionalists were wrong to argue that the ninth and tenth centuries represented a Byzantine apogee? Even if revisionists were merely making a case that success is to be determined solely by economic criteria, this would not be the case: the evaluation of success, as emphasized, is with respect to *other societies* at any stage of development: from this point of view Byzantium, we have seen, was more successful in the tenth century even though it was certainly a poorer society than in the twelfth. Similarly Byzantium in the twelfth century, though enriched, was a less successful society in comparative terms – there is no questioning the commercial superiority of Italians in the empire by then.

To clarify this conceptual problem a distinction needs to be made between two declines. That of the Byzantine state, for which the critical period is the eleventh century, and that for the economy of a Byzantine-dominated geographical area, one which as Hendy's analysis has shown shifted westwards to become more European. The latter decline took a different form, one which paradoxically was not incompatible with greater wealth per capita: it was one of growing economic 'dependency' as what had formerly been autonomous trading and manufacturing zones, with their own bourgeoisies of a kind, were absorbed by a world-economy whose centres now were in the Italian peninsula. Braudel expresses well the type of process in which the eastern Mediterranean had become involved in connection with a later stage of its development under Ottoman rule: he writes of the Ottomans being 'drawn into the orbit of a powerful monetary economy, already sufficiently strong to disrupt old patterns but not yet strong enough to create new and truly modern structures'.[36] The year 1204 was not such an important date with respect to this different form of progressive decline, whose sources on the one hand lay in the dynamism of the western European economy and on the other in the imprudent policy of the Comnenian emperors in admitting Venetian, Pisan and Genoese merchants to the imperial trading space on such favourable terms.

A transitional state, between Antiquity and the medieval world, one too whose quixotic obsession with preserving the imperial ideal caused it to clash continuously with new economic, social and political developments, thus, not altogether surprisingly, can be seen to have experienced the types of decline associated with both types of civilization. The first two of the three Byzantine declines on which we have focused were declines of the ancient type. 'The result was to cleave the whole unity of the Byzantine state in a conflict between civilian and military branches of the imperial order, strikingly similar to the fatal split which had preceded the fall of the Roman empire', writes Anderson of the social problems lying behind the Manzikert debacle[37] – and the third a decline of a 'European' kind, one whose consequences – loss of autonomy, loss of profits, domination from outside – were not as visible or as dramatic, but were no less, in their own way, profound: centuries of backwardness were to be the fate of the eastern Mediterranean.

For the further understanding of this third type of decline and an assessment of the degree to which this Byzantine space underwent it, it will be helpful to conclude with further information on the extent of Italian penetration of the economy of the east Mediterranean before and after 1204. Did the area become a 'periphery' dependent on Italian capital, or a 'semi-periphery' with some autonomy being shown by its own commercial classes? This is the question which I shall seek to resolve.

The traditional interpretation is one of a development of an overwhelming Italian commercial dominance over the empire consequent on the granting of a number of trading concessions by the emperor. It is well summarized by Charles Diehl: 'the Venetians', he writes, 'found footholds and enjoyed privileged treatment throughout the Greek empire; they became the necessary intermediary for all traffic between east and west.' Diehl argues that their hold was strengthened by a considerable migration to the empire, a colony of 10,000 Venetians existing in Constantinople by 1171. The pro-Byzantine bias in his work causes him to portray the Italian presence in an unfavourable manner: they 'wormed their way in everywhere', he writes, and made 'no effort to disguise their mercenary greed or their arrogance'. That their impact was indeed becoming great by the twelfth century is suggested by growing xenophobia towards them on the part of the Greek population, which included a massacre of the inhabitants of the Italian quarter of Constantinople in 1182. One is reminded of similar reactions to both Jewish and Italian mercantile intrusion in Spain during the sixteenth and seventeenth centuries. Diehl's interpretation of 1204 is that it had been preceded by an increasing realization by Venetian merchants that they would have to conquer Constantinople if they wanted to consolidate their commercial position in the east Mediterranean. An additional sign of Greek weakness was the pitting of rival Italian cities against each other – it is this interpretation which Diehl gives to the empire's grant of trading privileges, rivalling those of the Venetians, to the Genoese and Pisans from the second half of the eleventh century. Such policies may have checked Venice's commercial monopoly but they were to the 'detriment of the Empire, since the number of its exploiters was . . . increased.'[38]

From 1204 this Italian colonization of the eastern Mediterranean became a reality. In the partition of the empire which followed Constantinople's capture, the Venetians focused their ambitions on territories which would consolidate their naval power – they took possession of three-eighths of Constantinople, the island of Crete – the key we have noted to dominating the Aegean – of Negroponte (Euboea), which became their main base in the Aegean between Crete and Constantinople, and Modon and Coron on the southern tip of the Peloponnese in the Ionian Sea, which became the 'two eyes of the Republic': all vessels returning from the Levant were ordered to stop there to give information on commerce and pirates. At the northern end of the Ionian Sea the Venetians took Corfu in 1206. This had soon to be returned, but in view of their firm hold on the port of Zara in Dalmatia, captured with the help of the Fourth Crusade in 1202, they were in firm control of the Adriatic, Ionian and Aegean Seas. As Lane writes, they had 'undisputed maritime preeminence in the eastern Mediterranean'. They had used the Crusades, it is evident, to consolidate their trading monopoly. There seem to be no grounds for questioning the extent of this achievement or for doubting its implications. The Byzantine fleet had been almost totally neglected: 'of the Byzantine navy', Lane says, 'there remained but twenty rotten and worm-eaten vessels, nothing with which to challenge Venetian command of the sea.'[39] Venetian naval power and commercial strength ensured a virtual monopoly over the 'rich trades' which were crucial at this stage for economic hegemony. This position of monopoly the Venetians were to defend relatively successfully for some four centuries. The priority in their foreign policy in the east Mediterranean was throughout – as their choice of possessions in the Byzantine empire shows that it was from its inception – to safeguard this vital route for the 'rich trades'. As Braudel notes graphically in his *Mediterranean* of the network of possessions which Venice had assembled in the Adriatic and Ionian Seas by the sixteenth century, 'these islands, running along the axis of her power, were Venice's stationary fleet.'[40] The Venetians had effectively, in their turn, created an empire, but one of a different type from the Byzantine – a first 'world-economy' which was dominated from within Europe according to Braudel: 'a scattered empire, reminiscent, though on a very different scale, of the Portuguese and later the Dutch empires in the Indian Ocean, a trading-post empire forming a long capitalist antenna; an empire 'on the Phoenician model', to use a more ancient parallel'.[41]

The Byzantine return to control of Constantinople in 1261 resulted again in Genoese merchants being favoured at the expense of the Venetians. They were given customs exemption in the empire and control over the important site of Galata for their colony, as well as permission to establish settlements in Asia Minor and at Caffa in the Black Sea, which became a monopoly area for them. Again, to spite the Venetians, the extent of foreign predominance over Byzantine trade had been increased. Effectively the Byzantine empire's eastern maritime sections (Black Sea, western coastline of Anatolia) were now dominated by the Genoese, and its western ones by the Venetians. Both powers indulged in crude gunboat diplomacy to ride roughshod over any attempts by the later Byzantine emperors to check their power. The picture is one of colossal profits being made by the Italian powers with Byzantium barely benefiting from the huge expansion of trade which had occurred as a consequence of the Mongol opening of direct trade routes to the Black Sea. Diehl cites the example of the contrast between the respective yields of the Constantinople and Galata customs in the early fourteenth century to make this point – 30,000 against 200,000 *hyperpera* annually. As a Greek chronicler recorded at this time, 'The Latins have taken possession not only of all the wealth of the Byzantines, and almost all the revenues from the sea, but also of all the resources that replenish the sovereign's treasury.' A fact that seems to encapsulate the depths to which the empire had sunk, and the basis for the overwhelming Italian primacy, is the sale of the empire's second city in 1423 to the Venetians for 50,000 ducats.[42]

The discussion among Byzantine historians concerning the extent of Italian domination does not thus relate so much to a continued autonomy of the Byzantine state, but rather it concerns the Greek inhabitants of the empire and the extent to which they participated successfully in this increasing commercialization of the eastern Mediterranean, or were excluded because of poverty or archaic attitudes to commerce. The picture which emerges is an imprecise one in view of the lack of Greek documentation. A study by Angeliki Laiou on the Genoese links with the Black Sea shows a near-total exclusion of Greek participation except with respect to the provision of some short-haul shipping. Interestingly, we are later going to encounter a similar division of labour in a decadent Portuguese empire.[43] She concludes, 'The Byzantines participated in the economy of exchange; some made money out of it, but they did not control it; their economic activities were secondary and tied to the dominant Italian merchant capital.' However she does detect some autonomous mercantile activity in parts of Thrace (exporting of grain) and also among the Byzantine aristocracy and the emperor himself. There is evidence, she shows, of a high degree of interaction between Greek and Italian merchants.[44] Kazhdan, in an article on Greek and Italian cities, argues that the traditional contrasts drawn between them – the former as centres of consumption and the latter as centres of production – has been overdrawn, and he compiles a list of sectors in which Byzantine cities and their inhabitants showed commercial initiative, including manufacturing (especially silk), housebuilding, speculation in urban property and agricultural enterprises such as viticulture, as well as evidence for the existence of Greek commercial companies, participation by the Greek aristocracy in trade and close interaction between Greek and Italian traders. There appears to have been a growth in Greek cities, partly as a consequence of the steady loss of rural areas to the Turks. As other outlets were closed off, a greater participation in trade may have been enforced.[45] Hendy and Harvey, we have seen, have traced such a commercialization process back to the eleventh and twelfth centuries. The answer would seem to be that the existence of a strong commercial tradition in the area, one which had been weakened during the Byzantine Dark Ages but had been in recovery since the eleventh century, ensured that Byzantium was never entirely passive in its role in the emerging European-dominated world-economy. 'Semi-periphery' rather than 'periphery' would seem, thus, to be the label which applies.

The study by Angeliki E. Laiou of the place of Italy and the Italians in the political geography of the Byzantines during the course of the four-teenth century is perhaps the best way to encapsulate the metamorphosis which had occurred in the position of the empire in the two centuries following 1204. Her study demonstrates over a fifty-year period, as Byzantine losses in Asia Minor mounted and western intrusion in the western marches of the empire became more aggressive, a shift from ignorance to growing interest in the states of the Italian peninsula. The changed attitude, she concludes,

> is a measure of the weakness of the Byzantines and a measure of the colonization of the old Byzantine empire; to put it euphemistically, it is the measure of the inclusion of Byzantium into a broader Mediterranean world whose center of gravity was in Italy, and whose motor was the policies of the great Italian maritime republics. It was an unequal world; the ties that bound Byzantines and Italians did not bind them with equal force.[46]

# 5
# Italian Declines

The noble *otia* were now opposed to the vulgar *negotia*. Lawyers set themselves apart from notaries, physicians separated themselves from surgeons . . . eventually all those involved in mercantile activities or in manual trades, and their sons, were excluded from high circles.

Carlo Cipolla

As emerged in chapter 3, Italy's path from the fourteenth century was a complex one. A peak in performance was achieved then which was not again attained, it has been argued, during the Renaissance.[1] The claim is made by Robert Lopez, who characterizes the Italian economy as having experienced a kind of ageing process. The 'vigour' of the period of reconstruction following the fall of Rome had gradually been lost as a richer and more conservative society developed. A typical feature of the change was a transformation in the life of the merchant, who became more sedentary, commercial decisions coming to be taken in offices, with walls lined with account books, rather than on the move, as they had been, on Europe's expanding frontiers: 'The robust, but more inflexible body of maturity had replaced the lean, but more pliable frame of youth', Lopez writes.[2] Other characteristics of the more static society which had emerged were a growing concentration of wealth, a reluctance to take risks, an abandoning of trade by merchants for lives of leisure and a tendency for capital still in commerce to be used in a predatory manner, exploiting other more dynamic societies rather than in creating wealth in Italy. There was a consequent failure to provide adequate levels of employment and, linked to this, rising levels of inequality. In Florence in 1399, for example, beside the Medicis with their half-million-ducat fortune, there were 3,000 *miserabli* who were too poor to pay any tax at all, and two-thirds of taxpayers paid less than a florin.[3] The very brilliance of the Renaissance is linked by Lopez to decline: the value of culture, he argues, 'rose at the very moment that the value of land fell. Its returns mounted when commercial interest rates declined.'[4]

On the other hand, as we have seen, there was no definitive turning-point in Italian and Mediterranean fortunes until the seventeenth century, Italy gaining from some of the consequences of the Black Death: an increase in inequality of income boosted the demand for the luxury goods, in the manufacturing and trading of which it specialized, while particularly high urban death rates reduced the extent of competition in the provision of these services. Then, in the sixteenth century, following a short boom in Antwerp, economic leadership returned for a while to the Mediterranean, we saw, with the rise of Seville, the financial domination of Genoa and a revival in the Mediterranean spice trade.[5]

The establishment of the chronology of the Italian decline from the late Middle Ages is thus fraught with difficulties. It should be added too that there had been an earlier period of decadence for southern Italy – this time largely at the hands of Italians themselves in the nascent commercial centres of Lombardy and Tuscany. As emphasized in chapters 1 and 2, the economic changes with which we are concerned are not comprehensible on the basis of political units which came into existence centuries later. The motor for them, we have argued, was located in the economic centres of the 'world-economy' and the operable micro unit within this 'world-economy' was the region. In this chapter we shall thus study the incidence of movements in the 'world-economy' at the regional level. I shall provide short descriptions of the events in the four principal segments of the country – the south, including the kingdom of Naples and Sicily, Venice, and its state Venetia, Milan and the state of Milan, and finally Genoa. I shall consider these four areas in succession as their declines took place approximately in this order – though the declines of Venice and Milan were nearly contemporaneous. The procedure will throw some light too on the macro process, the 'world time', of which these Italian regions were now victims rather than beneficiaries.

## Kingdom of Naples and Sicily

Areas of southern Italy were at the forefront of the emergence of an independent, Italian mercantile tradition from the eighth and ninth centuries, as we saw in chapter 3, with important trading centres developing in Byzantine enclaves to the north and south of Naples, at Gaeta and Amalfi in particular and also, facing the Adriatic, at Bari and Barletta.[6] Like Venice, these commercial centres, were 'interstitial', but with an additional advantage over Venice in that their southern position enabled them to profit from Islam as well as from Lombardy and the Byzantines.

It was Islam which was initially the dominating force in the area, as we have seen: the Arabs conquered Sicily in 827, and their influence extended over the whole of the west Mediterranean, as is shown by their incursions into Provence and their sacking of Pisa in 935.[7] Islam's period of unity – of strong, centralizing caliphs – came to an end in the ninth century, with the decline in the power of the Baghdad-based Abbasid dynasty. Disaggregation until the Ottomans was then the pattern. However, the disaggregated sections of Islam to which southern Italy was most close were the empire's most dynamic parts until the tenth century and beyond. A sign of this is provided by demographic data: whereas the population of the Near East (including Anatolia) was nearly static at some 26 million between the years 600 and 1000, that of Islamic Africa, including countries down the west side of the Red Sea such as Ethiopia and Somalia, was in full expansion, and rose from some 14.5 to 21.9 million.[8] Trading in the zone was intense – a letter written in late summer of a year in the eleventh century from Alexandria reports that 'until today [from the beginning of the trading season], there arrived from the island of Sicily ten ships, each carrying about five hundred persons' – five thousand potential traders! The colonization of Sicily by Islam, like that of Spain, brought with it what was most advanced in European culture at the time – including sophisticated horticultural techniques and an introduction to two of the four principal textile fibres – flax for linen and cotton. Silk cultivation and weaving already existed on the island, a fruit of its prior Byzantine connection. A brief look at map 1 (see pp. 40–1) is sufficient to reveal what must have been the key element in the two principal commercial successes in the area, those of Gaeta and Amalfi: the towns were admirably situated to take advantage of the north–south routes which predominated, through Palermo and across Sicily, to gain from the links with North Africa and the spice trade.[9]

On the basis of these advantages the two towns experienced a growth process very similar to the early stages of that which took place slightly later at Venice. The extent of Amalfitan commercial influence was demonstrated by the existence of colonies of its merchants in the Levant, the ports of North Africa and Cairo as well as in Byzantium. The ports were also the principal activators of the commercial flows between Campania and Sicily.[10] The favourable conditions were, however, to be gradually eroded as a consequence of the area's experiencing, as Byzantium was doing, some of the 'fruits' of Europe's recovery during the eleventh century. These took the form of the establishment of the Norman influence in the area, with Robert Guiscard's becoming Duke of Apulia and Calabria in 1059, and the arrival of the Genoese following their sweep down the Mediterranean – Corsica and Sardinia had been captured by them in 1015 and 1016, and by 1088, as we saw, they were challenging Arab hegemony in North Africa with the capture of al Maddiyah, near Tunis.[11] Norman dominance in the area gradually increased – Messina was captured in 1061, Palermo eleven years later, and in 1130 Roger II united Sicily and Apulia. A year later Amalfi fell, and in 1139 so did Gaeta and Naples. Integration within the Norman kingdom was bound to affect Amalfi and Gaeta, which thereby lost their status of interstitiality. Their destinies were now joined to those of a dynasty whose principal ambitions were territorial expansion in the central and western Mediterranean.[12] Coinciding as it did with the expansion of the commercial interest of Genoa and Pisa, and the rupture which must have occurred in their Sicilian trades, it was not surprising that the influence of the two entrepôt towns steadily declined.

The exact sequence of events is in fact complex and it is now disputed that Amalfi and Gaeta experienced immediate eclipse. They were first edged out of the more valuable long-distance trades with the Orient. Initially this was engineered by peaceful means. Agreements with Pisa in 1126 and, later, Genoa in 1302, were designed to ensure a division of labour: the Amalfitans would enjoy the monopoly of the redistributive trades in the interior areas of southern Italy, but the spices would be handled by the northern cities. The development of a direct route to the Levant already, of course, undermined the previous Palermo–Africa trade, whereas Messina thrived as a consequence of the sharp shifts in trade routes, becoming a boom town largely populated by Italians. Force, though, was ultimately discovered to be the more effective agency: Amalfi was sacked by the north Italians in 1135 and again in 1137. It retained, though, an important role as a distributive centre for an extensive region: there had been a local as well as an international diaspora of Almfitans along the south-western Italian littoral at Ravello, Scalea, Maiori, Minori and Atrani, in interior areas of Italy, such as Benevento, as well as to the Adriatic at Bari, Durazzo and elsewhere.

Amalfi also expanded its commitments in the Tyrrhenian Sea, shipping and selling salt, grain, silks, cottons, dyestuffs, wine and other products. There was thus effectively a second stage in the existence of Amalfi. Arguably, then, there was no absolute decline, but if the wider scale and longer term, are considered, then it can be seen that though Amalfi's prominence had been in a period of a shrunken Europe with little international commercial integration (the scale of its expansion is consistent with this: as Abulafia comments 'the Amalfitan Levant trade simply does not present to view that massive, rapid expansion that we see with Venice, Genoa and Pisa'), it had at least exercised a certain dominance and leadership within this area. In contrast, with the commercial revolution of the eleventh to thirteenth centuries, and Genoa's and Venice's opening up Europe-wide trades for themselves, and with the fairs of Champagne outflanking it and its fellow south Italian ports, it was effectively reduced to a commercial centre of secondary importance only. Abulafia expresses this spatial shift – an enlargement of the Italian trading zone as a consequence of reconquest and extension of the commercial revolution was occurring – well: 'In this sense, the developments in Amalfi', he writes, 'are not simply part of the history of the Mediterranean; a commercial revolution which now took in the continent of Europe left Amalfi on the outer edge of the new, rapidly expanding western economy.'

Political changes worked against Amalfi and Gaeta too. They had become heavily involved in Norman royal finances in Sicily and on the mainland – an early and probably damaging consequence of loss of interstitiality. In this respect, and also in that of trade between Sicily and Campania, the revolt of the Sicilian Vespers of 1282, which gave rise to an Aragonese take-over there, and the separation of the two halves of the kingdom, 'were in some respects the Waterloo' for Amalfi.[13]

Amalfi's case is of interest: the town's rise, process of 'maturation' and then decline, as the scale of the European economy expanded, represented a first example of what was to be an often repeated pattern. It is the first decline in southern Italy of which we need take note – one involving relegation from the first tier of commercial activity to a position lower down the pecking order, as the commercial empires of Genoa and Pisa expanded. A second decline – or more accurately the second and conclusive stage of the first – was the transformation of southern Italy and Sicily into a dependent region, specializing purely in primary products, importing most of its manufactures, and with its trade handled predominantly by merchants from outside the area. A third was to see the collapse of the prosperity which even this humble role had brought.

David Abulafia and the French historian Henri Bresc interpret the further commercial deterioration largely in terms of trade dependency theory. The lightly populated islands of the Tyrrhenian Sea, including Sicily, and southern Italy, were the natural expansion area for northern Italy and Aragon, which were nearing the height of their medieval demographic and commercial expansions, and had no open frontiers on their own territories to expand into. The resultant commercial expansion, and colonization, consequent upon advantage being taken of these contrasting situations of population density, and hence extent of economic opportunity, resulted in the superior capital resources and technical expertise of the northerners dominating the southern areas and transforming them into complementary adjuncts to their north Italian economies: zones of monoculture, producing principally staple foods and raw materials and excellent markets for their industrial products.[14] Historians who have taken similar lines to these include Maurice Aymard, who writes of the two areas as 'two societies, two unequally developed economies', and Braudel who describes Sicily as the 'Canada or Argentina of the western countries of the Mediterranean', a role which it had played 'since Antiquity . . . with varying degrees of prominence but without interruption'.[15]

Abulafia, in various studies, describes some of the mechanisms whereby the foreign merchants acquired such a commercial grip on the area. Florentine merchants, for example, emerged to prominence during the period of dominance of the house of Anjou (whose claims to the throne over those of the Hohenstaufens, who had inherited from the Normans, had received papal backing in 1265) as a consequence of the support which they had given this dynasty in its conflicts with the Hohenstaufens. A range of concessions, including permission to export raw materials, grain and oil were the quid pro quo for this. Once established in this manner as the regime's principal financial backers, the Florentines' hold in the area gradually strengthened: further loans which they provided were generally repaid in the form of fiscal concessions, or in the grants of the proceeds of some form of royal tithe or tax, and they thus developed into the principal economic force in the kingdom. They made inroads, too, into the royal administration, Florentine culture becoming the culture of the Angevin court and their participation in the purchase of grain, livestock, olive oil and other commodities drew them into the heart of the kingdom, enabling them to commercialize their cloth.[16]

The example is representative. The other political regimes in the area had their financial backers – the Pisans and Luccans in the case of the Hohenstaufens, and the near-continuous political rivalry and warfare caused a regular need for finance and a susceptibility to making such concessions. The tradition was to endure too: Braudel emphasizes the near-identity of the contracts drawn up by King Manfred of Sicily in 1261, permitting Genoa to export corn, and those signed by Philip II, as Sicily's sovereign, in the second half of the sixteenth century with a range of states.[17] We have already noted a similar involvement of Amalfitan merchants in the affairs of the Norman dynasty.

Maurice Aymard, in a detailed study on cloth sales in the area between the fifteenth and eighteenth centuries, supplements Abulafia's insights into the political dimension of commercial penetration with practical details of the commercial connections which were made. The centrality of staple products to the economy of the kingdom, he shows, caused the timing of their marketing to become the principal commercial events of the year, generally in the form of fairs. Goods were paid for in advance, and the terms of the credit granted came to set the level of interest rates in the area. The large-scale transactions in staple products were followed by those in a range of other import and export trades, likewise generally handled by Genoese, Pisan or other northern merchants. The relationship between acquisition of staple products and disposal of imported cloth very often took the form of direct barter.[18] These practices were not, of course, unique to southern Europe. Wallerstein, we have noted in chapter 2, argues that they were universal in relationships between 'core' commercial centres and 'semi-peripheral' or 'peripheral' primary producers, and emphasizes their significance for that process of underdevelopment with which we are concerned. He writes that 'it would not be extreme to talk of a system of international debt peonage [which] . . . enabled a cadre of international merchants to bypass (and thus eventually to destroy) the indigenous merchant classes of eastern Europe (and to some extent of southern Europe) and enter into direct links with landlord entrepreneurs.'[19] Aymard's and Abulafia's research is consistent with a view of a politically initiated process of commercial decline of this type.

That, however, southern Italy and Sicily were already in the late Middle Ages effectively deprived of any autonomous capacity to react to new economic opportunities has been emphatically denied by S. R. Epstein. This view we shall have to consider in the light of our argument for a three-stage progressive decline. Epstein shows that, contrary to what would have been expected, Sicily's economy in fact proved far more flexible than Tuscany's, recovering more rapidly from the 'crisis of the Middle Ages'. This dynamism he attributes to successful regional specialization between three zones enjoying distinct comparative advantages. The west and south-west of the island became predominantly an area of grain monoculture, whereas the east, while drawing its basic subsistence from its own territory developed systems of polyculture, including silk, viticulture, flax, timber, oil and some cloth production. Labour was similarly mobile and moved particularly towards the east, which developed high population densities. This prosperous eastern half of the island also interacted vigorously, via the port of Messina, with Calabria, livestock being exchanged for timber. Rapid shifts in the relative sizes of the principal towns demonstrates the flexibility and responsiveness to economic opportunity. The development was facilitated, clearly, by the relative ease of communications in the area, which had the advantages of sea transport. Enabling agencies for the developments were institutional factors: the relative weakness of urban power, and thus of guilds and local monopolies, and the Aragonese reforms of 1392–8 which removed internal fiscal barriers to regional specialization.[20]

In support of his argument Epstein provides demographic data showing on the one hand a remarkably rapid recovery in Sicily from the impact of the Black Death – the population of the island which had stood at some 850,000 in 1282 had sunk to 255,000 by the 1370s to recover to 350,000 by the mid-fifteenth century, to between 500,000 and 550,000 by 1500, and to rise to over a million by 1600. In contrast Tuscany's population, which may have stood at between 665,000 and 720,000 in 1330, and fell to between 275,000 and 280,000 by 1427, recovered far more slowly: the fastest rates of recovery in rural areas at 0.82 per cent per annum were slower than the average rates in Sicily, which were close to 1 per cent per annum, and Florence's place in the pecking order of Italian cities fell from third or fourth to between seventh and ninth.[21]

In contrast to Sicily, Epstein demonstrates that Tuscany's recovery was held back by rigid institutional restrictions and by the financial and political dominance of Florence. A growth in the power of Florence following the Black Death might, it could have been thought, have contributed to some centralization and rationalization. Epstein argues that such a view is based on false suppositions about the character of Florentine government, which had no interests wider than those of the 100 or so rich patricians whom it effectively represented. In the absence of any such rationalization, the existence of a stronger state in fact represented a deterioration from the medieval situation of competing city-states in the area. Florence merely created a hierarchy of domination – it dominated the smaller towns and the smaller towns dominated their hinterlands. High rents, taxes and food demands from the cities impoverished the countryside and prevented rural recovery. Inequality in wealth was very pronounced. Rather than depending on wealth creation, Florence's rich were relying on exploitation. 'Florence's financial supremacy', Epstein writes, 'was . . . not the direct effect of its economic pre-eminence; financial capital was concentrated in the hands of the Florentine oligarchy by the purely political mechanism of taxation and forced exactions upheld by military force.' In such circumstances any type of spontaneous and rapid rural recovery was virtually inconceivable. As Epstein puts it, 'Institutional inertia and political expediency . . . together with exploitative relations between town and countryside, created a set of powerful constraints in the rural producers' commercial opportunities.'[22] The Italian historian Luzzatto's similar views on the exploitive relationship which grew up between the major cities and their hinterlands from the fourteenth century will be recalled from chapter 3: there is no doubt that Epstein's analysis represents one of the principal variants of Italian decline.[23]

Epstein's studies suggest certain generalizations concerning the character of the Sicilian economy which may be of relevance to its longer-term development as well as serving to throw light on another example of expansion followed by decline and dependency – the Spanish – which will be discussed in the next chapter. Firstly, he demonstrates a dynamism in the area to which the exceptional disruption of the Black Death must have contributed. It can be compared to the dynamism in Spain which followed the Reconquista, as it can to the momentum built up in Europe as a whole during the recovery period which began in the tenth century. The degree of autonomy which he emphasizes in the development of the area would have been contributed to significantly by the general European demographic crisis, which would have deprived the island of a great number of its Italian merchants, and the general commercial recession which diminished the circle of domination exercised by international trade. Aymard notes a similar recovery in local trades and local industries in the kingdom of Naples during the economic recessions of the fifteenth and seventeenth centuries.[24] The openness and flexibility of the Sicilian economy, the lack of municipal and guild power, however, even if not fully exploited by foreign merchants at this stage, meant that the area was open to such intervention, and evidently more open at a later stage than the regimented Tuscan economy.

In addition, important though the autonomous element may have been in Sicily's growth during this period, it seems unlikely that the contemporary shutting off of opportunities in the eastern Mediterranean, and reallocation of Genoese investments to the west Mediterranean, which coincides so exactly with the acceleration in the Sicilian recovery, did not play a role in some areas of the island. The revival of sugar production in Sicily and the extension in that of sweet wine, two of the developments which Epstein represents as part of the Sicilian *élan*, were consequent upon the Genoese and Venetian loss of their east Mediterranean colonies which had previously been the principal Mediterranean sources for these commodities.[25] Jacques Heers provides plentiful evidence for regular Genoese participation in the wheat trade from Palermo, and Messina was a regular port of call for Genoese ships in search of silk as well as wine.[26] Is it not possible that these international links were as, or more, significant than, for example, the Messina links with Calabria? Epstein plays down the importance of the export trade in grain, arguing that it never involved more than 15 per cent of output and below 10 per cent for most of the later Middle Ages.[27] However, as Kula argues, it is the percentage of the commercializable surplus, not of the total production, which is the crucial variable, and this was substantial.[28]

In the sixteenth and seventeenth centuries the international, European economy, whose development had been restricted during the crisis of the Middle Ages, moved to the forefront again. What is more, its potency was far greater than in the Middle Ages, for Europe was by now more populated (81 million in 1500, exceeding the fourteenth-century peak, and 100 million by 1600),[29] its economic integration more perfect and the voyages of discovery had provided a basis for expansion into a real world economy. Although the area showed continuous possibilities for autonomous development – and variety in the experiences of Naples and Sicily shows the importance of treating each case individually[30] – its fate can, on the whole, be quite convincingly accounted for in terms of developments on the wider canvas. There were some losses to the area from these – the sugar and wine trades suffered from the growing competition of Andalusia and the Atlantic islands off the west coast of Africa, which were being opened up by Genoese capital, and the Ottoman advance caused difficulties for Messina's trade with the Levant. The Ottoman expansion had once again split the Mediterranean though, this time, the area was firmly to the north of the barrier and Philip II was busily fortifying the coastlines of both Sicily and south Italy against the Muslim advance.[31] From the north, however, came ample compensation for these lost trades. The sixteenth-century demographic expansion and resultant food shortages, and that last expansive period for the Mediterranean economy discussed in chapter 3, occasioned a heavy demand for the south's staple products. Sicily and southern Italian agriculture faced both rising local demand, with population in both countries doubling, and became the granaries for the Mediterranean, political factors this time playing in their favour, for the growth of Istanbul was absorbing the wheat surpluses of the eastern Mediterranean and Black Sea. Braudel, we noted, provides evidence of these trends in his *Mediterranean*.[32]

In addition sheep-farming was extended in south Italy with the collaboration of Venetian capital seeking raw materials for its burgeoning cloth industry (to be discussed below). 'Foreign' capital thus returned to the area and, consistent with the higher level of performance at which the European economy was now functioning, it was on a scale far greater than in the Middle Ages. The Genoese dominated above all: a contemporary recorded that 90 per cent of silk purchases by foreigners in Sicily were made by them, and by 1585 there were some 8,000 Ligurian merchants in Sicily. The involvement of many Genoese in the area became a permanent commitment – figures for 1636 show Genoese owning some 1,200 of 2,700 rural centres in the kingdom on Naples.[33]

This situation of rapid commercial expansion came to a sharp halt during the seventeenth century, and this resulted in a collapse in the demand for the area's staple crops. The demographic stagnation and decline, experienced in particular in Castile and northern Italy, and the improving supply situation for northern grain, caused a fall in the demand for grain. Industrial collapse in northern Italy then precipitated a rapid decline in the silk trade of eastern Sicily from 1640, and also in the demand for wool. The difficulties of the kingdom of Naples were to be more severe, as is shown by population levels, which fell from some 2.5 million in 1600 to about 2.25 million in 1648, and by a further 20 per cent, following a serious plague outbreak in 1656, to about 1,800,000, against Sicily's experience of demographic stagnation, at a level of some 1 million. Western Sicily, Epstein argues, managed to remain reasonably prosperous on the basis principally of grain sales within the island. It was only the eastern half which experienced something of a structural crisis. Epstein indeed posits that had a broader market been allowed to develop in Naples, a solution might have been found for the crisis in the same sort of manner as in northern Europe, on the basis of market development consequent upon higher levels of economic integration.[34]

In conclusion, there appear to be three principal stages in the declines of southern Italy and Sicily. A first took the form of the loss of its commercial entrepôts as a consequence of the incursions of the Normans, Genoese and Pisans, and the relegation of its merchants to a regional, distributing role only. From this point the area gradually became a subordinate part of a trading zone whose capitals were in northern Italy: this was a second decline. It contained no equivalents of Barcelona, Genoa, Milan, Florence or Venice. There were fluctuations in the intensity of the domination by the north, such as the decrease experienced during the late Middle Ages, but the economic achievement of the area during these years, although impressive, did not restore it to a position of international primacy, and its continued lack of strong, autonomous commercial centres, and its very openness, laid it open to a revival in the kind of commercial exploitation which it had experienced before the Black Death. The economy of Tuscany, for all its grievous faults and inequities, was certainly free from any danger of a dependency of that kind. During the sixteenth century prosperity was achieved on the basis of this subordinate position in the international economy – though there must be some doubts about whether it would not have in fact been better off if its isolation from major international trade currents had been maintained.[35] However, during the seventeenth century crisis came. This time its very masters in northern Italy were losing their hold, and the area thus became on the one hand (worst of fates) dependent upon an area which itself, increasingly, was dependent, and on the other had to rely henceforth on the more casual comings and goings of Atlantic shipping.

The speculation that the area might have been better off without its sixteenth-century burst of prosperity is justified by the form taken by its decline. The expansion had been organized in an unhealthy manner. In addition to the intrusion of foreign capital and enterprise on such a scale, this unhealthiness had both technical and social aspects. With respect to the former, the increased grain production had been achieved on the basis of extending the cultivable surface rather than technological progress. Grain had been grown everywhere at the expense of the traditional Mediterranean polyculture. The result of this was declining returns and an upsetting of the delicate ecology of the area. The deforestation which had taken place on the hills caused soil erosion, and drainage problems affecting the plains reduced some areas to malarial marshes. The social problem consisted in the sharpest of polarizations in wealth. Both in Naples and Sicily, these commercial developments favoured large landowners, above all from the nobility and the Church, which owned 70 per cent of the land in southern Italy. Peasants were reduced to a totally dependent proletariat. The preference of the landowners for urban life in Palermo or Naples had the consequence that there was also a physical separation between property-owner and agricultural worker. In these circumstances social control over rural areas collapsed, banditry becoming rife.[36] The areas, thus, illustrate well Braudel's characterization of the social dimensions of decline to which reference was made in the first chapter.

Rapid population growth occurred in the area during the eighteenth century, totals for Naples rising to nearly $3\frac{1}{2}$ million by 1750, and close on 5 million by 1790, and those for Sicily to 1,660,267 by the latter date.[37] There are, however, few signs that much in the way of an economic recovery took place. Indeed the region's economic structure was such as to make dire poverty and glaring inequality a permanent feature. The agriculture of the region, which provided the only basis on which growth could take place, was deprived of any source of investment by an exploitive landholding structure and urbanization pattern. Though its livelihood came from the land, the region's elite preferred to reside in the city. Naples was the largest city of Europe, containing between 440,000 and 540,000 inhabitants, but its economy depended almost entirely on rural transfers. Heavy excise duties on the export of silk and olive oil (which forced down production costs), tithes, rents, taxes and income from rural properties were all transferred to Naples. So starved was the interior of credit, as Patrick Chorley shows, that a system known as *contratta alla voce* was introduced to advance cash to farmers so that they could plant, cultivate and harvest their crops. The credit was granted only at high interest rates, which led to further transfer of resources to the city. A credit mechanism for exercising commercial control over primary product producers which had been first introduced by Italian capitalists had become an entrenched economic institution, either by process of inheritance by local merchants and landowners or by that naturalization of Genoese merchants to which reference has just been made. Mercantile accumulation of capital there may have been, but it was in the hands almost entirely of importers and exporters in Naples, whose economic actuation was passive rather than active – they merely delivered the local product to foreign traders – and whose fortunes were a source for the reinforcement of the aristocracy rather than a threat to the status quo. 'This', Chorley writes, 'it seems to me, was one of the main mechanisms of stagnation in ancien régime economies of the "feudal" type.'[38]

## Venice and Venetia

Turning to Venice, we come to a commercial power which had been party, we have seen – if to a lesser degree than Genoa and Florence – to the commercial subordination of southern Italy. We return to the city's history in the fifteenth century, in the face of the expansion of Islam in the eastern Mediterranean.

Venice initially adjusted quite successfully to the threat. Its prosperity had always depended on its situation as an interstitial power, and from some points of view it was better equipped at retaining its trading monopoly in the area, now that the expansion of the Ottoman empire and later the rise of Habsburg power restored to it some of its status of interstitiality, than it had been in coping with the open competition of Genoa in the thirteenth and fourteenth centuries. Initially, too, the Ottomans, not a naval power, were more interested in land than sea conquest, and their first attempts to put to sea were easily defeated in 1416 and 1429.

With the fall of Constantinople, however, conditions became more tight. In 1484 the Venetian trading posts in the Black Sea were lost. In addition, the conquest of Greece and Anatolia had provided the Turks with a maritime population. This they soon put to good use, defeating the Venetians at sea for the first time in 1499. As they gradually extended their power round the Mediterranean, Syria was conquered in 1516, Egypt and Rhodes in 1517, and a foothold was established in North Africa in 1522. Following defeat of a combined Spanish, Genoese and Venetian fleet in the Ionian sea in 1538, the Adriatic was penetrated, Venice losing possessions in Greece and Dalmatia, and Turkish galleys reaching Ragusa. At the same time Venice's monopoly in the spice trade was challenged by Portugal and Antwerp, and there were additional challenges to the republic on land. France had invaded north Italy in 1494, defeating Venice in 1509, and the Habsburg dynasty had inherited a string of territories the length of Italy, from Milan and Genoa in the north to the kingdoms of Sicily and Naples in the south. Venice's situation could hardly have been more insecure during these years. The challenge to Venetian sea power by the Ottomans was supplemented by that of the Habsburgs, critical of Venice's trade relations with its Protestant opponents in northern Europe, and while the Battle of Lepanto (1571) signified reconciliation in this dispute and scotched the Turkish naval threat, it brought no real reprieve to Venice, whose resources were too stretched. It was followed by the loss of Cyprus in 1573 after three years of resistance. In addition, the reduction of Turkish naval power and the shift of the Habsburg war effort away from the Mediterranean after the battle gave the green light to generalized piracy by Mediterranean seafaring populations of all kinds, and increasingly by northerners, principally the English and Dutch. Particularly damaging was local piracy in the Adriatic by the Uskok-Slavs who used the Habsburg port of Trieste to sell their plunder. The historical parallel with the earlier harassment and displacement of Byzantine shipping in the east Mediterranean by Venice itself and other Italian states is emphasized by W. H. McNeill: 'English, Dutch and Algerian pirate-traders did to the Italians what the Italians had done to the Greeks half a millennium before: all but drove them from the seas.'[39] This reversal in Venice's position provides a sharp insight into the profound character of its decline.

The Venetian Levant trade, afflicted by these problems, touched a low point. It was restricted to Egypt where the decadent Mameluke dynasty's

incompetence added to difficulties and costs. The Ottomans had inherited the prosperous trade routes of the Black Sea, Danube basin and
Balkans. The crisis did not last long, however. By their conquest of
Egypt, the Turks in fact eased the situation for the Venetians, for they
confronted the Portuguese in the Far East, occasioning a revival in
the overland spice routes. Further, Turkish expansion to take control of
Iraq in 1534 brought the straits of Hormuz under their control too, and
reopened the trade routes between Baghdad and northern Syria, the port
of Aleppo flourishing. In a curious historical repetition, the Venetians
were drawing similar advantages to those that they had gained, together
with the Genoese, from the 'order' established in the Near and Far East
by the Mongols in the thirteenth century: by 1580, 80 per cent of the spice
trade was passing through the Mediterranean again. Their fortunes also,
as we have seen in the penultimate chapter, were boosted by the politics
of the Atlantic sector. Portugal's trade there was being harassed by
privateers following its merger with Spain in 1580, and, as we stressed,
the impact of the collapse of Antwerp's banking sector, the opening of
the 'Spanish road' and the selection of Genoa as banker to the Spanish
crown caused an Indian summer in the Mediterranean. The rerouting
of trades to the Mediterranean brought abundant Spanish silver to
northern Italy, which was invaluable as an entry product for the Levant
trade. The extent of Philip II's change of approach is shown by his
offering the monopoly of the Lisbon pepper trade to Venice in 1584 and
his chartering to the city the responsibility for its postal services with the
east. Even in these years of apparent revived fortunes for Venice,
however, there were clouds on the horizon. Firstly, as we have seen, the
northern powers were developing autonomous Levant trades, avoiding
the Venetians' monopoly. France in 1536 made a treaty with the Turkish
sultan and was rewarded with the same trading conditions as theirs, and
by 1550 Marseilles had developed as large a trade as Venice's in Syria.
The overland spice trade may have become the major one again, but
Venice was only taking a slice of it. A smaller-scale incursion, but an
ominous one, representative of the new distribution of forces in the
Mediterranean, was that effected by a number of minor commercial
centres including Messina, Ragusa, Zara, Spalato and Leghorn and the
former Venetian dependency of Ancona. Venice's periods of warfare
with the Turks (1537–40 and 1570–3) gave a particular fillip to such
involvements. The English, too, were active in the trade from the 1570s
as a consequence of the disruptions in their cloth entrepôt in Antwerp.
They drew direct advantage from the Venetian–Turkish war of 1570–3 to
gain favourable trading conditions from the sultan and founded a Levant
Company in 1582. War with Spain excluded England from access to

Portuguese spices, giving an added stimulus to the Levant link. The same disruptions, on the other hand, sent some English trade in Venice's direction: goods were rerouted to Hamburg, whose central European trade route to the Mediterranean via Leipzig, Nuremberg and Augsburg had its outlet in the Adriatic. Involvement by the Dutch soon followed, a first direct voyage to the Levant taking place in 1595, though until 1609 their trade was of minor importance.

Drawing up a balance sheet on the situation at this stage, on the one hand it is clear that Venice's monopoly had been broken. Its 'interstitiality' had become a relative one only, applying to the Ottomans and Habsburgs, and it itself was the 'empire' for these smaller, dynamic commercial centres and the emerging French, English and Dutch traders. On the other hand, Venice's position in the eastern Mediterrean, close to the Levant, its exceptional commercial and industrial experience and its vast accumulation of capital enabled it to sustain its position as the most powerful commercial force in the area. As late as 1599 its share of a large trade at Aleppo valued at 3 million ducats was a full half. The continued dominance reflected that late burst in prosperity of northern Italy and the Mediterranean. A sign of the favourability of trading circumstances for Venice was the arrival in the city of a stream of foreign merchants – Greeks, Germans, Milanese, Florentines and Jews, particularly from the 1570s. The latter were especially prominent and had two principal sources – from the east, where Sephardi Jews had been playing an increasingly prominent role in developing overland trade routes, across the Balkans, with Europe and from Iberia, where so-called 'Marrano' Jews (who had accepted nominal conversion to Christianity) were suffering from growing religious intolerance, above all in Portugal. The Jewish population of the Venice ghetto rose from 900 in 1552 to at least 2,500 by 1600. These Jews played the key role in Venice's developing overland trade routes to Constantinople to replace the insecure sea route round the Balkans. The phenomenon was not confined to Venice, other Italian centres showing renewed tolerance of Jews in view of the advantages to be drawn from their capital and trading skills. Leghorn became the centre with the largest concentration. The Jewish and other immigrations were clearly important contributory elements in the expansion. On the other hand this curious revival in the role of the Jews as the principal financial and commercial intermediaries in the Mediterranean, after the some six centuries of relative marginality, was a clear reflection of the decay of Italian enterprise. Again there are parallels with the prior Byzantine decline characterized by a growing participation of Italian merchants in both internal and external trade.[40]

The cause of the relative lack of Dutch penetration in the Mediterranean in the sixteenth century (the French and English were the main
rivals for Venice) was on the one hand their lack of a competitive fine
woollen industry to supply the Levant market, and on the other their war
with Spain and the consequent economic blockade which was imposed
by Philip III in 1598 on all Dutch trading within his empire. The ban led
to the exclusion of Dutch shipping from much of the west Mediterranean
as well as the Iberian peninsula, and also, crucially, excluded the Dutch
from access to the silver which, in default of cloth, was their only means
of financing Ottoman imports. However, the same restriction, in the long
run, was to contribute to the Dutch ability not just to challenge but
totally to supplant the Venetians. The embargo had the consequence
of diverting their shipping from the Iberian peninsula and Mediterranean to the East and West Indies. The event and date, which, Israel
provocatively (the target being Braudel and his dislike of the 'history
of events') argues recast Dutch destinies, likewise recast those of Venice;
for the Dutch, unlike the Portuguese, were efficient monopolists and
cornered the Far Eastern spice trades. No spices were to be had in
Aleppo in 1605, it was reported. With the Dutch–Spanish truce of 1609,
the Dutch returned triumphantly to the Mediterranean equipped now
with Spanish bullion as well as spices from the East Indies, and in
a position to provide the most competitive shipping services available.
Within months they added to their monopoly over the purchase of spices
another over their distribution in the Mediterranean, usurping the position which had been the principal *raison d'être* for the great Mediterranean commercial centres for centuries, and delivering spices even to
Genoa and Venice themselves.

The remaining trade in the east Mediterranean in the seventeenth
century (no longer in spices but consisting above all in the exchange of
woollen cloth for raw materials – cotton and silk being particularly
prominent) was to be monopolized, in turn, by the Dutch (from 1609 till
1621, when the truce with Spain came to an end), the English (1621–47),
the Dutch and English (1647–1680s) and the French (from the 1680s).
The exclusion of the Venetians from the new global trading system which
the Dutch had established meant that they were at a disadvantage in the
trade. They had difficulty in obtaining access to a number of the products
essential for trading in the Levant, including bullion, tropical products
and spices (a revolution) acquired in the east and now diffused in the
Mediterranean. With respect to the other fundamental key to obtaining
such products – cloth exports – the Venetian republic, like other Italian
producers, was finding it increasingly difficult to compete with northern
producers. In the eighteenth century the decline was to reach even

greater depths: the raising of Trieste in 1719 to the status of imperial port, and the foundation of a Levant company in Vienna were to challenge Venice's hegemony even in the reduced space of the north Adriatic. The city's commercial network had been pruned to an area not dissimilar to that from which it had started its expansion nearly 1,000 years previously.[41]

This growing failure of the cloth industry, and also the earlier one which we have registered of its shipping, are signs of internal weaknesses in the Venetian economy, aggravating the difficulties occasioned by the deteriorating international context for its trade.

Venice's naval power began to decline in the first half of the sixteenth century. The last sailings of her fleets of galleys, which were owned and administered by the Venetian government and had symbolized her power and monopoly in Mediterranean waters, were for North Africa in 1532, for northern Europe in 1535 and for Egypt in 1564. The degree of the curtailment in the Venetian state's role is shown by the fact that by the end of the century the only regular shipping service that it was providing was across the Adriatic, to the port of Spalato. However, as Frederic C. Lane has shown, it would be wrong to write off the Venetian shipping industry entirely on these grounds. In the fifteenth and sixteenth centuries there was a revolution in shipping design characterized by the growing dominance of the large, armed sailing ship over the galley. The decline in galleys was a reflection of this and of Venice's moving over to the use of sailing ships. In fact Venice's shipping industry sustained itself well throughout most of the sixteenth century, faring better than it had during the second half of the fifteenth century, when it had suffered severe competition from Spanish, Portuguese, Ragusan and even English shipping. The recovery was probably helped by the Atlantic and East Asian trades making such demands on the resources of Atlantic shipping that it was prevented from competing in the Mediterranean. However, from the 1570s a growing inability on the part of Venice's shipbuilding industry to keep up with the demand for its services became apparent, and the republic was forced to rely increasingly on buying foreign ships and licensing them to carry Venetian trade. The fundamental problem was a shortage of timber, particularly of oak, which affected other Mediterranean trading nations too. It was effectively insoluble, and Lane argues that the inability to match northern Europe, with its access to the vast timber resources of the Baltic, was a key element both in the decline of the maritime republic – if it could not build ships it could not prosper – and in that of the Mediterranean as a whole: 'In analysing the shift of economic leadership from the Mediterranean to northwest Europe', he concludes, 'one should consider not only the migration of technique . . . but also the depletion of the natural resources of the Mediterranean regions.'

Assessing whether the decline in Venice's fleet was a key element in its commercial decline is, though, problematic. The city's loss of influence in the Mediterranean carrying trades was more a consequence of increased competition than of shipping failure. The original dominance had been an artificial phenomenon, born of privilege in a period of restricted commercial and technical know-how. By the early seventeenth century it was arguably a more sensible policy to allow nations to service Venice's shipping requirements in view of the republic's diminishing commercial dominance rather than to attempt to revive its shipping industry. Mercantilist measures passed by the Venetian Senate in 1602 against the entry of foreign shipping into Venice were to occasion a severe commercial crisis. On the other hand it is possible that the decline of the shipping industry, which was nearly a total one – in 1650, for example, it was reported of Venice that 'ships are not made here and very few bought' – deprived Venice of an industrial tradition which, while it could not have restored the city's medieval grandeur, would, on the other hand, have represented an additional resource available to it as the wider opportunities closed down one after another.[42]

Venice's emergence as a major industrial centre came fairly late in its history. Its specialization was in trade and shipping, and it had always relied on others both for its own industrial requirements and for industrial products to export to the Levant. In 1500 its cloth industry was turning out only some 2,000 pieces of cloth a year. However, during the sixteenth century, there was an impressive expansion, to a maximum of some 30,000 pieces a year at the end of the century, making Venice possibly Italy's principal industrial centre. The growth, however, as a study by Domenico Sella has shown, was to a great extent compensatory to losses being made elsewhere. The first of these losses was that just referred to in Venice's spice trade consequent upon the opening of the direct sea route to the East Indies. The expansion of the cloth industry coincided with this change and was probably in part caused by it, as merchants looked for other outlets for the capital which they had previously deployed in the spice trade. The second consisted in the collapse of cloth production in Lombardy and, to a lesser extent, Florence, consequent upon the warfare in Lombardy and Tuscany following the French invasions in the first third of the sixteenth century: the production of cloth in Brescia, for example, had declined from 8,000 pieces to 1,000, cloth production at Como came to a near-halt, and the deterioration of Milan's industry is revealed by the decline in the number of entrants to membership of the drapers' guild from 158 in the second decade of the century to fifty in the 1520s and fifty-nine in the following decade. The extent of demographic loss is illustrated by the experience of Piacenza, where population fell from 16,000 in 1500 to 7,000 in 1535. Venice was spared involvement in these conflicts, and it was not only its cloth industry which benefited from this: its population grew steadily too, as the city became a refuge for the displaced population of the Lombard plain, from 115,000 inhabitants in 1509 to 168,000 in 1562.

The decline of the new Venetian cloth industry during the seventeenth century was nearly as abrupt as its growth had been: its output decreased to less than 10,000 pieces of cloth by the 1640s, and a mere 2,033 in 1700, less than its starting-point 200 years previously. Why the failure? A first point to record is that some of the factors which had occasioned the extent of the growth in the first place came to apply less during the second half of the sixteenth century: the spice trade had revived, causing a revival of investment there, and cloth production had recovered in Lombardy and Tuscany from the damage inflicted by the French invasions. Florence in particular benefited from the Venetian–Turkish war of 1570–3 to expand its trade. On the other hand, these local explanations, while they serve to account for growing competition during the late sixteenth and early seventeenth centuries, do not do so for the near-total collapse which then followed, for it is one in which nearly all industrial areas in Italy shared. This was a failure against the rising tide of north European competition. Why the inability to compete? A range of factors were involved: inflexible guilds, high wages, rising commercial costs as the scale of Venice's Levant trade declined, the existence of inflexible industrial regulations and, finally, the institutional restrictions preventing the emergence of the *verlager* or *marchand-fabricant* or 'gentleman-clothier', with a total control over the entire manufacturing process, which was judged increasingly necessary to ensure high-quality production. These factors prevented an adequate response to the innovative and cost-cutting industries of competitors.

The industrial challenge from the north represented, in fact, a bigger problem for some of Venice's industrial competitors within the peninsula than for Venice itself, for the city had never been primarily an industrial centre. Indeed there is evidence that the final collapse in the city's cloth production in the late seventeenth century is linked to a general recovery in other sectors of the city's economy: 'Venetian capital, enterprise, and manpower', Sella concludes, 'were being channelled once again into traditional fields, in which either the city's locational advantages were crucial, or exquisite workmanship necessary'.[43] Cloth production moved instead to areas of the Terraferma where conditions were more favourable to it, particularly to Treviso, Vicenza and Bergamo. Work by the

Italian scholar S. Ciriacono is helpful at this point in clarifying the different spheres which we need to investigate if a full understanding of the Venetian industrial response in a period of decline is to be understood. He firstly raises an important geographical issue, that in discussions of Venetian decline it is not just the experience of Venice itself which needs to be discussed but also that of Venice's very considerable territorial state, which extended from Lombardy (Brescia and Bergamo) to Friuli and included a section of the Trentino. Secondly, he makes a clear distinction, one again which has a geographical side to it, about the types of strategy open to the Italian economy in a period of economic reversal: there was a low-cost road towards survival which involved expansion in labour-intensive rural production, and there was also a luxury one, dependent upon profiting from the comparative advantage which Italian cities still possessed in certain highly skilled trades. We shall need to assess the response made to these two sorts of challenges.

With respect to the second, the luxury strategy, one of the most general developments of this kind in Italy was the movement into silk production. It was undertaken successfully for example in Florence, which departed from its traditional intense woollen cloth specialization. Venice, too, developed a silk industry but never fully protected it from competition as the interests of its consumers and its exporters (who could as well commercialize an imported product as a locally produced one) tended to outweigh those of its manufacturers. There was a similar failure to back fully a number of attempts from the late seventeenth century to introduce new production techniques in a range of trades – dyeing, silk weaving, velvet manufacture, silk lustring, woollen cloth production in the Dutch style. (There were similar attempts being made in commercial and industrial centres throughout southern and central Europe during these years as a concerted effort was made to catch up on the technical advances of northern Europe.) The consequence of these failures is that Venice effectively failed to become an important centre for luxury industries, with a few exceptions such as printing and publishing: the luxury textile industries it sustained were dependent technologically on those of Lyon and Florence, and showed particular weaknesses in the fields of dyeing, finishing and weaving.

The first strategy, the low-cost one, can also be tested on the basis of the silk industry. The lower qualities of production were permitted to diffuse from Venice and various towns achieved considerable success in their manufacture. In 1713 Vicenza above all was prospering on the basis of its production with 400 looms, and Bergamo contained 323. The expansion at Vicenza continued: it contained 1,100 looms by 1781, exceeding the count of Venice, which had experienced a sharp decline in its industry since the 1720s when it may have been quite substantial, and Padua, specializing in silk smallwares (braid), contained 6,000 (smaller) looms. So there was some success in this field, but it was a limited one only, and Ciriacono expresses doubts that its extent was sufficient to make up for the industrial decline in the capital arguing that the consequence of this relatively poor industrial base was that Venetia later was forced to concentrate on the so-called 'rough' stages of the silk process (mulberry growing, silkworm rearing, winding and yarn processing), leaving the weaving and finishing processes to be carried out elsewhere.

Ciriacono also argues that it was Venice's domination over Venetia which was in considerable part responsible for this failure. The capital exercised both commercial and industrial monopolies. With respect to the first the textile centres of the Terraferma were required to purchase their raw materials in Venice and were excluded from certain trades. For example, the silk producers of Vicenza were denied access to the Levant market and were thus restricted to working for Germany. With respect to the second, the production of only certain types of generally lower-quality cloth was permitted outside Venice itself. An example of the type of priorities which were being exercised is provided by the permission given to a Flemish artisan who had introduced an important new cloth type at Bergamo to set up a manufacture there *provided that he produced the same amount of cloth in Venice too*. It was only in 1760 that general freedom was granted to produce all types of silk cloth outside Venice, and even then there were some exceptions to the concession. Such guild restrictions were of course general in Europe with its strong urban industries, but in the case of Venice the extent of its own production was not such as to compensate for them. It is clear that the city's industrial guilds, while not strong enough to impose fully their priorities within Venice itself, where importing and exporting interests dominated, were powerful enough to hamper industrial diffusion in the extensive Terraferma. On the other hand, the extent of the damage inflicted should not be exaggerated. As Peter Musgrave's excellent monograph on the region of Valpolicella demonstrates, the extent of Venice's control over the Terraferma was limited – it was a loose federal structure rather than an empire – and restrictive measures, such as those just described, were more honoured in the breach than in the observance.[44]

Venice's 'seventeenth-century crisis' was thus not resolved as an earlier had been by a transfer of resources on any scale into industry. More significant changes, in contrast, occurred in the spheres of finance and farming. Our analysis of the city's experiences will conclude with these two themes.

A growth in the degree of financial instability in the city paralleled the increasing vulnerability of its commercial base. Between the year 1551, when the bank of Antonio Priuli failed, and the 1580s, most of the city's banks were forced to cease business. Banks' liquidity related closely to commercial circumstances in the Levant as they lent for long-distance trade and their directors, too, used bank resources for trading purposes. A spate of failures occurred before, during and after the Venetian–Turkish war of 1570–3. A further cause of instability was the growth in the practice of lending money to the Spanish crown, and here the Spanish bankruptcy of 1595 caused a sudden loss of confidence. A preference for rentier-type investment outlets of this kind was, however, a growing trend. The financial difficulties were enhanced by the lack of a central bank to provide stability to the financial system, but the response of the authorities to the situation was heavy-handed: on the one hand the activities of private banks and Jewish finance were restricted – they were blamed for the difficulties – and on the other, substitute state credit organizations which were founded (the Banco della Piazza di Rialto in 1587 and the Banco del Giro in 1619) were too cautious in their lending policy and provided no adequate substitute. The true cause for the difficulties was revealed by the timing of what must have been the heaviest spate of bankruptcies yet experienced, for a total of 2,007,356 ducats, between 1608 and 1610, the years following the truce when the Dutch finally captured the spice trade. The spice trade with the Levant had been persevered with to a bitter end. From this point the flow of capital into rentier placements gathered momentum principally with the financing of the Spanish government's debt, but also that of the French crown which was handled from Lyon, the Genoese acting as the intermediaries.[45]

The other means of disinvestment, by the purchase of land, is described by Brian Pullan as the 'most fundamental volte-face on the part of the Venetians': a city whose *raison d'être* had been its sea trade, and whose very existence and long survival had been consequent upon its isolation from the land, came to depend increasingly on its rural hinterland, the Terraferma. The premise for this development had been Venice's becoming a major, territorial state between 1405 and 1527 by its occupation of Padua, Verona, Brescia and Bergamo. Initially the relationship of the capital to its new landed resources had been very much that of a conqueror towards a tribute state. However, from the second half of the sixteenth century, land buying and land improvement (via drainage in particular) by Venice's merchants began to increase to become a major activity. Declining profits in the Levant trade, and rising population levels in the region, causing high food prices and a good return on agricultural investment, appear to have been the determinants of the trend. It is of this aspect of Venice's development that Braudel, we noted, writes of 'a classic pre-capitalist cycle . . . coming to an end': 'one has the impression', he writes, 'that the huge fortune of Venice was being withdrawn from commercial enterprise and invested for good or ill in loans at interest in the Besançon exchanges and above all in the countryside and costly land improvement schemes.'[46]

Demographic details serve to summarize the structural changes in Venetia consequent upon the shifting basis of its material existence. By the last third of the sixteenth century, the total population stood at some 1,700,000. Between 1576 and 1577 there was a serious outbreak of plague leading to a loss of between a quarter and a third of the total. However, as was generally the case in pre-industrial societies, empty spaces proved relatively easy to fill, and by the 1620s the early 1570s peak had been attained again. A further and more severe plague outbreak in 1629–31, however, repeated the damage: the total population fell by some 40 per cent to some 1,020,000. Recovery was again achieved relatively rapidly, and the peak figure had been reached again by the 1690s, but the population losses and resultant labour shortages appear to have contributed to damaging further the urban economies of the area. While the rural areas had recovered their pre-1629 population levels by the 1660s, urban areas remained well below them. A process of deurbanization was taking place. The urban percentage which had stood at 23.6 in 1548 and 20.5 in the 1620s had fallen to 16.5 by the 1690s and was to slip further to 14.9 per cent of the total population by 1790.

In absolute terms, it is true, urban numbers grew in the eighteenth century, for the total population was rising rapidly, the net increase being some 600,000. The urban dominance over rural areas – no power had been passed from Venice to its hinterland – meant that Venice and other cities in Venetia lived off the land as Naples did. 'Agriculture now', de Vries writes succinctly, 'bore directly much more of the burden of maintaining the privileged classes.' As in Naples, too small a share of the profits from agriculture was returned in the form of investment by the predominantly urban landowners. W. H. McNeill's expression of the new relationship is more forceful and has even more historical depth: he argues that the sort of exploitation which had been exercised over the whole Mediterranean was now being imposed on a limited number of farmers to support the luxurious lifestyle of the Venetian elite. The social price, thus, for decadence, and the form decadence had taken, can be argued to have been high. Venetia in the eighteenth century was among the most densely populated and poorest parts of Italy.[47]

On the other hand, terms of comparison (Venice against best practice elsewhere) can sometimes be too harsh. Peter Musgrave's study on the region of Valpolicella shows a rural society which, within stable structures, adapted and prospered during the century following the plague and demographic losses of the 1630s. On these grounds, of prospering without having to undertake major structural changes, he judges its economic system to have been more efficient than those of the northern economies. His study provides food for thought. It demonstrates that any agrarian difficulties that there may have been in Venetia cannot purely be attributed to Venice, whose influence was strong only on the nearer territories of the Terraferma, including Vicenza and Padua. He shows, too, that an additional cause of the crisis was probably Malthusian. The levels of population density achieved on the eve of the 1631/2 demographic catastrophe were as high as were ever to be achieved. The study documents considerable progress from soon after the collapse, with the introduction of new crops, though all within a strategy of risk minimization. However, the collapse of the experiment from the late eighteenth century and its strong manifestation of what was a general north Italian phenomenon, an extraordinarily high degree of absentee, urban landownership, must cause some doubt about the optimistic conclusions which he draws. Standing still in a period of change elsewhere in Europe is indeed a skilful operation, but it is ultimately a risky one and if, as it appears, it was also to the economic advantage of only a small minority of the local population, its social cost, too, needs to be taken into consideration.[48]

Recapitulating on Venetian development, perhaps the most fundamental change in the city's destiny was the acquisition of a territorial state on the mainland during the fifteenth century. From then its interstitiality, which had been the key to its success, was lost and Venice itself became prey to the costs and challenges of empire, in the form in particular of its struggles with the Turks, and then of northern challenges in the Mediterranean, but also within Italy. The possession of land additionally, as we have seen, contributed to aristocratizing its elite and, in the long run, provided it with an alternative to competing in the international arena. If there was a turning-point in the city's destinies it could be argued that it was the 1570s. Lepanto, which represented a last great effort to play the part of a major power in the eastern Mediterranean, the loss of Cyprus in 1573 and then the plague of 1576–7, which killed 45,000 of its inhabitants, represented crises from which there was to be no full recovery. The population figure for Venice on the eve of the plague (180,000) was not exceeded until the 1920s. Disinvestment from trade into land on a major scale by the city's elite can be traced from this decade, as can, we have seen, an increased reliance on foreign capital and enterprise. However the financial crisis of 1608–10, following the renewal of Dutch competition in the Mediterranean with the truce in the Spanish War is another benchmark of a most fundamental kind. There had been difficulties in the city's 'mother trade', the spice trade with the Levant, before then, but this crisis was definitive: rather like Amalfi, though the process had taken far longer, Venice was now completely outflanked by a commercial entrepôt to its north. The plague of 1630/1 and the quixotic war (1645–69) with the Turks over Crete, which had been the very key to Venice's empires since 1211, were additional landmarks on what was already a downward path.

The character of the city and its elite changed in conformity with their new sources of livelihood. The aristocratic government, now disconnected from trade and living off rents, prioritized policies assuring social stability – hence the attention given in Venice to charity and to conserving the guilds. The priorities were unlikely to be challenged in view of the lack of a dynamic Venetian mercantile class, since foreign entrepreneurs, confined to their trade buildings or ghettos, made little political impact. Such policies in themselves represented a further contribution to stagnation, slowing, as McNeill notes, 'adjustments in the allocation of resources, labor and capital alike'. McNeill communicates the full taste of the extent of the transformation, and of its social and cultural implications, contrasting the city's openness and creativity up to and including the Renaissance with its conservatism from this point, writing: 'Landlords and tax-collectors who squeeze goods and services from a sullen and resentful peasantry have a far less stimulating experience of life, particularly when custom has made it unnecessary to resort openly to force. Men's minds quite naturally close up when new experiences cease to be a normal part of life.' Of the city he writes 'Venice's urban economy came to depend very largely upon the city's role as a pleasure ground for rentiers where they could enjoy the amenities of life more fully than by living in isolation on their estates.' Only in vice, he adds bitterly, did the city holds its own with respect to innovation. The verdict is harsh, but the conflictive social history of Italy from the eighteenth century is surely in great part to be attributed to a failure on the part of the elite of the kind which he is implying.[49]

## Milan and Lombardy

Milan, and the state of Milan, of which it is the capital, provide a rare, in fact unique, example of an inland area of Europe which achieved high levels of urbanization and prosperity in the medieval period. As Domenico Sella writes in his inspired study on the region, 'the progress achieved in agriculture, the clear lead Lombardy possessed in a number of manufactures, and the strong commercial orientation of both its agricultural and industrial sectors convey the definite impression of an economy and society that, at an unusually early date, had developed many of the traits we normally associate with an advanced stage of modernization.'[50]

Geographical features provide the main cause for this progress. The fertile plain of Lombardy, irrigated by the River Po, lies between two mountain ranges, the Apennines to the south and the Alps to the north. Its climate, terrain and soil are thus highly varied. 'Between these two ramparts lower Lombardy is a complex of hills, plateaux, plains and river valleys', Braudel writes – and this variety provided a natural stimulus to agricultural specialization and trade. Vines and even citrus fruit were grown in the hills, mountain areas specialized in livestock and the fertile alluvial plain was devoted to winter pasture (at a premium in the Mediterranean), grain, rice from the late fifteenth century and intensive cultivation of a range of crops including flax and silk worms. As a German visitor in the late sixteenth century recorded,

> pasture is ever plentiful thanks to the abundance of irrigation, for in this territory one can see three or four canals built with great ingenuity one above the other . . . Whereby three or four times a year and even five is hay mowed in the said meadows. And this is why milk is produced to make cheese in such quantity as to seem unbelievable to those who have not seen it.[51]

To this advantage drawn from varied climate and terrain was added that of position with respect to trade routes. There were easy connections to the other plains of northern Italy, Venetia and Piedmont, but above all Lombardy was well placed to act as a linchpin to Europe's principal, overland trade routes. What Braudel describes as the 'German isthmus', or the trading zone between the Mediterranean, over the Alps, and the North and Baltic Seas – those links whose establishment represented a vital and distinctive element in the 'commercial revolution' of the Middle Ages – had their principal southern outlets in and adjoining Lombardy, via the Mont Cenis, Simplon and St Gotthard passes. The trading sphere, Braudel continues, was 'certainly an active zone, the outstanding example perhaps of what the fairs of Champagne must have been in the twelfth and thirteenth centuries – an early and potentially explosive form of north–south contact'. What is more, the shape of this vast trading area was like an inverted cone, with its point in Milan: the very dispersed trades involved were forced to converge by the obstacle of the Alps whose narrow passes channelled them into Milan. Milan, likewise, was the inevitable point of departure for the northerly currents emanating from its own hinterland and from Genoa and Venice – particularly from the former (Venice had the Brenner pass for trade with south Germany though the St Gotthard provided links with the Rhine, the Simplon with Lyon and Mont Cenis with the Rhône). The Alps brought other advantages too. They provided a virtually limitless supply for a range of resources – raw materials, such as timber, stone and iron ore, water and water power and also, crucially, people, serving as the demographic reservoir not only for Lombardy but for the whole of northern Italy.[52]

The advantages of geography and location, and the resultant intensity of commercial activity in the area, contributed to agricultural and industrial progress from an early stage. The intensive husbandry characterizing the alluvial plain of the Po can only be understood in these terms. It was the exceptional extent of commercialization which provided both markets for agricultural production and the capital for agricultural improvement. 'Man has entirely transformed this plain', Braudel writes, citing the drainage of swamps, the regulation of irrigation and water supplies, for which records go back to 1138, and the construction from the twelfth and thirteenth centuries of canals linking the Rivers Ticino and Adda to Milan and later connecting them with Lakes Como and Maggiore. Waterborne transport thus came to provide the basic communications infrastructure, just as it was to do later for Holland and England, the other two economies to achieve significant, internal growth before the railway age.[53] Manufacturing activities included the extractive industries, which flourished in the foothills of the Alps, and linen and fustian production at Lodi and Cremona, but Milan dominated above all with a large silk industry, introduced in the fifteenth century or earlier, the spinning of gold thread, a substantial wool industry, bleaching fields for German linens, and important leather, metal and armaments industries. Milan contained the highest concentration of industrial skills in the Mediterranean world: 'The greatness of Milan rests on its manufactures', it was reported in 1566; the city had 'an infinite number of craftsmen versed in all the mechanical arts, so that it can be called the nursery of manual skills', a Venetian observed in 1583.[54] Northern Italy had not only exercised a commercial dominance over Sicily and southern Italy, it had also plundered these areas of the technological inheritance which they had obtained from their centuries of Arab and Byzantine colonization.

Milan and Lombardy were thus in many ways the complementary, hinterlands to Genoa and Venice, and it is the interaction between the three centres which accounted for the extent of prosperity in northern Italy. In following the fortunes of Milan, thus, we are following those of what was not only a very important commercial and industrial centre but also the one most representative of the fortunes of Italy as a whole. Milan's was not a separate story – as in some ways Venice's and Genoa's were.

The area was dominated by its capital – Milan had a population of 120,000 at the end of the sixteenth century – but it was the prime example of, and pioneer in, that process of intensification and diffusion of commercial opportunities, described in chapter 3, which reached its height during the twelfth to fourteenth centuries. The exceptional degree of urbanization in the area reflects this extent of commercial diffusion: the state's 1,200,000 inhabitants were 25 per cent urban, and, in addition to Milan, there were eight secondary cities, four of them, Cremona, Lodi, Pavia and Como, substantial, with populations of between 10,000 and 20,000, and some twenty significant market towns.[55]

Unfortunately sources concerning the performance of the area's economy up to the sixteenth century are very sparse. Exports of woollens and linens to Venice in the early fifteenth century stood at 48,000 and 40,000 pieces respectively[56] – substantial quantities to which would have to be added local sales and those to Genoa – but there is no way of establishing whether these quantities represented progress or regression from thirteenth-century levels. There are signs of some industrial diversification during Lopez's Renaissance depression – cotton was introduced into the area in the early fourteenth century, silk probably in the fifteenth.[57] Cipolla also gives evidence for technical progress during these years: weight-driven mills for grinding grain were introduced in Milan during the fourteenth century, and new methods for cutting stone in 1402.[58] Were these various responses to declining commercial opportunities? It seems possible that the local version of what Epstein shows took place in Sicily consisted in a tendency towards slightly more economic autonomy, which included import substitution in the form of diversification into manufacturing.

A necessary preliminary to considering the performance of the area from the fifteenth century is to provide a brief sketch of political developments. A strategic geographical position has its downside: vulnerability to invasion. The state of Milan was the best point of entry to Italy for invading armies: it was known variously as the key to Italy or the *faubourg* to Naples. The consequence was that it became a principal battleground in the struggle between the Habsburgs and the Valois –

French, imperial, Spanish and Swiss troops clashing in a series of battles at Marignano, Lodi, Pavia and Mortara. Peace at Cateau Cambrésis in 1559, on the other hand, reversed the situation: France finally accepted Spanish dominance in the area (Milan had been a Habsburg imperial fief since 1535), and the region was to benefit from its status as the 'Spanish road' – money flowed into the state, troops were stationed there, the military infrastructure expanded and orders for armaments were placed. Slightly over half a century of favourable political circumstances were followed, however, from 1613 by a period of disruption of similar length, the state either serving as battlefield or as launching pad for new military expeditions. The area was being drawn into that downward spiral shared, as we noted in chapter 3, by all parts of the Habsburg empire.[59]

These political disruptions in themselves, though, cannot be blamed entirely for the area's fate from the seventeenth century. They interacted with more deep-seated causes of decline linked to that ageing process of the Italian economy described by Lopez. From the late fifteenth century economic performance at all levels – agricultural, industrial and commercial – began to flag. The difficulties in agriculture were particularly significant, for it was success in this area which lay at the root of the region's prosperity. They manifested themselves in the area's demographic history: in addition to a severe plague outbreak between 1576 and 1578, there were repeated periods of subsistence crisis following on harvest failures, notably in the 1530s, 1540s and 1590s. Public concern about these is illustrated by the building of a public granary in Milan in 1572 and the imposition of restrictions on the export of grain. The demographic situation in the area showed decreasing resilience, Milan only replacing its plague losses with difficulty, a situation which was accounted for by a contemporary in terms of 'the defect of nutriment and sustenance sufficient for it'. These details confirm Peter Musgrave's evidence concerning Malthusian elements in the Valpolicella area's seventeenth-century crisis,[60] as they do Braudel's ecological explanation for the decline of the Mediterranean.

Industry too showed itself to be vulnerable. While it was favoured by the local availability of some key raw materials such as minerals as well as of good labour supplies, the high living costs occasioned by agricultural inefficiency pushed up wages, and its prosperity depended ultimately on the continued relative scarcity in Europe of technical skills as well as of privileged access to certain key raw materials, such as silk, cotton and dyestuffs, commercialized principally in the Mediterranean. However, from the late fourteenth century onwards, the skills and the raw materials were percolating north to south Germany. The first industry to notice the impact of this was cotton: a range of competitors developed in the towns of Ulm, Ravensberg, Constance and Augsburg. In the sixteenth century the challenge was extended to armaments, competition from the armourers of Augsburg, Innsbruck and Landshut forcing the Milanese workshops to concentrate increasingly on the quality end of the market. Demand for arms in the area was so high, on the other hand, because of the extent of warfare that there was no industrial collapse at this stage.[61] Wool production did not receive this war dividend. During the late medieval period the area had established its prominence in certain high-grade cloths, but in the early sixteenth century, as we have just seen, the bulk of the industry was forced to migrate to Venice.

With peace in 1559, there was a vigorous recovery, particularly in Como and Milan, but it was to be short-lived only for, from the 1580s, there was decline again, not only in Milan and Como, but also in second-ary centres such as Alessandria and Vigevano. Greater competition was being encountered within Italy, from Florence and Venice, and also from northern suppliers. Silk's position, in contrast, was barely chal-lenged during the sixteenth century, although dangers, it can be seen, lay ahead: Henri IV was prioritizing the industry at Lyon and Henry VII was taking similar action in England. Overall, however, the signs are that the area's key position in Spain's foreign policy, and the lengthy period of peace, resulted in its being a principal beneficiary from the Mediterranean's last burst of prosperity. An Englishman noted in 1549:

> As for the richnesse and beauty of the country, I am afeard to speak of, lest to him that never saw it I should seem overlarge in the due praising of it . . . Nevertheless . . . this much I will say: that such another piece of ground for beautiful cities and townes, fields, and pastures, and for plenty of flesh, fowl, fresh water fish, grain, wine and fruites is not to be found again in all our familiar regions.

This is not a picture of decline.[62]

The renewal of warfare in the area after 1609 revealed, however, how fragile the prosperity was. Incipient difficulties gave way to outright collapse in almost all sectors. Demographically the situation was grim. There were crop failures in 1629, 1635 and 1649, the first being followed by an insurrection in Milan and plague in 1630, immortalized in Manzoni's great novel *The Betrothed*. There was a consequent veritable collapse in urban populations: Milan lost half its inhabitants, Cremona's population declined from 37,000 to 17,000 and the state's population as a whole fell by about a third to 800,000. This was crisis on a scale only equalled by the Black Death. Something most fundamental had gone wrong as was evidenced by the depth of the agrarian crisis. Large stretches of land went completely out of cultivation, herds decreased in size, rents and land prices collapsed. In urban areas too the collapse in confidence was general: houses were unsaleable, building came to a halt, and the decline in industrial production was nearly vertical. The number of Milan's silk looms fell from 3,000 to 461 between 1606 and 1700, and wool production was virtually effaced in Milan (production down from 15,000 cloths in 1600 to about 3,000 in 1640) and in subsidiary centres such as Como (a decline from sixty firms in 1600 with output of some 10,000 cloths a year to four firms with 400 cloths), Monza (twenty firms in 1620, none in 1640) and Cremona (cloth-making guild membership down from 187 in 1615 to twenty-three in 1648). There were only a few exceptions to the gloom: continued prosperity in some luxury industries, such as ceramics and in the metal industries, still benefiting from the impact of warfare. Otherwise, more than crisis, it is a process of near total de-industrialization which was taking place, breaking sharply what had been predominantly an upward trend for some 800 years.[63]

Peace with the Treaty of the Pyrenees brought little in the way of recovery this time. The continuation of the depression is revealed by the further decline or stagnation of the population of the state's cities apart from Milan: Cremona which had had 37,000 inhabitants in 1600 was down to 22,000 a century later, Bergamo's population recovered but at 25,000 in 1700 was only slightly over its 1600 figure, Como's population was down to 9,000 in 1650 from its 12,000 in 1500, surpassing its previous peaks only during the eighteenth century. Industrial decline went even further. Wool production at Milan had fallen to a mere 100 pieces by 1709. Cremona's fustian industry, which had had an annual output of upwards of 60,000 pieces of cloth in the late sixteenth century, giving employment to 14,000, was reduced to a shadow of its former self with a few hundred workers. Silk, too, remained depressed with the number of silk mills in Milan declining down from 388 to 100 between 1674 and 1698. Silk cloth imports from the Lyonnais, reversing the previous division of labour between the regions, became a major item in a growing commercial deficit. Again it was only in luxury industries that there were grounds for optimism – the manufacture of ceramics at Lodi, of violins at Cremona and of silk ribbons, gold thread, embroidery and silk stockings in Milan, all did well. These, though, were not major employers, and the overall picture is clear enough: what had been Europe's greatest manufacturing centre had become principally important as an area of consumption. Milan's demographic recovery was to a great extent due to this. There were 140 drapers' shops in the city. Sella describes the metamorphosis which had taken place as follows: 'For nearly two centuries these cities served mainly as centres of consumption, feeding on a flow of agrarian rents and government expenditures. Between the urban economies of the late Middle Ages and the Renaissance and their industrial successors of the twentieth century there is . . . a gap, a striking discontinuity.'[64]

It is the abrupt character of the decline and the relative permanence of the de-industrialization which require explanation. The parallels with Venice are clear, and indeed the crisis, as I have emphasized, was general in Italian industry: Florence's cloth production was down to 7,000 pieces by 1646 (against 16,000 in 1600) and Genoa's silk looms to 2,500 by 1675. Lombardy's crisis was just a particularly acute variant of the general experience. Its difficulties, though, as argued above, were the most representative of those of Italy as a whole: it is their analysis that provides the sharpest insights into the complex causes for this key turning-point in Europe's economic, and particularly industrial, development.

Part of the explanation has already been provided. That process of diffusion of techniques in which only the Milanese had previously excelled had continued and accelerated. By 1635 the silk industries of Lyon and Tours were well established and competing in all quality ranges. England in 1624 was introducing the production of gold and silver thread 'after the manner of Milan', and France from 1590 armament manufacture 'à la façon de Milan'. With respect to wool production, on the other hand, it was not a case of technological diffusion. This was an industry in which there had been international competition for several centuries. In this case the explanation which I have given for Venice's failure applies in great part to the Milan area too. The seventeenth century was one of difficulties for cloth manufacturers everywhere. Elsewhere there was adaptation, but the industries of the state of Milan did not show the necessary flexibility to survive.

The failure has been accounted for in a range of ways: high levels of taxation, a change in values, perhaps influenced by Spanish rule, causing a contempt for trade, and, linked to such a change, industrial disinvestment and excessive buying of land. High wages and restrictiveness on the part of the guilds have also been blamed. Of these explanations Sella gives prominence to the last – guild restrictiveness. One of his grounds for doing so is the fact the crisis affected capital- as well as labour-intensive industries, silk-throwing as well as wool production deserting the cities for the countryside. Had the problem been caused purely by labour shortage or shortage of investment, one would have expected one or the other of these types of industry to have fared better. A guild explanation is valid for both types of industry. His argument, then, is that the monopolistic attitudes of the guilds, which had not had major economic consequences when skills were still in short supply and industrial techniques little diffused, had become intolerable now that conditions nearer to free competition had emerged: the adjustments necessary to confront international competition were blocked. It was principally a failure in product innovation, rather than one of excessive costs, which had occurred.

This attribution of the crisis to the conservatism of the urban guilds is consistent with the fact that it was not general throughout Lombardy. From the second half of the seventeenth century there was both recovery and a range of new initiatives in the countryside and smaller market centres. Sella's study is in agreement with Musgrave's here. The progress occurred in agriculture. Intensive farming techniques and specialization were extended, there was an increase in fodder crops and the size of livestock herds, industrial crops such as flax and mulberry production were developed, and there was a remarkable expansion in rice production with the areas devoted to it increasing from 3,500 petriches in 1549 to 180,000 in 1723. Rural industry also expanded. This was both of the capital- and labour-intensive kinds. With respect to the former, the silk-throwing mills lost to Milan had been transferred to the countryside, which in 1762 contained 748 of them to Milan's thirty-four, and there was a growth in papermaking. Labour-intensive expansion took the forms of growth in linen production: there were 1,500 linen looms scattered across the state by the eighteenth century. A fustian industry larger than that lost by Cremona developed in the towns of Gallarate and Busto-Arsizio, and by the mid-eighteenth century was producing 100,000 pieces of cloth per annum. Rural diffusion of both silk and woollen production also took place. The iron industry, always concentrated in rural areas, had continued to prosper.

Sella's diagnosis thus is that a structural crisis in the region occasioned by the monopolistic practices of its cities was responsible for the extent of the decline, but that by the second half of the seventeenth century the area was adjusting in a way which prepared it for its later leading role in the Industrial Revolution. The structural changes, which were similar to those which had been achieved earlier in northern economies, and on which indeed these northern successes had been based, were effectively being forced on the Mediterranean economy. Distinctive characteristics of the Milanese example, he argues, were firstly the wide social basis for the provision of capital and enterprise in these new developments. An example of this 'collectivism' is the extensive resort to sharecropping rather than fixed rental tenancy agreements, with landlords stocking farms. A second distinctive characteristic was the extensive transfer back to the 'real' economy of capital which had been accumulated in some way or another in the affairs of the crown. Pierre Vilar has noticed similar transfers in the case of Catalonia's contemporary recovery. The area's decline thus provides further evidence in support of Lopez's views of the qualititative inferiority of the economic development in Italy which followed the crisis of the Middle Ages, even though the weakness which the trends had induced were only fully exposed with the rise of effective competitors in the seventeenth century.[65]

## Genoa

Genoa's response to changing commercial conditions from the mid-fifteenth to the early seventeenth century was plotted briefly in chapter 3. A quotation from Brian Pullan serves to recapitulate: 'Genoa adapted to the new situation', he writes, 'by cutting her losses in the east, by exporting goods and services (financial, naval and military) to the Spanish–Portuguese peninsula and by becoming involved in oceanic navigation.'[66] We have also seen above the extension of Genoese participation in Spanish-ruled southern Italy and Sicily during these years. P. Coles's observation that the link between Italy and Spain involved a trade-off between Spain's political domination and an Italian economic one is acute: he writes of a 'marriage of interests, the Spanish crown battening politically upon Italy, Italian businessmen battening economically upon Spain'.[67] The bargain served Genoa's interests well, we have seen, during the period of transition from the Mediterranean to the Atlantic, but the question of the city's survival, once this transition had been completed, remains open.

Before discussing how Genoa handled decline, however, the relationship between the crucial role which Genoa came to play in Habsburg finances after the bankruptcy of Philip II (1556/7), and the trends in other parts of the Mediterranean during this period which we have been detailing here and in chapter 3, need discussing. Italy's capitalism was useful to Philip II for two principal reasons. Firstly, the continued strength of its commercial links with northern Europe meant that there were active balances in its favour in Antwerp and other north European capital markets, which could be used as a means of financing Spanish military activities in these areas in lieu of shipping bullion. The second set of reasons for Italy's utility lay in its continued wealth as a society, which meant that there were broad social groups with money to invest (it is significant that Charles V and Philip II battened on the two parts of Europe where accumulation had been going on longest) and the advanced nature of its financial institutions, particularly those of Genoa. These were the factors which enabled a small group of Genoese financiers to service the Spanish crown's financial requirements for nearly three-quarters of a century. As Braudel emphasizes, at the annual fair of Piacenza the wealth of northern Italy was tapped to provide the advances which the Spanish crown required to finance its costly foreign policy.

It can be seen, therefore, how Genoa's role fits in with so many of the trends which we have been describing – it was the ample possession of bullion, channelled through Milan, which was an important enabling factor for Venice to continue to play a dominant role in the Levant trade; on the other hand the vast loans subscribed to for the Spanish crown were an encouragement to that process of disinvestment from commerce which we have been documenting. In Genoa itself, the extent of royal demands on its financial resources caused disinvestment from some of the commercial activities which had been developed during the previous century: for example from 1568 there was a withdrawal from financing Seville's Atlantic trade, and English and Dutch shippers took over a number of Genoa's coastal trades in the Tyrrhenian sea. Braudel, we noted in chapter 1, drew attention to this in his explanation for the Dutch success: Dutch capitalists stepped into Genoese shoes in the Iberian peninsula. A shift was occurring, thus, from commercial to financial capitalism in the city, leaving spaces on the lower tiers of the economic ladder for the upstart economies of northern Europe. Finally the link with Habsburg finances brought instability: the royal bankruptcy of 1595 disturbed confidence throughout northern Italy, including Venice, as we have seen, and that of 1627 brought Genoese involvement in royal finances to an end, breaking the city's credit in the same way as the 1556 crisis had broken Antwerp's. The failure had particularly important implications for Genoa itself, but inevitably influenced too the whole of that credit network which had been drawn into financing the Habsburg deficit, adding to the precipitancy of Italy's decline.[68]

Survival, however, was likely to be easier for Genoa than the other centres which we have been discussing. The purely commercial character of the city, and the constant need that it had experienced to innovate and try new markets in order to survive, had resulted, we have seen, in a flexibility and mobility in approach which was unrivalled in Italy. Thus, despite the crisis in Spanish finances, other Genoese investments – for example the commercial network which it had set up since the mid-fifteenth century in the west Mediterranean – remained in place and were there for expansion should disinvestment from financial commitments be necessary. Also, unlike Venice, Genoa faced in the direction of an area in expansion, and during the seventeenth and eighteenth centuries it profited from this. It was not at any geographical disadvantage in relation to the rising commercial powers of northern Europe with respect to the new oceanic trades: it was no further from Genoa to the New World than it was from Amsterdam. In particular, it was more successful than Venice in expanding its manufacturing activities, introducing new industries, in particular calico printing and the manufacture of fine silks and paper. The products of these industries were commercialized within Italy and the south of France as well as exported to Spain for consumption in the national market or for re-export to the New World.

The financial specialization was also persisted in. The credit needs of the Spanish crown were again serviced on several occasions, and consequently Spanish silver continued to flow to the area. The city, however, astutely, withdrew from the position of principal banker to the Spanish court, leaving that position to be inherited by Jewish and converso bankers in the 1620s, redirecting its lending to governments in Italy itself and then to royal houses and states throughout Europe: France, Austria, Sweden, Bavaria, Lyon, Rome, Lombardy and Venice. France, Europe's major power, was the main new outlet, and by 1784 accounted for some 34 per cent of Genoese investments. Genoa, like London in the late nineteenth century, became a rentier city, its earnings from its loans amounting to a full half of its total income. The specialization caused problems following 1789 and the consequent toppling of regimes and royal discredit, but demonstrated its flexibility once again ('the policy of the Genoese merchants seems then to have been flexible, interrupted now and then, but adaptable to new circumstances – like that of any self-respecting capitalist', comments Braudel), when nineteenth-century Genoa found new specializations in steam shipping, mechanized industrial production and, following the Risorgimento, industrial banking, playing a dominant role in the new Banco d'Italia. As an Italian historian comments, 'Genoa made Italian unity . . . to its profit.' The city's superior survival capacity over Venice is illustrated by their respective population figures on the eve of the First World War: 272,000 against 161,000.[69]

It must be added, however, firstly that 'survival' in this way represents a long call from the previous position of economic hegemony which the city had exercised, and secondly that, as with Venice, the manner of the city's survival left much to be desired from the social and political points of view. With respect to the first issue, we can return to the points of Lopez with which we started this chapter. Genoa's comportment since the fifteenth century, if the town can be personified in this way, had very much taken on the characteristics of the rentier. It had increasingly lived off other people and peoples, in both the southern and western parts of the Tyrrhenian sea which it dominated. Its shipping dominance, like Venice's, had been lost, its shippers confining themselves to inter-port activities and relying on the Ragusans, Dutch and English for links with the Atlantic. Gradually, too, even in this 'predatory' form of capitalism, Genoa was to occupy second or third place to the Dutch and English. A strong contrast with Venice is consequent upon Genoa's lack of a large territory of its own. Whereas Venice's accumulation of capital was buried in its hinterland, Genoa was forced to be more outward-looking, but the exploitive character of the trend is in common. It is perhaps this exploitive character of its business activities which caused Genoa's aristocracy and government to manifest the same political sclerosis that characterized other Italian cities and states during the eighteenth and nineteenth centuries. There was no precocious 'bourgeois revolution' in the city, and Stendhal's Fabrice would have been as out of place in it as he was in Parma. The demographic history of the Genoese nobility, Samuel Berner writes, 'mirrors that of the Venetian nobility: steady contraction and an unwillingness to address the increasingly vexed problem of the large number of unemployed, poor nobles'. Berner concludes his chapter by stating that Italy's 'failed transition' resulted from shrinking opportunities due to intense transalpine competition and the political make-up of the Italian states. 'We now understand that the problem of underdevelopment is intimately linked to political organization: the "failed transition" of early modern Italy must also be understood in terms of this link between politics and economics.' The politics of Italy's decline have barely been touched upon here – it was between the eighteenth and twentieth centuries that the necessary political adjustments were painfully made to enable Europe's first economic power to adapt to industrialization.[70]

# 6
# Iberian Declines

One cannot improvise an enterprising commercial society: when the explorations paid off, Portugal and Castile had to turn to German, Italian and other foreign merchants for capital and advice, and they never quite made up for a delayed start.

R. S. Lopez, 'The Trade of Medieval Europe'

We have been trying to make of this republic a republic of the bewitched, living outside the natural order of things.

M González de Cellerigo, *Memorial de la política necessaria y útil restauración de la república de España*

Conceptual problems exist with respect to Iberian decline. It has been argued that the very notion of the decline is a 'myth' in that there was no original economic success from which decadence could have been experienced. Criticisms have been addressed at the vagueness of the decline literature: vagueness concerning the timing of any possible decay, about the type of decline (economic, military or political) and about the identity of the unit involved: was it parts of the peninsula, the peninsula as a whole, the Spanish European empire or the Spanish European and American empires? It has been argued convincingly that the peninsula's fate cannot be considered in isolation but only in the context of developments in Europe as a whole, in view of Iberian 'dependency' on more advanced economies. Finally, as a corollary to this last point, it has been asserted by Henry Kamen that Iberia during the sixteenth and seventeenth centuries is more accurately portrayed as being in a state of dependency rather than as undergoing decline.[1]

That the Iberian economy became dependent is, I think, unquestionable, but no economy starts its existence in this way. It is a state induced by a development process in which one of two trading parties comes out the loser. There have, however, clearly been difficulties in locating an era in Iberian history when its economy was not, to some extent at least, dependent, and this is a principal cause for the conceptual difficulties. A preliminary in this chapter will thus be the locating of such an era. Once located, the dynamics and stages of Iberian decline should be easier to identify.

Moving back in time, the closest such point of non-dependency is between the years 900 and 1150, the high-water mark of the seven centuries of Arab rule in the peninsula. Rather than being dependent at this stage, the Islamic kingdom of 'al-Andalus' was itself a dominating force, both culturally and economically. Its levels of urbanization were exceptional for the period, Cordoba, with its population of some 100,000 in the tenth century, being Europe's largest city by far;[2] it was a channel for oriental spices and luxury products, precious metals from Africa and slaves; it was a source for rare minerals like tin and zinc; it possessed an advanced agriculture, specializing in particular in olives, almonds, figs, lemons and grapes, and using intensive irrigation techniques for the production of saffron, madder, pastel, cochineal, flax and silk; it contained an important industrial sector, famed for its manufacturing of armaments, silk, glass, leather goods (the gold-embossed 'Cordobans'), fustians and paper. It was the most westerly outpost of a flourishing and powerful civilization, a central point of interchange between this civilization and the Christian world. The trade axis at the extremity of which it lay followed the North African littoral, passing south of Sicily, with Tunis an important port of call, and Almería the point of entry, to form a second prong in the Arabic Mediterranean commercial network to that, passing through Sicily into Italy, which was considered in the first section of the previous chapter.

There was no dependency at this point. Rather it was Arabic Spain which controlled the 'rich trades' and drew advantages from this. Barcelona, the closest powerful Christian commercial centre, prospered as an intermediary, rather like Amalfi.[3] Al-Andalus was 'civilization', the Christians, concentrated north of the Duero and east of the Ebro, the 'marcher lords', demanding tribute in return for commitments not to attack, yet constantly drawn south, attracted by the superior civilization. 'Until the mid-twelfth century', writes Olivia Constable, 'al-Andalus, and the peninsula in general, appear to have maintained this role as entrepôt and exporter.'[4]

The reversal of this situation came about, as that of southern Italy had done, as a consequence of reconquest. The Italian ports of Pisa and Genoa, particularly the latter, participated in this in Spain and, as they had done in southern Italy, and as the Venetians had done in the late eleventh century in connection with their provision of naval assistance to Byzantium, they demanded and received substantial trading concessions in return. With the gradual Islamic withdrawal, Italian capital (Florentine as well as Pisan and Genoese) filled a considerable part of the vacuum which was left. Italian merchants also served as the increasingly essential intermediaries in a Christian-dominated Mediterranean for the isolated, still unconquered kingdom of Granada. It was not of course a total evacuation by the Muslims. Left behind were both some of the Jewish traders who had played a large part in Islamic–Christian trade as well as a subject Moorish population (the 'mudejars'), among whom were both skilled agricultural and industrial workers as well as traders. However, Italian capital became the dominant force. A dependency thus came into existence for the first time. Constable leaves no doubt as to the character of the change which had occurred: 'Genoese and other Christian ports', she writes, 'came to fill the role which Spain itself had played in previous centuries, of procurer and distributor of eastern goods in the Western Mediterranean.'[5]

It should be added, of course, as was emphasized in the previous chapter in connection with the parallel process in southern Italy, that more was involved in the change than purely the supplanting of Arab and Jewish traders. There was a qualitative difference in the Genoese and Pisan role in that their links with inner and northern Europe meant that for the first time southern Spain was becoming fully a part of a larger, Christian economic area. David Abulafia's comment, which was quoted in connection with Amalfi in the previous chapter, could as well have been made of Andalusia: 'the developments . . . are not simply part of the history of the Mediterranean, a commercial revolution which now took in the continent of Europe left [Andalusia] on the outer edge of the new, rapidly expanding western economy.'[6] Equally, of course, southern Iberia was being withdrawn from the Egyptian-based Arab trading zone which, limited as it now was to the north and the west, was being extended south and east to the Red Sea and down the east coast of Africa, Alexandria, rather than al-Andalus becoming 'the frontier market between Muslim and Christian trading spheres'.[7]

The earliest growth of 'dependency' in the Iberian economy thus came with the Reconquista. As was to be the case later following the voyages of discovery, the Reconquista brought territorial gains and commercial opportunities which were too great to be fully exploited by 'Iberian' hands. Italian involvement was all the intenser as the Reconquista coincided with the height of the Italian 'commercial revolution'. It should be emphasized, however, that the term 'dependency' is not a precise one. Andalusia's was not as extreme an example of it as Corsica's and Sardinia's, subjected to direct rule by the Italians behind the departing Muslims. The nearest analogy would again be southern Italy and Sicily where, as in Spain, 'feudal' political regimes provided some checks to the incursions of north Italian capital.[8] It should also be noted that it is in Andalusia, not in the whole of Spain, that 'dependency' was developing: Castile, the kingdom of Aragon and northern Spain were not at this stage being infiltrated in this way, and within Andalusia the Italian presence was concentrated at Cádiz, Puerto de Santa María, Jerez de la Frontera and Seville itself, the towns providing access to the Guadalquivir valley, the core area of the Islamic civilization containing those resources listed above.

A further cause for the extent of the Italian involvement in the area was the Reconquista's opening of the straits of Gibraltar to Christian shipping and the development in the second half of the thirteenth century of a direct sea route to northern Europe. Spanish ports were used both as stopping points on this route and also as a source, and market, for traded goods. The types of shifts which were going on are well illustrated by the diverging fortunes of the cities of Almería and Málaga, both in the kingdom of Granada. The former had been the principal Arab port, well situated as it was for servicing the trades from Africa and the needs of the Moorish capital at Granada, and the latter was ideally situated as a provisioning and trading point on the now more important trade routes leading out of the Mediterranean. Almería stagnated while Málaga boomed. Again, however, it should be emphasized that the degree of Iberian 'dependence' on Italian capital occasioned by these new trading activities was limited at this stage and that the Italian presence brought opportunities as well as dependence. Iberian wool exports developed, replacing silk as the principal fibre traded, and extensive use was made of Iberian shipping by Genoese, Pisan and Venetian traders: in this case it was Italian resources which were inadequate for servicing the new trading opportunities which had presented themselves.[9]

Moving now to the issue of variations in the intensity of 'dependency' over time, the Malthusian-induced slowing down in population growth from the late thirteenth century, and then the collapse in numbers following the Black Death, caused international commerce to retreat everywhere, and particularly from more peripheral involvements such as those with southern Spain. This was noted in connection with southern Italy and Sicily in the last chapter. It also contributed to a slowing down in the Reconquista. During the thirteenth century, progress had been extremely rapid, Christian Spain doubling its territory between 1212 and 1264, but the final conquest of the kingdom of Granada was to have to wait for over two hundred years until 1492.[10]

On the other hand, an intensification in 'dependency' came about in the fifteenth century with, on the one hand, demographic recovery throughout Europe, which contributed to a new expansive phase in the still Italian-centred European capitalism, and, on the other, as noted in chapter 3, the Ottoman expansion in the eastern Mediterranean. Once again the Muslim–Christian struggle was setting the parameters for commercial life and, though this time it was Muslim rather than Christian successes which were the catalyst, it was again Christian trade which was boosted in the western Mediterranean. The vast stocks of Genoese capital, accumulated principally in the eastern half of the Mediterranean, were redeployed in the western half, and, beyond the Straits, in trade with Africa, the east Atlantic islands and northern Europe. Jacques Heers describes this geographical metamorphosis as a 'a veritable Genoese colonialism, not in the east this time . . . but in the west'.[11]

To this impact from these shifts in trade routes, and from the major involvement of Italian capital, was added from the late fifteenth century that occasioned by events consequent upon different causal chains: firstly the dynastic marriages which gave rise to Spain becoming the centre of a European empire, and secondly Columbus's voyages of discovery, which led to a second, and even larger empire, being built. The first step in the former developments, described by Perry Anderson as the 'the supreme artefact of feudal mechanism of political expansion', consisted in the union between the crowns of Castile and Aragon in 1469 following the marriage between Ferdinand, then king of Sicily and heir to the throne of Aragon, and Isabella, the heiress of Castile. This was followed by the marriage of the fruit of this marriage, Joanna (the mad) to Philip (the handsome), himself the product of another marriage alliance between the houses of Burgundy and Habsburg. The full harvest was reaped by Charles V (V of the Holy Roman Empire though I of Spain) in the sucessive inheritances of Burgundy in 1506, Castile and Aragon in 1516 and the Holy Roman Empire in 1519.[12]

It is on these stages of the peninsula's history that I shall be focusing in this chapter. To avoid incurring the type of stricture made by Kamen,

I shall stipulate what will be the principal objects of my analysis. I shall be attempting to clarify the dynamics of the process of decline which the Iberian (both Portuguese and Spanish) economies experienced during the sixteenth and seventeenth centuries. In this clarification, I shall be concerned with Spain's American and European empires, as well as with its international military involvement and the international trading system into which the Iberian peninsula fitted, but concerned with them here only insofar as they have implications for developments within the Iberian economy. Some of their implications for other parts of Europe have been considered in chapters 3 and 5.

# Portugal

## *External developments*

Overseas discoveries were to make most impact on Portugal, which was a smaller country than Spain and one which experienced no distraction from European empire.[13] The size and resources of the area which it had been allocated by the treaty of Tordesillas in 1494 were so vast in relation to its own territory that, bar short interludes during which the needs of the domestic economy were prioritized, 'colonization' became the determining influence on its history. The impact came earlier, too. The return of Vasco da Gama to Lisbon in 1499, laden with spices, occasioned an immediate economic revolution. This contrasts with the fifty or sixty years which passed before Columbus's discoveries brought significant economic returns.

The empire's history divides into four principal stages. A first, consisting in the establishment of trading posts in the East Indies and the consequent initial monopolization, and then profiting from a share, of the European pepper and spice trades, was described briefly in chapter 3. It lasted until approximately 1620. A second saw the growing importance of the Atlantic trades, particularly sugar production in Brazil, and lasted into the 1680s. A third phase was occasioned by the discovery of large gold resources in Brazil and was also contributed to by growing wine exports, from Portugal itself and from its Atlantic possessions. Finally, a last lease of life was drawn from Portugal's remaining, African colonies in the twentieth century as a consequence of access to their interiors being provided by railway construction.[14] Turning to the first phase, characterized by the novel partnership between Lisbon and Antwerp, we have seen that its progress was checked from the 1540s by financial crises in Antwerp and a recovery in the overland spice route with its outlets in the east Mediterranean. This development has often been felt to imply a Portuguese 'failure', for the original intention had been to cut the overland spice route. Such a view, however, is imprecise, for the recovery by no means brought the Portuguese trade to an end. Firstly, pepper and other spices continued to be imported, and though there was no monopoly, they represented a basis for achieving large profits for Lisbon's merchants. Secondly, with the faltering of the pepper monopoly, there was a broadening in the Portuguese trade to include the import of precious stones and, above all, textiles. For the period 1580–1640 records show that the latter – silks and cottons – were the predominant item in the trade, accounting for some 62 per cent of the total value of cargoes. The pessimistic views on the sea route to the east have arisen from focusing purely on the trade of the Portuguese crown, which exercised the pepper monopoly. In fact the bulk of the trade from the mid-century was in private hands, and its broadening to include other commodities was a sign of its vitality. A. C. Boyajian, the trade's historian for this period, writes that the 'expansion of private trade during the second half of the sixteenth century in fact gradually transformed the Portuguese overseas venture from a regime of plunder, tributes, and privileged trade of the king and a few aristocrats into a truly commercial empire, whose wealth derived from the private trade of merchants in Lisbon and across Asia and Africa, and the Americas.'[15]

A better measure for the trade's fortunes is provided by the records of the number of ships involved in it. The figures decline from a peak of 138 departures from Lisbon for 1500–9 to remain at a relatively stable level (this may mean progress as ship sizes increased), decadal sailings fluctuating between a low of 44 and a high of 96 until the 1630s. From this point there was a slump from which there was only slight recovery, the collapse being explained by military incursions of the Dutch, as we have seen.[16] The trade was never lost totally, but it had ceased to occasion a major transfer of resources to Portugal even though it enriched the many Portuguese who had settled in the east and others who moved to the Dutch Republic to continue with their businesses.

This success in dominating the East Indies trade for some 130 years illustrates a marked robustness in Lisbon's commercial community. The extent to which this strength was a Portuguese one (and thus a sign of commercial autonomy), or one of foreign merchants (and thus of dependency), is a complex one which must be broached at this point. Firstly it must be acknowledged that Portugal, like Spain, had benefited from Italian collaboration, both in its reconquest and in early colonial ventures in North Africa and the east Atlantic, from the first half of the fourteenth century. The early Portuguese colonization of the Canary islands between 1367 and 1383, for example, had profited in particular from the aid of the Genoese, with their prior experience of colonizing in the east Mediterranean. On the other hand, the involvement had a different character from that in southern Spain. Portugal, with its extensive coastline, was far more of a maritime nation than Castile, which had no Mediterranean outlet until the thirteenth-century conquests, and a limited one only until the fall of the kingdom of Granada in 1492. Nor were the ports of Portugal, bar those such as Lagos on its southern tip in the Algarve, so essential a stopping place for the Italian convoys trading with northern Europe as those of Andalusia. These factors gave a greater autonomy to the trading in the area and caused those Italians who did settle in Portugal (the Lomellini family being the prime example) to do so largely on Portuguese terms, so that they integrated into the Portuguese social and commercial networks rather than purely acting as agents for their home ports.[17]

A second distinction must be made between those trades in which the Portuguese and Italians had complementary skills or resources, in which collaboration occurred, and those in which they were rivals. The sugar and wine plantations in the Canaries, Madeira and Azores are an example of the former. Italian merchants provided a crucial input in terms of technical expertise and investment, establishing some of the largest plantations on the islands, and also playing a key role in the commercialization of the sugar, both in the Mediterranean and in parts of northern Europe. In contrast, in North and West Africa the Portuguese and Italians were rivals: both needed the wheat surpluses of the area, both wanted to corner the gold supplies, and Genoa's position as neutral intermediary between Christianity and Islam was jeopardized by Portugal's extending the concept of crusading reconquest to North Africa. Finally there was a substantial share of Portugal's trading which was quite separate from any Italian interests. This was that with northern Europe in fruit, wine, leathers and salt, and in sugar from the Madeira islands, around the Bay of Biscay, up the western coast of France, with Ireland and as far north as the Baltic, in return for grain, cloth, salted fish, timber and other northern products – what Jaques Heers describes as 'this sort of large-scale coastal navigation which links Lisbon to Bruges via all the French ports of call'.[18] Italian capital thus followed in the paths of Portuguese maritime expansion rather than preceding it, and its prominence in Lisbon was a consequence, rather than cause, of Diaz's and Vasco da Gama's pioneering of the direct maritime route to the East Indies and the city's being granted a monopoly of the trade. Portugal's capitalism, rather than being a dependent one, attained a remarkable degree of autonomy at an early stage. The country's coastal position and deficient agriculture gave rise to early development of trade, and the resources and the consequent influence accruing to its Lisbon merchants were the cause for their triumphing in what has been described as 'the first bourgeois revolution' in 1381. It is true that, following the discoveries, wholesale merchants from Italy, and Italian merchants situated in other commercial centres, and above all Antwerp, came rapidly to play a central role – as did international wholesale merchants from all over Europe – in the distribution of the spices and other imported products. The trade was not, however, entirely controlled by foreign capital. Wallerstein makes a useful distinction between the 'Eastern contract', the buying up of spices in the East Indies and the financing of their shipping to Lisbon, and the 'European contract', concerned with the redistribution of the spices round Europe. The foreign capital was principally devoted to fulfilling the latter contract, whereas Portuguese resources, with some assistance, were concerned with the former. The trade, like that with Madeira, the Azores and Canaries was again one in which a division of labour could take place between Portuguese and foreign commercial resources.[19]

In fact the strongest argument for Portuguese commercial expansion not being fully 'autonomous' at this stage is based not on the participation of Italians but rather on that of Jewish or New Christian capital. The size of Portugal's Jewish or New Christian population had been significantly boosted as a consequence of Spain's expulsion of the Jews in 1492. There was no inquisition in Portugal until the 1540s and the relative toleration caused the country to be the main refuge for the Spanish Jews previously particularly prominent in trading in Granada and Andalusia. The immigration was on a large scale. In 1497 70,000 Jews, mostly recently arrived from Spain, were submitted to forcible baptism in Portugal, becoming 'New Christians'. The total population of Jews and New Christians at the turn of the century was some 100,000, a very significant share of Portugal's total population (which stood at between 1 and 1.4 million) and an even greater one, it is certain, of the country's commercial and industrial classes. This migration induced by religious intolerance is comparable in its economic impact on that two centuries later induced by the French Revocation of the Edict of Nantes. If Italian capital was principally involved in the fulfilling of the 'European contract', that of the New Christians was involved from an early stage in the 'East Indian contract'. The participation of New Christians in the trade from its beginning is apparent from the extension in 1501 to the whole of Asia of a Portuguese prohibition on New Christians holding any form of administrative office, however lowly. The scale of the participation was large. For the end of the century Boyajian calculates New Christian participation in the provision of circulating capital for the Asian trade at 44 per cent, in the Cape trade at 75 per cent and that of Manila at 30 per cent.[20] Thus if the original base of Lisbon's capitalism was Portuguese, and bred on its mother-trades with northern Europe and in the east Atlantic, the country's gradually widening commercial horizons – North and West Africa, the east Atlantic islands and the route to the East Indies – and the religious intolerance of its neighbour, caused its progressive internationalization.

What was to be the principal force in the next phase of Portugal's commercial expansion, its trade with Brazil, emerged during the sixteenth century. The colony had been discovered by accident in 1500 but, as it lacked treasure and provided no access, as in the east, to established trades, and as, too, its tropical climate and vegetation and uncultivated soil made it an inhospitable area for Europeans, its utility was initially restricted to acting as a zone for penal settlements. From the 1530s, however, partly to anticipate growing French and English interest in the area, colonization of coastal areas was undertaken with the introduction of sugar plantations on the model of those established earlier in Madeira, the Cape Verde islands and São Tomé. Those on São Tomé, a tropical island, using slave labour, represented a particularly useful dress rehearsal for the Brazilian enteprise. The new plantations flourished, their production soon far exceeding that of the east Atlantic islands, a growth in output from 2,915 to 19,434 tons being recorded between 1570 and 1600. The Madeira islands, less well suited climatically to sugar production, were devoted exclusively to viticulture from this point.

With the colonization of Brazil, what had been a significant coastal African slave trade with Portugal and the Atlantic islands, became a major transatlantic one, with Angola the main source for the human cargoes. Thirty-five thousand slaves were exported between 1551 and 1575 and 77,500 between 1575 and 1600. Expansion in the sugar trade was rapid. The number of sugar mills in Brazil grew from sixty in 1570 to 346 in 1629 and 500 in 1670, and production of sugar by the mid-seventeenth century had approximately doubled from its 1600 figure. The trade gave rise to great shipping demands, some 300 ships being needed to carry the sugar to Europe, and to some industrial development linked with sugar processing in Lisbon. By the 1630s, with the faltering of the Indian trades, it had become Portugal's principal trade. Sugar, writes the French historian F. Mauro, 'substituted for spices as the product acting as the motor for colonial activity'. Additional 'colonial' exports from Brazil included brazilwood (used for dyeing), tobacco, cotton, cocoa and rice.[21]

Like the Asian trade, the American suffered from Dutch incursions. During the 1630s the slaving port of Bahia was captured and the Dutch took over most of north-eastern Brazil, setting up a slaving station on the island of Curaçao. An uprising of settlers in 1645, however, drove out the Dutch: gaining control of the sea was one thing, but achieving dominance over territories in which the Portuguese were by now well established was quite another. The number and fighting qualities of Portuguese settlers, and of the already substantial *mestizo* population, combined with anti-Jewish feeling (it was 'New Christians' from Amsterdam, exiles from Lisbon in many cases, who dominated the Dutch West Indian Company and who were among the principal Dutch colonists) and a boost to morale caused by the receipt of news of the outbreak of Portugal's war of independence against Spain, to defeat the Dutch.[22]

From the time of these wars, however, growing international competition caused the sugar trade to be less profitable. The Dutch were the catalysts. Though they had failed in Brazil, the experience which they had had of the profitable triangular trade with Africa and the New World encouraged them to introduce it to the West Indies. They played the role of middlemen, equipping Spanish, English and French plantations in the area with machinery, know-how and, above all, slaves, and then buying the proceeds for shipping back to Amsterdam and processing and distributing around their commercial network. The small island of Curaçao became the entrepôt for their trade.[23] The impact of the increased competition shows in a steady fall in sugar prices. These halved between the mid-seventeenth century and 1680. Portugal lost its principal markets. By 1699–1701 England was importing 371,000 cwt of sugar from the West Indies, and its traders, who had developed their own distribution networks, were dominating both their domestic and north European markets. As J. Child wrote in 1669 of the Portuguese, 'In my time we have beat their . . . sugars quite out of use in Europe . . . formerly their Brazil fleets consisted of 100 to 120 thousand chests of sugar, they are now reduced to about 30 thousand . . .'[24]

Mauro argues that this second phase in Portugal's imperial history was one of progress rather than of decline. Contemporaries, he argues, in their interpretation of Portuguese commercial progress, made too much of the role of the spice trade and the later 'mirage of gold', consequent upon the gold discoveries, and it was rather this colonial exploitation of Brazil which made the greatest contribution to Portuguese wealth. The trade had the advantages of involving less distance – one rather than two oceans to cross – and also of involving and enriching broader social groups. Brazil's expansion, he continues, was the most successful European colonial experience of the seventeenth century causing the Portuguese economy to be alone in escaping depression.[25] He is clearly right. Lisbon's continued growth (it had already mushroomed in the sixteenth century, from 30,000 inhabitants in 1500 to 100,000 in 1551) to 130,000 inhabitants in 1650 and 165,000 in 1700, attests the continued vitality of the empire,[26] and the Brazilian experience became Portugal's most typical and enduring one. However, economic growth is different from world economic leadership. During the 120 years in which the spice route had been intact, Portuguese merchants, while not quite exercising this, had certainly, in conjunction with other centres such as Antwerp, Seville and Genoa, been occupying positions at the commanding heights of Europe's trade. A period of 120 years' enjoyment of near uninterrupted monopoly in such valuable trades meant colossal capital accumulation. With the loss of the East Indian trading monopoly, the disruptions to established commercial circuits occasioned by the Dutch revolt, growing intolerance in Portugal to religious nonconformity, and finally the new opportunities which had appeared to open for Portuguese merchants consequent upon the union of the two kingdoms – participation in the American trade and in Habsburg finances – there was a gradual seepage from Lisbon of the New Christian and other foreign capital which had helped to place the city in such a prominent position.

During the 1620s Jewish and converso or New Christian capital, which formed as much an international network as Protestant capital was to do in the seventeenth and eighteenth centuries (we have recorded its growing importance in Italy and its prominence in Islamic trade had been increased by the Spanish measures), assumed the mantle from Genoa of acting as the principal financial resource of the Spanish crown.[27] Portugal's participation in Spanish destinies was causing it to experience characteristics of what, as we shall shortly see, was the Spanish style of decline. In short, to return to Mauro's point, the more confined and isolated Atlantic world between Portugal and Brazil was to prove a more comfortable space to dominate, but it could, and did, become a backwater, and the shorter range of Portuguese trade, by depriving the country of its internationalism, made it vulnerable to domination by the succeeding, presiding powers in the 'world-economy'.

The deterioration in the sugar trade coincided with other trends of a kind unfavourable to Portugal's long-term commercial interests. From the 1640s the traditionally close relations with England had become yet more amicable, trading treaties between the two powers being signed in 1642, 1654 and 1661. These resulted in what had been the Portuguese triangular trade becoming a quadrilateral one, with the English making increasing inroads into Portuguese commercial spheres by the provision of shipping services, trading in slaves and the disposing of manufactured goods in both Portugal and Brazil. The dependency was unfavourable to Portugal, and this fact, and the declining profits in the Brazil trades, caused protectionist measures to be introduced between 1675 and 1690, including import tariffs, government encouragement of import substitution and rationalization of the slave trade by the founding of a mercantile company on the Dutch model. The Portuguese were thus responding on the basis of the precepts of mercantilist writers, in the same way as Venice had done, to the excessive dominance of the northern powers in international trade.[28] The new stance was not, however, persevered with.

The causes for the reversal in strategy serve to underline the point made earlier about the sheer weight of the colonial influence on Portugal's destinies. Two developments took place which caused a continued preference for empire over switching to a prioritizing of the metropolitan economy. Firstly an upward trend in the sales of wines grown in Madeira and, increasingly, in Portugal, to Holland, England and the English colonies in the West Indies and America received extra stimuli as a consequence on the one hand of Colbert's trade war with Holland, which diverted Dutch wine purchasers to Spain and Portugal, and on the other of an English ban on French wine imports following the outbreak of the Spanish War of Succession in 1697. The scale of the expansion in viticulture was very considerable. There was, for example, a tenfold increase in exports of malmsey and brandy from Madeira between 1650 and 1718, and vines were planted and areas of traditional viticulture extended all over Portugal. The production of port was introduced from the 1650s, and the vineyards of the Douro valley in particular much extended from 1688. Secondly, during the 1690s, significant gold discoveries were made in Brazil. The changes, as Godinho notes, caused the 'industrialists' to give way to the 'seigniors of the Vineyards', and the latter's influence was to remain dominant in government circles throughout the first half of the eighteenth century. Protective measures were reversed, and Portugal and its colonies came to serve principally as suppliers of bullion and raw materials for the English expansion. It was a role, it is clear, which provided a perfectly satisfactory rate of profit for an influential mercantile and landowning elite within Portugal. The new relationship with England was confirmed by the terms of the treaties of Methuen in 1703 and 1713.

Our third phase thus opens with 'the "cycle" of sugar and tobacco from Brazil, of Setubal salt and Cadiz silver' giving way to that of 'port, madeira and Brazilian gold'.[29] It was an extremely prosperous phase, a boom even, known later as the 'golden age' of King João V (1706–50), with Portugal becoming, according to Braudel, the Kuwait of the eighteenth century.[30] The scale on which Lisbon was rebuilt after the 1755 earthquake can only be understood in terms of this prosperity. Maximal

figures for gold production were reached from the 1760s, the value of
shipments from Brazil to Portugal rising from £350,000 in 1700 to
£2,200,000 in 1760. The negative impact of the new trading patterns on
Portuguese industrial potential, on the other hand, is evident. The wealth
was principally used to finance imports of English manufactured goods –
the proceeds of the gold and diamond mines and the amount spent on
English exports rising in parallel to reach values of between £1,000,000
and £2,000,000 from the 1730s. The location of the journey's end for the
Portuguese treasure trail is revealed by Lisbon-minted gold coinage
becoming a principal part of the money supply in England and its
American colonies.

What is more, in addition to the trade nipping in the bud any possibility of Portuguese industrial development, its benefits to Portuguese merchants were only limited. As Stephen Fisher has shown, a sharp division
of labour existed between the trading activities of Portugal and its
colonies and the country's international connections. The former were
dominated by Portuguese merchants and ships, whereas the 'international' trading was almost entirely in the hands of foreign merchants.
Of the 232 Portuguese ships which entered Lisbon in 1772/3, for example, only five did not come from another Portuguese or colonial port. The
foreign dominance extended to the organization and financing of
European trading: 'The Portuguese themselves carry on no commerce of
consequence with any other European dominions', an English merchant
noted in the 1750s, 'the British, French, Dutch, Germans, Danes,
Swedes, Spaniards and most of the states of Italy having factories and
consuls settled in Lisbon.' Of these, it was the English, with their
command of the sea and strong trading relationship, who dominated in
the eighteenth century, even with respect to Portuguese links with Mediterranean ports, providing, for example, seventy-one of the 145 vessels
entering Lisbon from this source in 1772.[31]

In common with Spain, Portugal, from the 1750s under the administration of the 'enlightened' secretary for economic affairs, the Marquis of
Pombal, attempted to provide fuller support to the long-term prospects
of its 'imperial' economy. The peaking of gold production, awareness
of the colossal trade deficit with England and, again, trends in political
economy were behind this change. Some success was achieved. During
the second half of the eighteenth century, again in common with Spain,
progress, it is noted, was made in 'ensuring that the profits of the American dominions would accrue largely if not exclusively' to Portuguese
nationals, and a brief golden age opened for the two empires following
the ending of the American War of Independence. Exports from
England fell sharply. The naval rivalry between France and England was

allowing space for other nations to develop their economies. The trend, however, was not allowed to progress very far. On the one hand, from the 1780s gold mining recovered, trading with Asia expanded and Brazilian cotton began to find markets in Liverpool – once more the immense commercial scope of the Portuguese colonies was removing the need for prudence. On the other, and more fundamentally, from 1789 the golden age for overseas empires ended for all empires other than the British. Spain by 1823 had lost most of her colonies, and its domestic and imperial markets became saturated with English imports. In Portugal events took a slightly different course, for the royal family following the Napoleonic invasions took refuge in Brazil and there in 1816 the prince regent, Dom João, declared the colony a coequal kingdom with Portugal. There was a certain historical logic in this development in view of the disproportion which had always existed between the size of Portugal and that of its empire. As José Jobson writes, 'with the transfer of the court to Brazil, they sacrificed the European homeland in order to try save the colony. At this point, the colony ended its status by assimilating the metropolis.' Later, in 1822, Joao's son Pedro, during his father's absence in Lisbon, proclaimed Brazil independent and himself emperor. Finally in 1889 a revolution led to Brazil becoming a republic.[32]

This nineteenth-century crisis of empire caused a continual economic crisis within Portugal and provoked our fourth phase in Portugal's imperial development. Again a solution was not sought in the modernization and industrialization of the metropolitan economy, but rather in the creation of a new territorial empire in the remaining African possessions.[33]

## Internal developments

Portugal's interior history is characterized by near-total continuity. The only exception to this was that expansion in the export of commercial crops referred to above – principally olives and the vine – and it is worth emphasizing that this change was executed with some persistence and efficiency, with considerable introduction of machinery, import of foreign (largely French) viticultural expertise and very effective lobbying to ensure that tariff policy was suitable. The change did not, though, in any way shake the position of the landed aristocracy – indeed it reinforced it. This continued aristocratic domination was the key factor in Portugal's social and economic stagnation.

It was a large aristocracy, of some 150,000, or approximately 10 per cent of the total population, and its practice of primogeniture resulted in younger sons entering the Church, which can thus be regarded as its adjunct. It was a significant adjunct, as there were over 30,000 priests and 25,000 members of religious orders, and an expanding one, for the number of convents, for example, increased from 396 in 1600 to 477 in 1739. Between them the nobility and Church owned the bulk of Portugal's land – some two-thirds. Most of the rest belonged to the crown.

Royal possessions, which took the forms of land, feudal and fiscal dues, were largely farmed out to members of the nobility. In addition, the crown was grand master of three extremely powerful military-religious orders which dated from the reconquest, those of Christ, Santiago and Aviz. The manner in which the extensive possessions of these orders were administered provides a microcosm of the manner in which Portuguese society functioned as a whole. They were divided into what were known as commanderies – 400 in the case of that of Christ – which were granted, generally for two generations, exclusively to members of the nobility. They provided a range of different types of secular and Church-based incomes: tithes, rents, feudal dues, dues from olive presses, receipts on mills and so on. Some of the commanderies were very substantial. That of Crato, for example, which straddled the Tagus inland from Lisbon, contained some twenty-nine parishes and 30,000 inhabitants. The property rights of the crown and nobility extended beyond the coastline – shares of fishing profits were included in dues in coastal areas, and commercial ports, with their seagoing and commercial income, were included in some commanderies – the order of Christ, for example, owned the ports of Setubal and Alcacer. With commercial and colonial expansion noble incomes were boosted by involvement in colonization and colonial trading.

As for the peasantry, there was very little left for them. As Godinho writes, 'while here and there enjoying the remnants of common rights [the peasantry] had to pay tithes to the Church, dues to the seigneurs, tolls and rent-charges, so that it retained only a minor fraction of the fruits of the soil, which went to fatten a swollen class of ecclesiastics and nobles.' Social disorder was only prevented by the possibilities of emigration to Lisbon or abroad.

The comfortable monopoly enjoyed by the nobility was partly to be explained by the crown's drawing the bulk of its revenue from commercial and imperial sources, and thus not being overdependent on the internal resources of the kingdom. The king was a major entrepreneur in his own right, retaining monopolies in the import of the red dyewood, which gave its name to Brazil, and of tobacco exports to India, owning a third share in the Cacheo company, which was involved in a range of West African trades including slavery, and being a major participant, providing ships and capital, in the East India Company. With the formation of the Junta do Comercio in 1663 the crown also played the principal role in administering a fleet system for trading with Brazil. The king's relationship with the nobility was to a certain extent one of a first among equals: his income, though clearly far greater, came from a similar range of sources to theirs and was administered in a similar way. Religious orders too adhered to the pattern. The Society of Jesus was doing no more than following established practices when it carved out for itself a commercial and landed empire, in Portugal and the New World, establishing what was virtually an independent state in Paraguay and attempting to achieve monopolies in the maté tea produced there and in Chinese silk.[34]

## An explanation

Before considering the character and causes of Portugal's 'decline' it seems only right to emphasize some of the areas of its achievements. In doing so we shall provide some insights into the types of value judgements which lie behind much of the literature concerning decline. The Portuguese achievement in developing a maritime route to the east, and then in imposing its military power over the trade in an area extending from the east coast of Africa to Japan, was a quite extraordinary one, all the more so in view of the country's slender demographic base. It was certainly on a par with the near-contemporary Spanish conquest of America. Following the conquest, the Portuguese not only developed a regular trade between Lisbon and the east but were also the first European power to involve itself in the eastern home trades, many Portuguese families permanently settling in the east. Their cultural influence made a permanent impact, and they were responsible for the spreading of Christianity in the area: in contrast the austere Dutch Calvinism was to have few adepts. They were supplanted in the east by the Dutch, but the Dutch success was only on the basis of asserting stronger political control over the trade, ensuring that its profits should be channelled more effectively into the coffers of the Dutch East India Company. In terms of the general level of Asian trade, the Dutch influence, in contrast to that of the Portuguese, has been judged to have been negative.[35]

In addition to setting the parameters for European participation in the East Indies, ones which were later followed by the Dutch, English and French, the Portuguese also 'invented' the Atlantic trades. In Brazil they developed the first American plantation economies and from there introduced to Europe a range of tropical products, including tobacco and cocoa. They extended slavery to the New World, and theirs was thus the first 'triangular trade' between Europe, Africa and America. It is true that there were east Mediterranean precedents for such colonial practices, and thus the 'achievement' is more properly considered a joint Italian–Portuguese one, but we have seen that the Italians were operating within a Portuguese framework. On the basis of these developments the Portuguese economy was alone in Europe in escaping the 'seventeenth-century depression'. It goes without saying, of course, that 'achievement' here is being conceived of in a Eurocentric manner and in economic terms. The human price which was being paid in Africa and Asia for the success of small sections of Europe's population was huge.

The Portuguese, finally, hung on to their colonies with great persistence, never surrendering control of the direct trades with their possessions to outsiders, establishing solid setttlements and maintaining their political independence both from Spain in the peninsula and against Dutch, English and French challenges in Africa and Brazil. They were, with the British, Europe's greatest colonizers. 'The Portuguese is a pilot and a peasant', writes Frédéric Mauro. It is a perceptive categorization which, while identifying the specificity of the skills involved in the initial explorations and of the qualities which contributed to the resilience of Portuguese colonization, also hints at the types of resources which Portugal lacked.[36]

The failures consist, we have seen, firstly in the gradual erosion of Portugal's commercial position in the world economy. An initial position of unprecedented global predominance, in conjunction with Antwerp, had by the late seventeenth and eighteenth centuries given way to a situation in which Portuguese traders were confined principally to the Atlantic and operated in circumstances of dependency with respect to other European economies. Secondly, there was a failure within Portugal. The commodity make-up of Portugal's trade revealed backwardness: it exported primary products and bullion and received, in return, manufactures. The Portuguese interior had stagnated. Important export trades in wine and olive oil had been developed but these had merely served to reinforce the status quo socially. The country remained dominated by a powerful aristocracy, and harsh poverty was the lot of the peasant majority.

With respect to the first failure, the most fundamental of its causes was the slender nature of Portuguese resources, in terms of both capital and manpower, for exploiting the vast opportunities which had opened up for the country. From the very beginning, we have seen, a collaboration with foreign capital and enterprise was enforced. The collaboration took the form of a division of labour, with Portuguese resources being concentrated on exploiting the direct trading links with trading posts and colonies, and foreign capital and merchants handling the European end. This form of collaboration became the general pattern for all Portuguese commercial activities, we have seen, even when their geographical range had become more restricted. Manpower was required as crews, soldiers, colonists and administrators over a vast geographical space and Portugal's 1.5 million population was not proportionate to these demands. During the sixteenth century some quarter-million Portuguese emigrated – a high proportion. The resort to slave labour (in Portugal itself about 10 per cent of the population of Lisbon in the sixteenth century were slaves) and the colonies, as well as the policy of miscegenation in the latter, are to be explained by this shortfall.[37]

The consequences of this excessive burden on Portugal's commercial and human resources was, on the one hand, the progressive neglect of those European trades which had provided, as we have seen, the roots of its maritime and commercial traditions. For example the shipping requirements for its import trade quickly passed to other hands: whereas there had been an average of 150 Portuguese ships sailing annually through the Danish sound into the Baltic this figure was down to between ten and twenty-five by the 1620s.[38] On the other hand, the labour shortage contributed to a failure to exploit fully Portugal's domestic sources for agricultural growth, particularly in the south. With our advantage of hindsight we can see that a continued reliance on these traditional domestic economic activities could have provided a more satisfactory route to the twentieth century. The need to concentrate all its energies on its empire curiously ended up by narrowing down the range of competences possessed by the Portuguese economy: a specialization was enforced which in the longer term removed flexibility.

On the other hand, defeat in the east by the Dutch who were, with their population of some 1.5 million in 1620, no more numerous than the Portuguese, reveals that other than merely demographic factors contributed to the Portuguese failures. The preliminary for exposure to this threat was of course the merger with the Spanish crown in 1580. As mentioned, Portugal thereby participated in Spain's wars, and its far-flung coastal empire was a far more vulnerable target than the Spanish interior possessions. As Jonathan Israel has shown, the Spanish embargoes, especially those of 1598 (by then Amsterdam and Holland had taken the relay from Antwerp and the southern Netherlands) and 1621, following the twelve-year truce, acted as the catalysts for the Dutch intervention: the ships, capital and commercial expertise devoted to trading with Lisbon shifted to direct involvement in the African, East

Indian and Brazilian trades on a very large scale: 200 ships to West Africa, 768 ships to Venezuela and fourteen fleets totalling sixty-five ships to the East Indies between 1599 and 1608.[39]

However, exposure to such competition would no doubt have occurred anyway at some stage. The crucial failure was Portugal's inability to resist the Dutch challenge. A principal cause for this was the character of its social and political organization. The conduct of its trading with the East Indies reflected the traditional and uncoordinated character of this. Involved were, as we have seen, on the one hand the crown, with its pepper and other monopolies, and on the other, members of the nobility and private merchants operating on their own account, who were dominant from the mid-sixteenth century. Out in the east, this lack of cohesion resulted in private transactions within the oriental trading system rapidly coming to exceed in importance those with the mother economy. The set up can only be categorized as individualistic and disaggregated, reflecting the situation of shared sovereignty which characterized the running of Portugal's domestic politics. It was neither of a nature to maximize economic gains to the Portuguese state nor to ensure an effective and co-ordinated resistance against intruders.[40] By contrast, the Dutch trade, after a few years of similar uncoordinated and competitive involvement of different shippers, was entrusted in 1601 to the Dutch East India Company, which was a tightly organized, monopolistic trading organization, acting on behalf of a wide range of investors, and in receipt of military support from the Dutch government. Jonathan Israel refers to it as 'the Dutch Republic's most original commercial institution' and as a 'unique politico-commercial institution, and one that could be instituted nowhere else in the world'. It reflected on the one hand a capacity, probably unique at the time, for voluntary group collaboration on a scale larger than that of the city, and on the other a similarly precocious alertness to the links between military power and commercial success. Two great historians of the Netherlands emphasize these qualities. Israel writes of a 'tempering of civic particularism with a much greater measure of provincial collaboration than pertained in any of the S. Netherlands provinces' as 'an abiding pillar of strength to the future Dutch world entrepôt', and Jan de Vries of the Dutch Republic's 'pragmatic efforts to bind trading energies to the political strategies of the state'.[41] Portugal, as traditional a society as any in Europe, thus found itself, following its Spanish merger, confronting Europe's most modern state. In retrospect it can be seen that the failure was to have been expected.

In the Atlantic, problems were of another type. The military costs and capital requirements for harnessing the resources of Brazil may have been less, but the organizational and demographic tasks involved in establishing a completely new commercial and agricultural colony were clearly greater. They were resolved in legislation of 1534 by dividing the immense area up into fifteen 'captaincies'. These were granted to 'donatorios' who, at their own expense, committed themselves to populating and exploiting their areas in return for the most generous of fiscal and political privileges. Again, the parallels with the manner in which Portugal itself had been administered since its reconquest – by surrendering large areas of sovereignty to the nobility – are apparent. The greater success achieved by the Portuguese in Brazil in their struggle with the Dutch between the 1630s and 1640s reveals that such sorts of arrangements were in fact perfectly well suited to ensuring resilient, territorial settlements.[42] Portugal's failure did not lie there. It was in the commercial field. It was here that the Dutch and, later, English and French traders showed themselves to be at an advantage as a consequence of their greater capital resources, superior capacity for achieving collaboration among trading interests and closeness to what were becoming the most bouyant markets. The failure was also aggravated by the erosion in Portugal's mercantile base mentioned above. The Dutch, French and English enjoyed at this stage, too, the advantages of their 'interstitial' status – Portugal and Spain had borne the development costs and were bearing the administrative costs of their empires and of the colonization of the New World, whereas their rivals were in the comfortable position of being able to prioritize commercial transactions either in Iberian imperial markets or in their own small-scale West Indian colonies.[43]

Turning now to the second failure, that of the Portuguese interior to benefit from the years of commercial expansion, a first and major point will have emerged from the summary of the stages of growth in the global trading network. At various stages an awareness had developed of the disadvantages to the Portuguese national economy from overcommitment to trading interests, particularly in the late seventeenth century and under Pombal. In both these cases, however, renewed trading opportunities removed any need for adjustment. It was the sheer bounty of the colonial opportunities to which its early exploration achievements gave rise which represents a principal cause for the neglect of the domestic economy: the overseas possibilities were such for Portugal's elite that the need to prioritize alternative internal source of income was barely experienced.

It might, however, have been thought that the extent of commercial profit, and the growth of Lisbon, might, government prioritizing of wider economic development or not, have served to spread economic prosperity and provide commercial and industrial opportunity. This was not the case, and Lisbon remained throughout an enclave, relatively isolated from the rest of Portugal. This was not so unusual – it has, for example, been argued even for England two centuries later that the impact of its ports on the general economic development was minor. 'Commercial revolution' is defined as a radical transition, but one confined to the commercial sphere. However, the degree of Lisbon's isolation from the rest of Portuguese society was extreme, and exacerbated by political and religious policies. Thus its large converso population was forced into a position of *de facto* isolation by restrictions which excluded it from holding any form of public office or honours. The type of social integration achieved earlier by Italian merchants was not possible under such circumstances. The restriction of the right to administer 'commanderies' to noble families was a further barrier, one which applied in this case to Portuguese as well as converso traders. Clearly there was a potential conflict of interests between different social groups among the Portuguese elite.[44]

The divisions in Portuguese society between conversos and others became progressively more acute. In the 1540s an Inquisition was established, and between 1570 and 1590 it began to make an impact, conditions for Jews or New Christians becoming harsher in Portugal than in Spain. Thousands of conversos left – finding refuge up the west coast of France, in the Low Countries, in Spain itself after the Union in 1580, as opportunities opened up in Seville and Madrid, and in North Africa and Italy.[45] It is to this policy that Boyajian and L. M. E. Shaw attribute Portuguese decline. The Inquisition created a type of society, they argue, which was incompatible with the growth of capitalism. 'A society unable to accept New Christians as Portuguese', the former writes, 'was unable to come to terms with the commercial revolution in which the New Christians played a leading role for at least a century.'[46] Jonathan Israel's work on European Jewry, however, and on Iberian relations with Spain, demonstrates that there was another important strand to the story which requires elucidation. The 1598 blockade of the Dutch Republic, and the counterpart to this, the successful Dutch blockade both of the Scheldt and the Flemish coastline, isolated the Portuguese converso merchants from the trades on which they depended. This served as a further stimulus to their movement from Portugal, and they set themselves up in trading centres throughout Europe, both north and south. From their new locations they took up where they left off – participating in the Brazilian trades from Amsterdam for example and, when the Dutch were defeated there, shifting their investments to the West Indies, redistributing East Indian spices and northern European products in the Mediterranean from Venice, Genoa, Milan, Florence and above all

Leghorn, which came to hold the largest Jewish concentration in Europe – in many ways playing the role previously played by Lisbon. The embargo, rather than strangling Holland, had contributed to creating a new world trading system from which the Iberian peninsula was largely excluded. Insofar as it was not totally excluded, the conversos again played a crucial role: they were better placed than any other group to develop illicit trade routes to and from Spain, via the Basque country to Bayonne, where they were numerous, via Seville, or via North Africa.[47]

Portugal's exclusion from trading opportunities during these years, and its loss of a significant share of its mercantile class, weakened trading interests. It is to this, rather than to the activities of the Inquisition, that V. M. Godinho attributes the decline, reversing the causal priorities of Boyajian and Shaw. He argues that there were four principal dominant social groups in Portugal – the crown, the nobility, the urban bourgeoisie and the Church. The crown depended on the commercial bourgeoisie more than on the nobility, he points out and we have seen this to be the case from a breakdown in the crown's incomes – however, it did not entirely commit itself to it, competing with it in its own right as a trader and being influenced too by the strong prejudices of the religious establishment towards the cosmopolitan bourgeoisie. The declining weight of the mercantile influence in Lisbon was thus all that was needed to tilt the balance of forces in the direction of the Church and landed interests, thus preventing 'the flowering of a Portuguese capitalism' and explaining 'the politico-social opportunities open to the landed nobility'.[48]

## Spanish History up to 1500

Spain is five times as large as Portugal, and in the early fifteenth century was five times as populated. In addition it was, as Pierre Vilar emphasizes, the first European power raised to global dimensions.[49] Its rise and decline thus were on a different scale from its neighbour's, forming, indeed, the central events of sixteenth- and seventeenth-century European history.

Explaining Spain's complex trajectory during these two centuries is a difficult task. As mentioned in the opening of this chapter, what has to be disentangled is, on the one hand, the impact on the peninsula of the shift in the locus of Italian capitalism from the east to the west Mediterranean and to the Atlantic and, on the other, the interaction of this development with other forces for change – the development of Spain's European and American empires. To provide a sense of process I shall

**Map 2**    Iberia

provide what will effectively be a narrative account of developments. In this section I shall give a brief summary of the character of Spain's development and the salient features of Spanish society up to 1500. In the next I shall continue with the story, but on a thematic basis, recounting events relating to demography, agriculture, industry, trade and finance in turn. I shall then conclude the chapter with an attempt to interpret the Spanish decline.

In 1500 Spain had just completed a reconquest which had been going on for some seven hundred years. Such a long struggle was inevitably a major influence on all aspects of Spanish society: parallels indeed have been drawn with the impact of the frontier on American history. It had caused it to be warlike; Spanish social structure to be dominated to an exceptional extent by the nobility, which remained a warrior class; royal authority – in view of the need for a leadership role in the Reconquista – to be strong; and crusading religious values to be held with unique fervour.

More specifically the Reconquista had been conducted in three distinct sweeps down the peninsula – a Portuguese one, originating in Galicia; an Aragonese, with its roots in the Pyrenees and in Charlemagne's France, which passed through Catalonia as far as Valencia and then radiated across the Mediterranean, absorbing the Balearic islands, and, from there, blending with the prior Norman and Genoese expansions, across to the east Mediterranean; and, above all, a Castilian, accounting for most of the territory in the peninsula, with its source in Asturias, which was completed with the fall of Granada in 1492. Thus the Reconquista, while it conferred some common features on the peninsula, in view of its splintered nature also reinforced its principal political divisions.

The length of the period of reconquest was a further cause for regional differences. A distinction needs to be made between a slow reconquest, up until the eleventh century, as far as the River Duero, which gave rise to a relatively egalitarian process of colonization, then a more rapid, but barely opposed eleventh-century reconquest as far as the Tagus, which culminated in the capture of Toledo in 1085, and finally a far harder-fought consolidation and extension of this reconquest, converted into a Crusade, until the mid-thirteenth century. The circumstances of the later reconquest caused the position of the nobility and military orders to be an even more dominant social force south of the Tagus. In addition, the length of time during which different areas had been colonized was a further cause of sharp contrasts. The passing of nearly 500 years since the area north of the River Duero had been in Christian hands – and the coastal area to the north of the Cantabrian mountains had never been penetrated by Islam – had permitted there the consolidation of a society with strong links to the rest of Europe. Cultural and economic links with France in particular had received additional stimulus from the tradition of pilgrimage to Santiago de Compostela. Historians write of this area as the Spain of the 'camino francés'. In contrast Andalusia's 'integration' was more recent, and the repercussions of Granada's 1492 incorporation into Spain were only being worked out during the period which concerns us, as is attested to by the 1609 decision to expel Spain's remaining Morisco population.[50]

Spain's expanding frontier resulted in her not being exposed to the Malthusian problems experienced by densely populated inland areas of Europe. Conditions also contributed to an unusual degree of freedom among the Spanish peasantry, who were offered favourable conditions to colonize underpopulated areas. The impact of the frontier has been described as a 'whirlwind of freedom'. On the other hand the circumstances were not favourable to demesne farming and meant that Spain was not subjected to those types of pressures which led to a gradual improvement in farming techniques in densely populated parts of the continent. What was encouraged – in view of the space available and suitable climatic and physical conditions – was sheep-farming and cattle ranching. The thirteenth-century conquest of Estremadura and La Mancha, which possessed abundant pastures not only in autumn but also in spring, provided the basis for the development of ranching and sheep-herding on a transhumant basis, in a style and on a scale unmatched in western Europe, anticipating practices in the New World.[51]

The so called 'Mesta', which administered the transhumant routes over which the herds passed, was established in the 1260s. It was a guild-like organization which represented a rationalization of previously locally organized Mestas (the word meaning literally 'confluences') by the creation of three major national, transhumant grazing routes, one from León, through Zamora to Andalusia, a second from Palencia and Soria, through Segovia to the River Guadalquivir, and a third from Cuenca to La Mancha. The 'national' dimensions of the Mesta arrangements alert us to another distinctive characteristic of the emerging Spain: its material life, despite its unsophisticated character, was rationalized and organized on a national basis. Trade and traders followed the routes of the Mesta.[52]

The fact of colonization gave rise to an instability in the peninsula's population: there was a slow drift from north to south. Patterns of colonization were patchy. On the one hand some cities were rapidly occupied by Christians following reconquest – for instance Cordoba and

Seville, which grew to containing 25,000 inhabitants within a few years; and on the other hand in other parts of the peninsula there was near-continuity with the previous situation under the Muslims. In Valencia, for example, while the cities were inhabited by Christians, the rural areas remained Muslim. In Andalusia, it was a post-reconquest Muslim uprising which led to the expulsion of the Muslims. As a rule, the greater the opposition to conquest, the severer the policy towards Morisco populations. In many areas of Spain, rather than reconquest occurring, Muslim leaders came to terms with the advancing Christian forces, receiving *fueros* (or charters) guaranteeing them rights.[53]

The fact of reconquest, and the existence thereby over the centuries of new economic outlets and the possibility of booty, favoured social mobility and is held to have had psychological consequences on Spanish mentalities. Rather than the patient exploitation of small-scale gains on a high turnover, which had become, for example, the basis for profit in a 'mature' Italian capitalism, rapid gains and the fortunes of war were the preference of the Castilian elite, one to which the fragile nature of their rural incomes contributed. The attitude of the followers of El Cid, were expressed as follows by one of them: 'Great were the rejoicings there when the Cid won Valencia and entered the city. Those who had been on foot now became caballeros. And the gold and the silver, who can count it?' This was, as Angus Mackay argues, representative, and was exported, together with other 'institutions' of the Reconquista, to the New World.[54]

That the frontier with Islam had been as much 'Europe's' as Spain's had had the additional consequence of occasioning a curious modernity in political organization. Spain was an open society with regular contact with the most mobile and advanced social groups among its neighbours. Techniques of rule which had been worked out over centuries elsewhere were imported wholesale and applied in order both to further the reconquest and to discipline a warlike and disorderly nobility. Ferdinand and Isabella inherited well-developed notions of divine right and, in Castile at least, the most highly centralized political structure in Europe.[55]

With respect to this union it should be emphasized that Castile, though the more backward of the two crowns, was by far the dominant party. Aragon had been worse hit by the Black Death, its fifteenth century was characterized by the severest of political disorder, and its commercial empire had suffered from the very forces so much favouring the commercial development of southern Spain. The Genoese were the main commercial rivals and Barcelona was too far up Spain's Levantine coast to profit much from the developing Mediterranean–Atlantic trades. Indeed the development of the Mediterranean–Atlantic route via the straits of the Gibraltar diverted trade from Barcelona. The type of balance existing between Catalonia, part of the crown of Aragon, and Castile at this stage is suggested by their relative demographic weights: Catalonia with a population of 331,000 in the 1550s only contained one-twentieth of Castile's population and a twenty-fourth of that of Spain (in contrast to the ninth of Spanish population it contained in the 1960s).[56]

The greater stability of northern Spain, resulting from its early reconquest and longer cultural interaction with areas to the north of the Pyrenees, contributed to a fuller development there of a market economy. From the early thirteenth century, the export of wools to Flanders had begun, and during the fourteenth century, with the Hundred Years War and consequent frequent disruptions in English wool supplies, and also possibilities of negotiating trading agreements with the French, these trades, and also those in wine, the export of iron and salt and the import of manufactured goods, particularly Flemish textiles, had built up. Spain's Cantabrian ports were effectively at this stage, in contrast to their situation later, in an 'interstitial' position with respect to the warring parties in the Hundred Years War, and the shipping strengths of the area increased considerably, assisted by protective legislation passed by the Spanish crown. Favourable trading terms were negotiated with French and Flemish towns, particularly Bruges, Rouen, Bordeaux and Bayonne, and then defended against the rival shipping interests of the ports of the Hanseatic League. Cantabrian shipping showed itself equal to that of northern Europe, if not the better, as it had the benefits which could be drawn from Iberian contact with Mediterranean shipbuilding techniques and Spain's pivotal position in Europe's shipping services at this stage. The Basques, together with the Portuguese, as we noted in chapter 1, were the first northern invaders of the Mediterranean.[57] Predominating in this norther *élan* was Burgos, one of the few cities in Spain that had its own powerful mercantile class with sufficient resources to participate widely in commercial opportunities through the peninsula.[58]

Spanish Atlantic shipping successes were matched by progress in developing a Mediterranean fleet following the capture of Seville, again with the help of the Genoese, who provided a succession of admirals. The stimulus here was the continued Islamic threat and Portuguese rivalry in North Africa and the eastern Atlantic. Cantabrian vessels participated here too, playing an important part in the capture of Seville in 1248. They also played a major part in supplying the shipping needs of the west Mediterranean from the fourteenth century, their services being used by the Catalans, by Seville merchants, by the French at Marseilles and by the Genoese. Spain's predominance in the sixteenth century, both in Europe and globally, can only be understood if it is recalled that for a while it was probably the greatest maritime power on the continent.[59]

The meeting place for the commercial currents from north and south was the large fairs, the first of which were established in the thirteenth century in Andalusia, to be followed by those of Castile from the four-teenth century – that of Burgos established in 1339 and the famous Medina del Campo in 1321. It was the dynamic interaction between the two processes of expansion – that proceeding from the Mediterranean and that which had been generated between Castile, the Bay of Biscay and northern Europe – as the Iberian peninsula became the hinge of Europe, which gave a particular impulsion to the Spanish economy during the fifteenth and sixteenth centuries. Parallels could be drawn to the impact further to the east occasioned by the earlier overland inter-action between north Italian and Flemish capitalism at the fairs of Champagne in the thirteenth century.[60]

The qualitative inferiority of Iberian capitalism in the south needs, however, to be emphasized. There was a strong dependence on foreign merchants, and particularly on the Genoese, who had their own quarter in Seville. This development marked the first step in the development of Spanish 'dependence' noted above. The booming Andalusian economy from the very start was bringing more profits to foreigners than to Spaniards. The relationship between Italy and Spain has been referred to as a macro version of the *commenda* – Italy was the capitalist, pro-viding capital and enterprise, Spain brought the manpower, ships and seafaring skills. A sign of the lack of commercial development in Spain was the reliance on fairs, rather than on settled, urban financial centres, for commercial transactions. There was little interaction between com-merce and government finance, different social groups functioning in each. In addition to the dependence on foreign capitalists, there was a reliance internally on Jewish and converso finance. From the point of view of its state of commercial development southern Spain at our date of departure can probably not unfairly be compared to Italy in the seventh and eighth centuries, in the early stages of its recovery following the barbarian invasions.[61]

Further, profound weaknesses characterized agriculture. The recent date of settlement, the lack of demesne farming, the prioritizing of livestock over arable crops and the high fiscal burden consequent upon the successful centralization of government resulted in a general insec-urity concerning subsistence. Particularly during the second half of the fifteenth century, as the population touched new ceilings, there were frequent crop failures culminating in a prolonged crisis in 1469–73 and again in 1486 and 1491, and between 1502 and 1508. Worse, the food shortages of the first decade of the sixteenth century were not a consequence of adverse climatic conditions but of structural characteristics of Spanish agriculture: Vicens Vives attributes them to 'excessive protection to livestock farming, rural absenteeism, the expulsion of the Granadine Moriscos and . . . latifundism and the increase in the aristocratic class'.[62] Fifteenth-century Spain, before its Golden Age began, can be characterized as being already in the grip of social crisis, with what was probably excessive urban growth. Anti-Semitism has been linked to this crisis. The enforced and voluntary baptism of Jews after the fourteenth century and anti-Jewish pogroms had in fact only exacerbated the tendency to this phenomenon, for the conversos were consequently released from all legal restrictions on their activities, resulting in a strengthening of their hold on financial affairs. The strong position of converso capital, particularly in royal finance, was a further sign of the deficiency of the Castilian commercial classes. The resulting anti-Semitism reveals the existence of a dualistic society in which there were sharp cultural and social divisions between the modern and the market, handled by foreigners and conversos, and the domestic, predominantly agrarian material life. Thus there were strong parallels with Portugal. The founding of the Inquisition in 1478 and the expulsion of the Jews in 1492, however, in no way resolved these problems: they were populist measures, like the later expulsion of the Moriscoes, of an unsettling kind for the commercial life of the kingdom. One hundred and fifty thousand Jews were forced to emigrate, many to Portugal, as we noted.[63]

The commodity make-up of Spanish foreign trade provides another clue to the character of the Spanish economy. Although there was some industrial production, little of this was exported, and Spain's specializations were principally those characteristic of a dependent economy: the export of primary products such as wools, minerals and foodstuffs in return for manufactured goods. The openness of the economy, and the large size of the nobility with its high levels of consumption, made Spain Europe's best market for consumer products. The pattern was in many ways similar to that existing between western and eastern Europe: earnings from the export of primary products were spent on foreign luxuries.[64]

The completion of the Reconquista might have enforced consolidation, a stock-taking and a prioritizing of the more intensive development of domestic resources over conquest in the same way that this had happened in northern Spain. However, as Angus Mackay emphasizes, the immediate successsion of the 'age of the frontiers' by an 'age of empire' was to prevent this.[65]

## From 'Golden Age' to Decline

The weaknesses of the Spanish economy at the beginning of the sixteenth century should not, however, be exaggerated. Its viability was to be demonstrated by its dynamic response to the opportunities which the century brought in terms of new markets and rising prices. 'For the first three-quarters or more of the sixteenth century', I. A. A. Thompson writes, 'Castile's population multiplied, the arable was extended, agricultural production increased, the level of urbanisation rose, the manufacture of silks and woollens flourished in the great textile centres of Toledo, Granada, Segovia and Cordoba; wool exports remained buoyant until the 1560's, foreign trade until the 1590's, and traffic with the Indies until the 1610's.'[66]

### *Population growth*

Population growth was at its most rapid in the first two-thirds of the sixteenth century. Vicens Vives claimed that maximal growth rates in Castile were attained in the 1530s at some 65,000 per annum, to be reduced to 40,000 per annum between 1540 and 1595. Spain's total population may have grown from slightly over 6 million in 1541 to over 8 million in 1600, or by approximately a third. By this date, population density – at some 22 per square kilometre in Castile – was around the European average, though, in view of the harshness of natural conditions, the level achieved should be regarded as high.[67]

The turning-point in demographic trends took place at some time after the 1560s: population totals for cities which exist for 1560 and 1594 show higher figures for many small and medium-sized centres for the earlier date (as in Salamanca, Burgos, Avila, León, Soria and Medina del Campo). These towns, though, are concentrated in León and Old Castile: rather than a general urban decline at this stage, what was happening was that different areas were having distinct experiences. Large cities were benefiting at the expense of smaller ones (the population of Madrid, made capital in 1561, increased rapidly from 4,060 in 1530 to 37,500 in 1594; Seville mushroomed from 25,000 inhabitants in 1530 to 75,000 in 1591). Rural areas, likewise, registered diverging performances, a sample of 370 villages in New Castile for 1575–8 showing increases in 234 villages, stagnation in thirty-seven and decline in ninety-nine. A comparison made between population densities as well as average incomes in different regions between 1541 and 1591 provides additional nuances concerning the types of changes which were occurring. The heart of Castile – the provinces of Valladolid, Segovia, Avila and Palencia – still retained this dominance, showing the highest population densities at the second date. However, the extent of their demographic dominance had been slightly eroded, areas of New Castile, Madrid, Toledo and Cuenca recording the highest population growth, closely followed by the northern provinces of Burgos, León and Galicia-Zamora. By contrast income levels at the later date were high in the Mediterranean area and at their lowest on the Atlantic side, with Old Castile and central Spain lying between the two. The comparison suggests that a southerly shift in the centre of gravity of the Spanish economy was beginning to occur, the centre already gaining demographically and the Mediterranean littoral benefiting from the point of view of incomes.[68]

A slowing down in population became a sharp fall from the 1590s. Serious harvest failures in 1593/4 were followed by four years of plague between 1598 and 1602. 'The hunger coming up from Andalusia', a contemporary wrote, met 'the plague descending from Castile'.[69] As had been the case since the first appearance of plague in Europe, it followed the routes of trade. The difference in the sixteenth century, however, was that these trade routes were at their most intense in the Atlantic with Castile playing a linchpin role in the late sixteenth century. Plague entered Castile from the north, between Santander and the French frontier, and its impact was greatest in Old Castile, in a circular area comprising Valladolid, Madrid and Toledo and centred on the densely populated provinces of Avila and Segovia. It also entered Spain via Andalusia and Portugal. The overall demographic loss has been estimated at some 8 per cent of the population of Spain as a whole, and some 10 per cent of that of Castile. These losses in themselves are not believed sufficient for plague to be judged the prime cause of demographic decline in seventeenth-century Spain, but their particularly heavy concentration in Castile, unusually in rural as well as urban areas, and their being followed by large-scale out-migration – to escape plague and in search of new economic opportunities in the south – do contribute to accounting for a particularity of the Spanish demographic experience in the seventeenth century – the abruptness of the depopulation of Old Castile.[70]

These plague and Malthusian losses were added to by the self-inflicted damage of the expulsion of the Moriscos between 1609 and 1613. Some

270,000 people were involved, from all over Spain, and particularly from Aragon, which lost some 15 per cent of its population, and Valencia which lost over a quarter of its inhabitants. The impact on these areas in particular was very great. In 1638, in Aragon, of 453 localities which had been inhabited previously by Moriscos, 205 had been abandoned totally and 244 others were populated only in consequence of a transfer of population from Christian areas. It would be wrong, however, even if the immediate impact of the 1609 legislation was on these areas, to consider the consequences of the treatment of the Moriscos as purely a local phenomenon. The expulsion came at the end, rather than at the beginning, of the Spanish policy towards the formerly dominating Muslims of southern Spain. Following the Reconquista there were, according to Vicens Vives, some 1,000,000 Moriscos in Spain, mostly in Castile (500,000 in the recently conquered Granada, 200,000 in the rest of Castile) but also 50,000 in Aragon, 160,000 in Valencia, 10,000 in Catalonia and 15,000 in Mallorca. An uprising in Granada in 1568, that of Alpujarras, had led to the expulsion of the Moriscos from there. Some 300,000 left, mainly to Valencia and Aragon, but also to Castile and North Africa. On the eve of the expulsion there remained somewhat less than 300,000 concentrated particularly in Aragon and Valencia, but with close on 100,000 still living in Castile. Clearly a steady erosion of the Morisco population within the peninsula had been occurring for over a century, and clearly too, though Valencia and Aragon provided the chief redoubts and were to suffer the immediate impact of the 1609 expulsion, the greatest demographic change had been that occasioned by the reduction in the Morisco population of Castile before the expulsion from some 700,000 to less than 100,000. In the treatment of the Moriscos, thus, we not only have a contribution to the explanation for Spain's demographic decline, but also for the distinctive regional experiences in both the sixteenth and seventeenth centuries. The lower levels of demographic growth in southern Spain during the sixteenth century have a part of their explanation in the loss of the Morisco population there. The better performance of these areas in the seventeenth century, and the worse performance of Old Castile, have their explanation in the movement of population from central Spain to fill the gaps left by the prior Moorish population. Spain, as well as experiencing the ups and downs in demographic performance common to all Europe, was also undergoing the specific experience consequent upon the completion of its reconquest. The economic impact of the loss of 1 million Moriscos is incalculable: they were the heirs to nearly 1,000 years of a unique tradition, unrivalled in Europe, of irrigation agriculture and horticulture.[71]

The situation was, of course, even more complex than this, for Spain was losing population through other channels and the gaps were not being filled only by its own nationals. In addition to a decline in population being experienced in the sixteenth and seventeenth centuries, the actual make-up of the peninsula's population underwent considerable change. The additional losses were to the Americas, and also on the various military fronts throughout Europe on which Spanish soldiers fought. Estimates of the size of losses to America for the sixteenth century vary between 120,000 and 240,000, those on the battlefields of Flanders at some 2,000 to 3,000 a year from the 1560s. The new capital of Madrid also drew extensively on the demographic resources of Old and New Castile. The persecution of Jews led too to a steady decline here. Contributing (in addition to the inhabitants of the north and Old Castile) to filling these gaps were, above all, French migrants. A calculation for 1680 reveals 70,000 French in Spain, 16,000 of whom were in Andalusia. The levels of immigration into Catalonia were particularly high, some 20 per cent of Catalonia's population in the late sixteenth century consisting of so-called 'Gascons'. Italians, too, played their part, though in this case it was an immigration purely of social groups of higher status, which came to play a key economic role in the peninsula: there were some 10,000 Genoese in the kingdom of Castile in 1600, and a significant concentration in Aragon as well. The Flemish provided substantial numbers of immigrants, particularly under Charles V, and the Portuguese too, we have noted, entered Spain in numbers following the union of the two kingdoms in 1580. In the French case, by contrast, it was an immigration both of merchants (principally to Andalusia) but also of the poor, with the latter in the majority in the north-east, providing an important contribution to the Catalan agricultural and industrial labour forces.[72]

Such demographic disasters and population losses, if severe, were not, on the other hand, without precedent in the sixteenth century, and so do not provide a total explanation for the collapse in Spanish population by nearly a quarter, from a figure of some 8.5 to about 6.5 million. A portion of the blame must be attributed to a failure in the birth rate. A decline in baptisms is registered from as early as the mid-sixteenth century in Castile, and then is experienced at a range of dates stretching into the 1620s in other parts of Spain. On the other hand Catalonia's demography was kept relatively buoyant by this French immigration (Catalonia was alone too in escaping the turn-of-century plague), and elsewhere, where there was economic opportunity, demographic recovery was recorded. The aggregation involved in considering national demographic variables conceals demographic performances far better than the average as well as others which were far worse.[73]

This selective character of the demographic recession is revealed by the history of the towns. Firstly, operating still at the aggregate level, if towns had grown at above-average rate during the period of expansion, they lost more than the average during the period of decline. The number of Spanish cities (using a threshold of 10,000 to define city status) had increased from twenty to thirty-seven between 1500 and 1600, but during the seventeenth century it fell back to twenty-two, the percentage of population living in such centres having risen from 6.1 to 11.4 but falling back again to 9. The total numbers living in cities of over 10,000 changed as follows: 1500, 414,000; 1550, 639,000; 1600, 923,000; 1650, 672,000; 1700, 673,000. Recovery only came in the eighteenth century with 767,000 in 1750, finally exceeding the 1600 peak of 1,165,000 in 1800.[74] Secondly, disaggregating, it is clear that some urban areas suffered far more than others. Tables 6.1–6.4 reveal two quite distinct stories: on the one hand a demographic crisis in Old Castile whose only parallel in European history is to be found in the post-Black Death collapse; on the other hand more continuity in eastern and southern Spain, with the latter sustaining an unusual density of urbanization through the seventeenth century despite some losses.[75] As on other occasions in this work I shall use these demographic details as a proxy for detailing economic performance, and shall comment briefly on what

*Table 6.1*  Demographic performance of cities of Old Castile and northern Spain (in thousands; −10 = less than 10,000)

|  | 1500 | 1550 | 1600 | 1650 | 1700 | 1750 | 1800 |
|---|---|---|---|---|---|---|---|
| Avila | ? | 16 | 14 | 6 | 5 | −10 | −10 |
| Bilbao | −10 | −10 | −10 | −10 | 6 | 7 | 11 |
| Burgos | −10 | 22 | 13 | 3 | 9 | −10 | 9 |
| Medina del Campo | ? | 16 | 14 | 3 | 5 | −10 | −10 |
| Medina del Rioseco | ? | 11 | 10 | 6 | 7 | −10 | −10 |
| Ocaña | ? | ? | 13 | ? | ? | −10 | −10 |
| Palencia | ? | 8 | 12 | 4 | 4 | −10 | 10 |
| Salamanca | ? | 20 | 25 | 15 | 12 | ? | 9 |
| Santiago | 4 | 1 | 1 | 10 | ? | ? | 25 |
| Segovia | ? | 22 | 28 | 16 | 8 | −10 | −10 |
| Valladolid | ? | 48 | 40 | 15 | 18 | 19 | 21 |

each table reveals to us about the stages in the different regions' growth over these some 200 years.

The lack of data for the period before 1550 is unfortunate, but it is probable that Burgos's experience is a representative one. The area experienced, it is evident, very rapid demographic expansion, with a probable doubling in its levels of urbanization. The details for the second half of the century demonstrate that this area was also precocious in its decline, Burgos and Valladolid already experiencing sharp falls in population, and the fair towns of Medina del Campo and Medina del Rioseco stagnating. By contrast, the industrial centres of Segovia and Palencia and the university and administrative centre of Salamanca were continuing to grow. The first half of the seventeenth century witnesses deurbanization on an extraordinary scale, at its most severe in Avila, Burgos, Medina del Campo, Palencia and Valladolid. Industrial centres were thus failing as well as commercial and administrative ones. Segovia, Salamanca and Rioseco's falls only appear 'moderate' against the collapses in population elsewhere. Only the near-coastal towns of Santiago and Bilbao experienced growth.

Turning to New Castile, there is again the lack of data for pre-1550, though table 6.2 records Madrid's extremely rapid emergence before it was made capital in 1561. There is only a single case of decline before 1600 but, like the declines in Old Castile, it is a sharp one. Elsewhere, however, rapid demographic progress is recorded. From 1600 the area's experiences appear to be influenced principally by the rapid growth of Madrid, which absorbs population from Toledo in particular, though industrial decline causes the demographic collapse of Cuenca.

The high level of urbanization of Andalusia throughout is worthy of emphasis. For the first half of the century it is the growth of Seville which stands out. Unlike Old Castile, there is no significant demographic

*Table 6.2* Demographic performance of cities of New Castile (in thousands; $-10$ = less than 10,000)

|  | 1500 | 1550 | 1600 | 1650 | 1700 | 1750 | 1800 |
|---|---|---|---|---|---|---|---|
| Alcazar de San Juan | ? | 20 | 10 | ? | ? | ? | 10 |
| Badajoz | ? | ? | 11 | ? | ? | ? | 10 |
| Cuenca | ? | 14 | 25 | $-10$ | $-10$ | $-10$ | $-10$ |
| Madrid | $-10$ | 30 | 49 | 130 | 130 | 109 | 167 |
| Toledo | ? | 30 | 50 | 20 | 20 | ? | 25 |

*Table 6.3* Demographic performance of cities of Andalusia
(in thousands; −10 = less than 10,000)

| | *1500* | *1550* | *1600* | *1650* | *1700* | *1750* | *1800* |
|---|---|---|---|---|---|---|---|
| Alcala la Real | ? | ? | 10 | ? | ? | ? | 12 |
| Andujar | ? | ? | 12 | ? | ? | ? | 12 |
| Antequera | ? | 10 | 16 | 19 | ? | ? | 15 |
| Aracena | ? | 6 | 10 | 7 | −10 | ? | 10 |
| Baeza | ? | 18 | 21 | 12 | 7 | ? | 10 |
| Cádiz | 2 | −10 | 5 | 7 | 23 | 60 | 70 |
| Cordoba | 27 | 33 | 45 | 32 | 28 | ? | 40 |
| Ecija | ? | 17 | 32 | 20 | 10 | ? | 28 |
| Granada | 70 | ? | 69 | ? | ? | ? | 55 |
| Jaen | ? | 22 | 22 | 18 | 20 | 22 | 28 |
| Jerez de la Frontera | ? | 18 | 27 | 17 | 13 | ? | 35 |
| Lucena | ? | ? | 18 | ? | ? | ? | 18 |
| Moron de la Frontera | ? | 13 | 13 | ? | 30 | 32 | 36 |
| Osuna | ? | ? | 10 | ? | ? | ? | 14 |
| Ronda | ? | 8 | 8 | ? | ? | ? | 15 |
| Seville | 25 | 65 | 90 | 60 | 96 | 66 | 96 |
| Ubeda | ? | 13 | 19 | 12 | 10 | ? | 14 |
| Utrera | ? | ? | 11 | 11 | 8 | ? | −10 |

decline in the second half of the sixteenth century: on the contrary rapid growth is registered in Antequera, Aracena, Cordoba, Ecija, Jerez, Seville and Ubeda. From 1600 there is crisis, but in no case on the scale of Old Castile. Sharp declines are experienced by Baeza, Aracena, Ecija, Jerez, Seville and Ubeda, moderate declines by Jaen, and continuity or moderate growth characterize the experiences of Cádiz, Antequera and Utrera. A later decline than the Castilian also meant one that carried on further into the seventeenth century, as can be seen in Baeza, Ecija and Jerez – and Segovia in Old Castile followed this pattern.

Eastern Spain was spared the extremes: gradual growth in the first half of the sixteenth century gave way to something of an acceleration in the second half of the century, though only Valencia's performance was the equivalent of the degree of upturn elsewhere. Valencia's decline was also the sharpest, but even in its case the degree of deurbanization is

*Table 6.4*  Demographic performance of cities of eastern Spain
(in thousands; −10 = less than 10,000)

|            | 1500 | 1550 | 1600 | 1650 | 1700 | 1750 | 1800 |
|------------|------|------|------|------|------|------|------|
| Alicante   | −10  | −10  | 11   | 11   | −10  | −10  | 13   |
| Barcelona  | 29   | 35   | 43   | 44   | 43   | 50   | 115  |
| Cartagena  | 4    | ?    | 8    | ?    | 12   | ?    | 33   |
| Murcia     | 10   | 13   | 17   | 20   | 25   | 32   | 40   |
| Orihuela   | −10  | ?    | 10   | ?    | ?    | ?    | 19   |
| Palma      | ?    | ?    | 10   | ?    | ?    | ?    | 14   |
| Valencia   | 40   | 37   | 65   | 52   | 50   | ?    | 80   |
| Saragossa  | ?    | 18   | 25   | 30   | 30   | ?    | 40   |

insignificant when comparisons are made with Andalusia and Castile.
Stagnation rather than urban loss characterizes the experiences of the
area in the second half of the century before its exceptional performance
in the eighteenth century.

## Agriculture

The information which we possess on the progress of agriculture during
the sixteenth and seventeenth centuries goes some way to accounting for
this pattern of demographic development. During the first half of the
sixteenth century there was a process of expansion, the area under cultivation being extended and commercial crops such as the vine and olive
expanding. Behind this development were rising prices, accountable for
in terms of the arrival of American bullion, and growing demand consequent upon population growth, rapid urbanization and the trade with
America, and an elastic response to this situation by agricultural producers as a result of landlords offering more land for rent (rather than
relying on seigneurial dues) and a general preparedness to lend money to
farmers for clearing land or financing the growth of new crops by means
of *censos* (loans made on the security of land). The expansion was,
however, on an extensive rather than intensive basis and there was no
rise in yields. On the contrary there was movement on to marginal lands
of low productivity, and growth in grain output was at the expense of the
number of sheep (a decline from 3 to 2 million) and cattle, mules replacing oxen as the principal working animals. The relationships between
graziers and arable farmers was conflictive rather than collaborative, as

might have been the case given the advantages derivable from mixed farming. Yields were declining because of excessive cropping. 'The land is becoming exhausted and the fields are not as productive as they once were', a contemporary noted in 1578.[76] In these circumstances, increasing difficulty was experienced by cultivators in repaying the debts which they had incurred during the period of expansion.

As much as land shortage (and there were still vast stretches of virgin land), it was a failure in techniques and institutional developments that was to blame for the problems. The conditions of expansion do not appear to have lasted much beyond the mid-century as demand for foodstuffs from America went into decline, the imposition of a *tasa* (price limit) on grain prices checked the growth in farming profits, and production costs (rents, wages and interest on loans, above all) rose. Some problems may have been self-created: the strong links between country and town had led to the diffusion of urban consumption patterns, farmers may have overspent on consumer goods, and, when difficulties arose, did so on litigation. Difficult weather conditions exacerbated problems: there was a period of exceptionally wet weather from 1589 to 1598 and one of drought between 1603 and 1614. Again, however, it has been judged to be inadequacies in agricultural technique which rendered farmers particularly vulnerable to such climatic variations. In these conditions the payment of interest on loans became burdensome, land began to be withdrawn from cultivation, and unemployed peasants and agricultural workers to drift to the towns. The turning-point, like the demographic, would appear to have occurred at some stage between 1560 and 1580.[77]

Institutional changes and the financial crisis of the monarchy, with which we shall concern ourselves below, exacerbated difficulties. The extent of the crisis and its duration can only be understood in terms of the interaction between something local and specific, the difficult but not yet disastrous circumstances of Castilian agriculture, and Castile's increasingly central role in the Habsburgs' imperial endeavours both across the Atlantic and in Europe. The point is stressed by the Catalan historian Jaume Torras: 'Between the American treasure and the politics of chimerical hegemony in the Mediterranean and in Europe', he writes, 'one has to interpose, however, some mediations internal to the society and economy of Castile.' From the time of the bankruptcy of Philip II it was increasingly within Spain, and within Spain from Castile, that Habsburg foreign policy had to be financed. Taxes in Castile increased threefold between 1560 and 1590, and the desperate search for credit led also to the sale of *baldios*, waste land nominally belonging to the crown, from 1560, and at an accelerating rate from 1580. Peasants were having to buy what previously they had enjoyed free. Common land owned by the municipalities was also liquidated, for they too were having difficulty in meeting fiscal demands, and this resulted in a change in its use. From serving the community at large it was loaned out or became the property of the highest takers. This trend received a particular impulse with the adoption of a new purchase tax from the 1580s, the *millones*: in return for their acceptance of this new fiscal burden, communities were given *carte blanche* to do what they wanted with any of their resources. Their actions favoured the rich. Llopis Agelán writes of an acceleration of differentiation within the peasantry and the rise of local 'bosses' as 'two of the most singular features of the social and economic development of seventeenth-century Castile'. Torras reaches a similar conclusion, writing of a 'process of dispossession of poor peasants and of concentration of lands in the hands of wealthy lenders'.[78]

The hesitations in agricultural growth were thus much exacerbated by social and institutional factors. 'The depression can only be understood in the context of the changes which took place in the Castilian agrarian system, changes which were not predetermined, but were in great part the result of specific historical circumstances in the different areas', Llopis Agelán insists. Such was the fiscal pressure, and the difficulties occasioned by loss of access to common land and the resultant need to clear waste, that land was deserted. Benefit could not be drawn from rents when they declined in the seventeenth century.

> Someone who works has to support himself as well as the señor who has inherited the land and the señor who rents the land, and the collector of the tithe, and the agent for the loan, and the others who make requests; and from the above one can understand why the ratio between those who work and those who are idle is so low; it works out at one to thirty.

The contrast between Spanish power and apparent vast wealth and this seizing up of its society at its very roots was striking and commented on: 'the whole trouble stems from the fact that they have scorned society's natural foundations', wrote de Cellerigo, the Spanish *arbitrista* (term used for contemporary commentators who were aware of Spain's crisis and made suggestions as to how it might be reversed), a quotation from whom provides one of the epigraphs heading this chapter, 'and that they have adopted the destructive attitude of all commonwealths: the belief that richness lies only in money . . . Wealth has not sent its roots deep because it has never come down to earth.'[79]

What is impressive is both the extent of the decline and also the duration of the depression. Work on grain production in New Castile, for example, shows that the upward trend in grain harvests reached a peak in approximately the 1570s to be followed by steady decline until the end of the 1630s, by which time production was barely half of what it had been at its height. Recovery did not start until the 1670s but was very slow – only an eighth of what had been lost being recovered by 1680: the 1570s peaks of production were not again attained until the nineteenth century. 'In Castile', Llopis Agelán concludes, 'economic growth ceased for approximately 150 years.'[80] Wool exports conformed to these trends. They had peaked between 1571 and 1579 at an annual average of 4,025 tons, fell to 2,587 tons between 1589 and 1594, stabilized then for some seventy years before experiencing a further fall to 1,840 tons betwee 1664 and 1670, and then recovering gradually to exceed the 1570s peak during the 1750s. The hiatus is again some 200 years. The only exceptions to the grim picture were on the one hand the fortunes of non-transhumant sheep-herding – the stock of sheep expanded with the decline in arable farming – and on the other agricultural progress experienced by the northern littoral, in Galicia and Asturias, with the introduction of maize.[81] Here lies the explanation of the demographic vitality of this area, for example the growth against the trend in Santiago, but the progress achieved was on an autarkic subsistence basis, and of little service to the development of a market economy. Similarly in the south and south-east, grain shortages were experienced, but coastal situations permitted food imports and promising specializations in exportable wine and wine derivatives (eau-de-vie) and olive oil.[82] Difficulties were experienced in the seventeenth century, but the records suggest an experience of stagnation rather than one of decline and a later crisis than that of Castile (post-1650). South-eastern Spain's pattern is similar, with few signs of difficulties until the 1640 revolt of the Catalans.[83] The crisis in Castile, however, it should be emphasized again, was acute and long-lasting. The forms which social and institutional development had taken, and the investment practices consequent upon the availability of fixed-return incomes on government debt, had created structural problems which were to take centuries to resolve; and attesting the depth of the problems was a feeling of helplessness with respect to their solution: 'Those who can will not; and those who will, cannot', recorded de Cellerigo.[84]

## Industry

Industrial performance too followed the pattern which has been emerging, though, as the demographic details suggested, with somewhat of a lag. Two principal loci in the Spanish cloth industry had emerged since the completion of the majority of the Reconquista in the fourteenth century: a southern one, concentrated in Cuenca, Toledo, Ciudad Real, Murcia, Cordoba and Baeza, and a Castilian one, in Segovia, Palencia, Soria and Avila. It was the former which led until the sixteenth century, but the northern industry, with Segovia as its capital, became dominant from this point. Segovia employed 20,000 workers in 1515 and its annual production rose to over 16,000 pieces in the 1580s, making it one of the largest cloth-producing centres in Europe. As with agriculture, the extent of growth and, in addition, the predominant form of organization of production – the *verlagsystem* dominated by wealthy merchant investors – was influenced by the buoyant demand situation in the peninsula and the monetary abundance occasioned by bullion imports.

An additional stimulus to the dominance of merchant capital over the industry was occasioned by the crown's promotion of the guild system in New Castile and the imposition of production regulations. Both measures favoured the larger-scale producer with capital. The extent of the dominance of urban capital over the industry was increased following the reversal in 1566 of legislation obliging foreign merchants to export their positive trade balances with Spain in the form of Spanish commodities. The Spanish merchants, who had been the principal intermediaries in these transactions, found themselves suddenly with idle capital on their hands which they turned to cloth production. The urban control exercised by such merchants over rural production was a further means, in addition to the payment of *censos* and rents to urban landowners, by which the countryside was exploited for the benefit of the towns. At the same time there were limits to the entrepreneurial control exercised by such merchant manufacturers, with guilds surviving with the support of royal protection to protect the interests of artisans and oppose innovation.

The fortunes of the industry turned at the end of the century: in addition to suffering from a decline in demand consequent upon the agrarian depression, peace with England in 1604 and the Dutch Republic in 1609 removed the effective protection which it had been enjoying and exposed it to a competition which it was in no way equipped to withstand. The response of the guilds was defensive, as in Italy: they were not prepared to accept the necessary technical and organizational changes to confront northern competition. The industry's entrepreneurs were no more effective: faced on the one hand by these difficulties, and on the other presented with the new possibilities of participating in the export-import trade, introducing foreign cloth and exporting raw materials (principally wool), they chose the latter course, disinvesting on a major scale. A study on Segovia's notarial contracts, which had shown an upward shift in the percentage of transactions relating to cloth production from 40 to 80 per cent between 1550 and 1570, records a drop in this figure to a mere 5 per cent by 1630. Segovia's production had fallen about 3,700 pieces, to less than a quarter of its 1580s level, by the end of the seventeenth century. Other areas of Spanish industry, for example silk production at Valencia and Toledo, suffered similar near-total eclipses, the timing for the decline being between the 1590s and 1620s. The suddenness and scale of the collapse are parallel to those recorded for northern Italy in the last chapter.

Although some of the difficulties were inevitable – textile industries throughout Europe were in trouble – the extent of the Spanish collapse, like the Italian, was a consequence of local conditions. Wages were high, there were labour shortages, and Spanish industrial organization managed to combine an unhappy mixture of extreme individualism in financial priorities with obstruction of technical or organizational change. Merchant manufacturers dominated production, excluding the artisan from access to raw materials or direct participation in the marketing processes, while guilds opposed technical change. Finally the government failed to provide protection, following the pattern which we have observed in Portugal of favouring agrarian interests, supporting the export of wool to industrial competitors rather than looking after its manufacture. James Casey characterizes the débâcle as one of 'the nemesis of "power without responsibility", of the incomplete capitalisation of the textile manufactures'. The description is an excellent categorization of the behaviour of an entrepreneurial class whose monopoly had served to drain artisanal workers of their autonomy and savings, and which later used the proceeds of its capital accumulation to promote exporting activities which deprived artisans of materials with which to work, and importing ones which competed with such Spanish cloth as was still reaching the market.[85] As with agriculture, a burst of prosperity had created no permanent basis for enrichment but had rather destroyed industrial traditions leaving a legacy, again for centuries, of social polarization and inability to generate new initiatives.

## Trade

With respect to trade, two principal areas of Spain need to be taken into consideration: the north with its links to Flanders; and the south and east with their Mediterranean outlets and the growing Sevillian trade with the New World. A basis for the prosperity of both was in fact the interaction beween each other's trade currents. However, as was seen in chapter 3, the Flanders–Bay of Biscay links were the dominant ones until 1557, the first bankruptcy of Philip II, whereas Seville–Mediterranean links came to dominate from this point into the seventeenth century.

These Flemish–Spanish commercial links had been strong since the fourteenth century at least, as we noted above, and they received an extra stimulus following the accession of Charles V. The new king encouraged economic links between his different possessions, and to these commercial links were added financial ones as his bankers, the Fuggers, made Antwerp the main centre of their activities. The boom in Flanders was all the greater in that it built on the momentum already established by interchanges with Portugal and on Antwerp's entrepôt role for English cloth, Baltic commodities and the metals of southern Germany. The stimulus of European empire was being added to the role of commercial core, and under the dual stimulus Antwerp experienced its greatest burst of prosperity between the 1530s and 1550s, attaining a population of over 100,000, more than double its 1500 level. American empire added yet a further dimension. As Braudel points out, the immense project of colonizing and trading with the New World required the collaboration of others, and the Flemish were initially the principal collaborators. As Cantabrian shipping resources were transferred to the American trade, Flemish shipping filled the gaps in the carrying trades and was also contracted by Charles V for Mediterranean duty. In addition, fleets needed to be equipped and the colonies to be supplied. Antwerp was the intermediary in obtaining naval stores and a range of manufactured goods. Finally, from the 1530s, as the flow of silver from the New World began to pick up, it served as a second return product to wool exports for the Flemish imports.[86]

These developments we have covered in chapter 3. What concerns us here is their impact on interior Spain. This is evident. A prime explanation for the buoyancy of demographic and agrarian conditions, and for the rapid urbanization of Old Castile during the first half of the sixteenth century, lay in the enormous prosperity of the Iberian–Flemish trades which were channelled into the Castilian interior. The exceptional prosperity of this area, accompanied by the earlier rapid growth in its cities, is accountable for in terms of its being at the heart of these dynamic interactions between the different sections of Charles's empire. The sudden and extreme deterioration in conditions in Castile from the 1570s is, similarly, to a significant though unquantifiable extent, explicable in terms of the increasing difficulties experienced by these trading routes following the beginnings of the Dutch Revolt in 1568. The fortunes of the fair town of Medina del Campo provide the most sensitive register of the changes. Its population, which had stood at 16,000 in 1550, had sunk to a mere 3,000 in 1650. The sharp reversals in Burgos's and Segovia's – northern Spain's commercial and industrial capitals respectively – fortunes also reflect the changing trading circumstances and their impact on Old Castile. What had been Europe's principal commercial highway had become a cul-de-sac.

A preliminary to assessing the fortunes of the second, southern, commercial zone is to emphasize the imperial links which connected it to a range of different territories in the west Mediterranean, including the Balearic islands, Sardinia, the duchy of Milan (Spanish from 1535) and the kingdoms of Sicily and Naples. As was the case with his Burgundian inheritance, Charles V had encouraged the economic integration of these areas with the peninsula. However, the Italian wars between France and Spain and, in addition, the channelling of silver and the spice trade through Antwerp caused the prosperity of the area to be checked until the mid-century. This relative marginalization is a further explanation for the strength of those commercial currents which had brought such hectic expansion to Castile during this half-century. Barcelona's merchants, for example, looked to Castile and to Medina del Campo for most of the sixteenth century for their principal commercial and financial operations. The failure, thus, in Antwerp and Castile could be of potential benefit to this effectively rival, southern trading bloc. It was to be so all the more emphatically as the Spanish crown redeployed its financial and foreign-policy activities to the Mediterranean. Genoese merchants were chosen to succeed the Fuggers as Philip II's bankers following his bankruptcy in 1557 and, from the 1570s, following the outbreak of war with both England and the Dutch, Spanish bullion for expenditure in Flanders was directed on an easterly route out of Spain, through Barcelona to Genoa, and thence over the Alps as the so-called 'Spanish road' was developed. As Pierre Vilar writes, 'the exchange fairs of Piacenza triumphed while those of Medina del Campo died.' To these financial activities were added the benefits of peace in northern Italy following the treaty of Cateau Cambrésis in 1559 and the revival in Venice's Levant trade noted in the previous chapter.[87] In southern Italy the expansion had started earlier. There, following the conquest of Naples by Alfonso the Great of Aragon in 1442, a process of rationalization and market integration had taken place, Naples growing and the nobility losing power, and this had been followed by a growth in silk and grain exports as the area was integrated in the sixteenth century with the other Mediterranean Habsburg territories.[88]

The impact for southern and eastern Spain, and for the western Mediterranean and Italy, of these changes was all the greater in that they coincided with the period of most rapid expansion in the American trade. The shipping involved in this rose from a tonnage of some 3,000–4,000 a year to 15,000 between 1565 and 1570, 25,000–30,000 in the 1580s and peaked at just over 45,000 tons in 1608, while bullion imports increased from 350,000 kg in the 1560s to peak at 2.75 million kg in the 1590s. A further boost followed from the 1580 union with Portugal, which brought the East Indies, much of Africa, and Brazil under Spanish rule. Recognition of the turning-point and the new geographical distribution of Spanish power was given brief recognition by the raising of Lisbon to the status of Spanish capital for a few years in the 1580s. As we saw in chapters 3 and 5, a short Indian summer followed for the Mediterranean economy, lasting into the seventeenth century.[89]

A high degree of complementarity between the Spanish and Italian economies was a further element favouring commercial expansion. Genoa had developed since the fourteenth century into a major manufacturing centre and, like Florence, Venice and Milan, it drew on Spanish supplies of wool, wheat, olive oil, wine, fruits, minerals, leather and silk. The concentration of the American and East Indian trades in Seville and Lisbon provided additional bases for trade in both directions. Wool was the principal Spanish export, and a study by Jonathan Israel on all Spanish wool exports for the period from the 1560s to the mid-seventeenth century illustrates the contrasting fortunes of the Flemish and Mediterranean trades. The latter had had the dominant exporting current until the 1570s, at up to 20,000 sacks a year, but from the Dutch revolt exports slumped below 10,000 sacks while those from east Spain – Alicante, Cartagena and Tortosa being the export points – and Andalusia expanded. Exports to southern France were high, as well as those to Italy, until the French Wars of Religion.[90] The records for silk production suggest a similar pattern. In the Murcia region, for example, where silk cultivation had been introduced at the turn of the century, production and exports peak in around 1600 after a particularly rapid expansion in the late 1580s.[91] It was not purely the primary sector, however, which was growing. The textile industry in the areas around Cordoba and Baeza/Ubeda, benefiting from expanding American demand, grew more quickly even than Segovia's, Cordoba's production reaching peaks of over 18,000 pieces of cloth in the 1580s, when the number of looms recorded in the city in the 1590s was 832. Silk production, too, prospered in this area, Cordoba containing 2,000 looms as late as 1630,[92] and, at the other extreme of the peninsula, Barcelona's cloth industry expanded, with colonial imports including dyestuffs. The ports of Barcelona, Valencia, Cartagena and Malaga all benefited from this trading activity. 'Barcelona', a contemporary commented in 1582, 'is overflowing with wealth', and the prosperity endured well into the seventeenth century, a commentator in 1620 registering the fortunes which had been made by some sixty commercial houses during the previous fifty years through trade with Italy and Sicily.[93]

On the other hand the extent of capital accumulation within the peninsula was limited by the overwhelming dominance of Genoese finance in all commercial and productive spheres. In the previous chapter emphasis was placed on the degree of dependency created in the Sicilian and Neapolitan economies by the intrusion of Ligurian capital. The same pattern applied in southern and eastern Spain, but with even greater intensity, as the Genoese shifted resources to the peninsula to profit from the exceptionally favourable economic situation there, intervening in all areas, including shipping and exporting to the New World, manufacturing, exporting and importing, the slave trade, royal finances, farming and tax-collecting. Spain, Scammell argues, represented to Genoese plutocrats what the Terraferma was coming to do for the Venetian elite. The investment served to stimulate economic activity, but a price was evidently charged: 'in exchange for their services they exacted financial, commercial and industrial privileges . . . and exercised in short an extensive, informal empire', Scammell writes. The Genoese were ubiquitous, from the fairs of Castile, to Seville and to the equipping of the expeditions of conquistadors in the Caribbean and Peru and New Spain, from involvement in farming and cloth production to retailing and finance. Even a city like Barcelona, with its own bourgeoisie, played merely 'the role of a staging-post' in the expansion. This second phase in Spain's commercial growth had been concentrated in what was, as we noted above, the area of the peninsula with the weakest commercial traditions. The degree of Iberian dependency had been decisively increased.[94]

The period of expansion came to an end during the first two decades of the seventeenth century. The stages in the decay of the Amerian trade is registered by the declining shipping tonnages plying between Seville and America. Seville's Casa de Contratación, founded in 1510 to serve as a form of government agency for promoting and monitoring the American trade, had been given the monopoly in 1573. These tonnages averaged 15,000 in the 1630s, well down on the peaks at the beginning of the century, and then fell steadily to bottom out at just under 3,000 tons for the first decade of the eighteenth century. Bullion imports fell too, though less drastically, to a level of 2 million kg for the 1620s before experiencing some recovery in the 1630s.[95] Trade with Italy also declined. That in wools collapsed with the crisis in the Italian cloth industries, falling to half its 1570s level by 1664–70.[96] Exports in silk from southern Italy suffered even more seriously: those from Cosenza, the principal producer, declined from levels of between 430,000–560,000 lb in the 1540s to 1570s to less than 85,000 lb by 1639. It is evident that it is the west Mediterranean as a whole which is the proper unit for assessing the development of these years.[97] Manufacturing experienced a similar scale of decline to that recorded earlier in Old Castile: the number of silk looms in Cordoba, for example, had declined to a mere fifty by 1680, and the position of the woollen industry was even feebler, boasting a mere five looms producing some 100 pieces of cloth a year.[98] Levels of poverty grew, reaching crisis point between 1647 and 1652, which gave rise to hunger riots in eighteen different localities in Andalusia. Details of agricultural performance are complex. Production and price data for grain, wine and olives for the seventeenth century in Andalusia show a predominant tendency towards stagnation, with conditions deteriorating after 1650. However, consistent with the demographic data for the region, and for southern and eastern Spain generally, the crisis appears to have by no means matched that suffered in Old Castile.[99]

The principal cause for the decline in the American trade lay in the New World: the sharp decline in the continent's demographic resources consequent upon the brutality of the conquest and the decimation of the Indian population as a result of their exposure to European diseases. The destruction first took place on the islands of the Caribbean and then continued on the mainland. Population levels declined from being roughly equal to Europe's at the time of the discovery to a mere tenth of the earlier figures by 1600. Mexico's population, for example, fell from a pre-Conquest level of perhaps 25 million to not much more than 1 million by 1600. The negative impact on Spanish trade of these demographic trends was exacerbated by the character of economic and social change in the New World. Settlement there had taken the form of *encomiendas* – similar to feudal estates – rather than plantation economies, and this, combined with the development of its own urban system consequent upon the profits from mining and an expansion in manufacturing, gave rise not to complementarity with the metropolitan economy, as was the case with the Brazilian developments, but to growing self-sufficiency. The Spanish empire was not a trading one like the Portuguese, but a product of conquest and the subjection of a different civilization. What demand there was from the empire came increasingly to be not for foodstuffs, the principal export in the early years from Andalusia, but for manufactures, in the production of which Spain was at a disadvantage with respect to north European producers. In 1695, for example, the shares of manufactured goods for the American trade exported from Cádiz were distributed as follows: 25 per cent from France, 21 from Genoa, 19 from the Dutch, 11 from the English, 7.6 from Hamburg and a mere 3.8 per cent from Spanish suppliers. The Spanish trade by its fleet system with the New World had thus been fully 'colonized', and Cádiz was more an international commercial centre rather than a Spanish port. In addition there was an increasing 'direct' trade, via contraband, with the Spanish possessions as the Dutch, French and English occupied the more peripheral islands of the Caribbean. Labour shortages in the New World also halted growth in mineral production. The population of the mining town of Potosí, for example, the centre of the Peruvian mining industry, which had topped 100,000 in the late sixteenth century, had sunk to a mere 10,000 a century later.[100]

Portuguese trades too, as we noted above, were being prised away from Iberian control, the catalyst for the change being the trade diversions enforced by the eighty-year war with the Dutch. The end of the 1609–21 truce was decisive. The Dutch and other northern powers had been acting as shippers on behalf of Genoese capitalists and Spanish exporters. With renewed trade embargoes, and with an increased involvement of the Dutch in Iberia's extra-European markets, the Dutch and later the English came to intervene in the Mediterranean on their own account, provisioning Spanish and Italian markets with cloth as well as the spices which had formerly come from Lisbon. Alicante's counter-cyclical growth through to 1650, which was noted above, was an un-healthy sign for the Spanish economy, as the quality of its port, and its convenience for supplying the Spanish interior, made it a preferred point of import for Dutch, English and French shippers. Its performance con-trasts with the formerly expanding commercial centre of Valencia, whose trade was in sharp decline.[101] Both the motors for the Mediterranean's Indian summer – foreign policy in the Italian peninsula, silver and trad-ing opportunities in the New World and Indies – were failing. Southern and eastern Spain, like southern Italy and Sicily, were slipping down the economic hierarchy as their former dominators, the Genoese, them-selves in decline, were joined by the incursions of French, Dutch and English capitalism.

## Taxation and finance

As noted above, Castile had developed a centralized government with extensive fiscal powers. However, the costs of empire were to swamp these resources. The change of scale is impressive. An impression of it can be gained by comparing the revenue of the Spanish crown in 1510, which stood at some 32 million maravedis, with the treasury's total debts in 1556, estimates for which vary between 7,500 and 11,000 million. The size of the debt grew progressively as the table 6.1 shows. The discrepancy between these figures and income was not as great as the

*Table 6.5*   Estimates of debt in millions of
ducados

| | |
|---|---:|
| 1556 | 20 |
| 1573 | 50 |
| 1581 | 80 |
| 1598 | 85–100 |
| 1623 | 112 |
| 1667 | 180 |

comparison made above as new fiscal sources and American silver had
increased revenue. However, the disproportion was still very large:
revenue according to Braudel stood at some 13 million ducats in 1577, or
about one-sixth of the debt, and the gap grew steadily larger, the 112
millions of debt in 1623 representing at least ten years of revenue.[102] The
silver imports from America, even at their height in the 1590s, were little
more than a palliative, given the extent of the gap. Vilar calculates that
debt interest charges then not only exceeded the crown's portion of the
treasure but also the total private influx.[103] The costs of empire, it is
evident, were far beyond the resources of the Spanish crown to finance.
Hence the royal bankruptcies at approximately twenty-year intervals in
1557, 1575, 1596 and 1607.

Our concern is with the consequences of this continuous financial
crisis on the Iberian economy. Two factors need to be taken into consideration. The first is the impact of growing levels of taxation as attempts
were made to balance the books; the second is the effect of the growing
reliance on largely foreign lenders to finance the large deficit. With
respect to the first, it is from the accession of Philip II that Spain became
exposed to the brunt of the monarchy's fiscal demands. In the Cortes
of 1573–5, tax demands were multiplied. For example Cordoba's and
Segovia's by two and a half, Seville's by three. The burden was all
the greater in those towns which by the late sixteenth century were
experiencing demographic decline. Thus Segovia's families were by 1584
paying six times as much as some twenty years earlier, and the tax burden
on twenty-three communities in the territory of Cordoba went up from
4.5 million maravedis in 1557–61 to 13.6 million in 1590–5. New taxes
were also introduced – the harshest being the new excise tax, the
*millones*, initiated after the defeat of the Armada in 1590. The more
effective centralization in Castile than in the other possessions of the
Spanish crown caused it to be the principal victim.[104] The injustice of this

situation lay behind attempts in the 1620s and 1630s to increase fiscal control over Portugal and Catalonia – a process which contributed to the revolts in the two areas in the 1640s: the issue of finance thus lay at the heart of Spain's political as well as economic problems. We have also seen, though, that the extent of taxation had implications for the very structures of the economy. The excessive fiscal burden, inequity in its distribution – hidalgos and clergy being exempt from most taxes – and the inefficient ways in which taxes were raised contributed to destabilizing the very basis of the Spanish state, its agricultural system. Later the royal bankruptcies and devaluations undermined credit generally. Individuals as well as muncipalities were affected. Taxes to be raised had been apportioned to different towns, which themselves had been forced to rely on credit to pay them. The debt of Cordoba in 1580, for example, stood at twice the annual yield of the *alcabala* purchase tax. In the space of a century there had been a shift from exceptional monetary abundance to general discredit. The damage to the country's credit system was another reason for the depth and duration of the crisis.[105]

Indebtedness, both at the central and local level, relates to another facet of Spain's economic problems: the issue of *juros* (interest-bearing bonds) by the government absorbed an increasing share of available capital, depriving agriculture, industry and trade of resources. The growing weight of income coming from such sources contributed to reinforcing a hidalgo mentality, characterized by a preference for unearned income over active involvement in business.[106] The virtuous circle which had been behind the short 'golden age' had been succeeded by a downward spiral in which the different areas of difficulty interacted with each other.

As foreign bankers provided the bulk of the Spanish crown's credit, the payment of interest on debt resulted in the regular transfer of resources out of Spain. Initially it was German bankers, the Fuggers and Welsers, who benefited most, and we noted above their replacement by the Genoese following the 1557 bankruptcy, and the resultant transfer of resources to northern Italy. The Genoese involvement in fact preceded 1557, and over the period 1519 and 1556 their contribution to crown finances was already larger than that of the Germans, slightly under 15 million ducats of the some 40 million borrowed, against the Germand 13.5 millions. The domestic Spanish part stood at about half of these figures, just under 7.5 million ducados. The losses in interest paid were considerable: The Venetian ambassador calculated in 1595 that the Genoese had received some 24 million ducats during the previous sixty-four years, but they were not limited to this. As had been the practice in relationships between private financiers and the state since time immemorial, economic and fiscal advantages were extorted from the crown in return for loans, or in lieu of loan repayments. Thus the Fuggers, for example, in lieu of directly paid interest, were given the yields on the tax farms on the three great Castilian ecclesiastical orders.[107] This effective mortgaging of the peninsula's resources in return for credit recalls the similar practices in southern Italy from the twelfth and thirteenth centuries to which reference was made in the previous chapter. It was on a large scale. From 1519 to the end of Charles V's reign, 518 *asientos* (contracts between the crown and businessmen) were granted with a value of 59 million ducats, and by 1575 Philip II's concessions already exceeded those which his father had made. Very few of the concessionaires were Spanish. Bennassar argues that this sacrificing of Spanish interests to outsiders was eased by empire. The fact, for example, that the bankers of Augsburg were included in imperial territory attenuated 'the impression that Castile was being exposed to pillage by foreigners'. Wallerstein emphasizes the way these concessions demonstrate the hollowness of Habsburg political power – a surrender of sovereignty was involved with 'long term effects on the politico-economic strength of the king'.[108]

The widespread xenophobia in Castile in the seventeenth century is clearly attributable to growing awareness of the drain on Spain to other countries occasioned by its indebtedness and dependency. If the existence of *juros* had an impact on individual investing practices, the large scale of royal finance, and the discredit to which bankruptcies gave rise, was most destructive to the overall credit of Castile. The final demise of the fair of Medina del Campo is attributable to the 1596 bankruptcy.[109] The rapidity of the growth of Madrid – itself most destructive in the excessive demands which it placed on the declining demographic resources of Castile – is also attributable to the scale of the crown's imperial financial, as well as administrative, efforts. Running an empire was bringing few benefits to the peninsula.

## Interpreting Spanish decline

Many explanations have been offered for Spanish decline. Kamen, we noted at the beginning of the chapter disputes the very utilization of the concept for a country which never 'rose' in the first place. Elliott drew attention to the fact that the decline was one predominantly experienced by Castile, with peripheral areas faring better. C. R. Phillips, on the other hand, argues for the broad applicability of a Malthusian model to the crisis for all regions of Spain.[110] For Bennassar the failure consists in the misallocation of the capital accumulated from the Americas, with resulting destructive rather than constructive consequences for the surpluses. James Casey argues for the applicability of the concept of a 'failed transition': capital had been accumulated and markets developed, but the process of rationalization came to a halt and there was no interaction between capital and labour: the 'transition was frozen', he writes:

> peasants and artisans were both pauperized, but they stayed by and large in control of agriculture and manufacture, a handicap for further growth. The classes which had the wealth remained prisoners of the past, trapped in the service of a horribly costly and inefficient agrarian monarchy . . . The wreckage of the old without anything better to replace it – that was the real significance of the crisis in Spain.[111]

For Parker and Wallerstein, Spain was paying the price of the possession of an excessive empire. Parker judges that it was the chance accession to Portugal, with its vast empire, which was the turning-point, giving rise to a clear and massive case of 'imperial over-stretch'.[112] Wallerstein considers the task that the Habsburgs set themselves, to dominate politically such vast expanses of territory, was beyond the administrative possibilities at their disposition: 'Spain did not erect (probably because she could not erect) the kind of state machinery which would enable the dominant classes in Spain to profit from the creation of a European world-economy', he writes, 'despite the central geographic-economic position of Spain in this world economy in the sixteenth century.' As a result of this failure, Spain's degree of dependency increased, Wallerstein adds, describing the two peninsular states as 'conveyor belts for the interests of core powers in the peripheral regions'.[113] Kamen reaches similar conclusions, citing the contemporary who wrote of Spain becoming 'the Indies for the foreigner'.[114]

It is not the case that any of these views is incorrect. They relate to different aspects of an extremely complex reality. It is to be hoped that this chapter will have thrown light on some of its components. To recapitulate: the origins of 'dependency' in the Spanish economy were traced back in the opening of this chapter to the period immediately following the Reconquista. It was, though, it was emphasized, dependency to a limited degree only, mostly confined to parts of Andalusia, making little impact on Old Castile, where commercial and industrial development was well entrenched after an early reconquest, and less accentuated than that experienced by other zones bordering on the Tyrrhenian Sea.

The completion of the Reconquista, the discovery of America and the creation of the Habsburg empire gave rise, it has been seen, to a period of great prosperity, above all in Old Castile, characterized by rising population, agricultural production, trade and industrial development. This expansion, though, was soon brought to a halt by a first crisis in the Spanish economy in the second half of the sixteenth century. Behind the failure were, on the one hand, the decline in the trade artery which had crossed Castile, linking Seville and Andalusia to the Meseta and, from there, to the burgeoning capitalism of Flanders. On the other was a developing failure in the region's agriculture, demographic crisis and demographic drift, as a steady southward migration in the peninsula's population took place consequent on the departure of the Moriscos and as the new opportunities opening in Seville added to losses from plague and famine. Industrial crisis followed the demographic and agricultural one. Actions of the state – its tax-collecting, its privileging elite groups at the cost of producers, its establishment of apparently fully safe investment outlets for rentier capital, its demands for manpower for its warfare, its promotion of the capital, Madrid – exacerbated the crisis, interacted with the commercial and agrarian crisis, causing a steady downward spiral, turning what had been the most populous and by far the most civilized and densely populated part of Castile into a depopulated, depressed zone characterized by the sharpest of social divisions, and setting the scene for some 300 years of stagnation. It is this interaction between external circumstances and this internal cycle which accounts for the depth of the crisis and its duration.

Southern Spain, thus, and, to a lesser extent Aragon, benefited in part from this early failure of Castile, as trade routes as well as population were moving south. Here, there was little sign of failure until well into the seventeenth century. The crisis, when it comes, is in part a distinct one, that of the Mediterranean economy whose Italian facets were surveyed in the last chapter. The demographic data bear witness to this spatial and chronological distinction as well as its generally milder (if still severe) characteristics. It is in the case of this second crisis that the issue of dependency is relevant, whereas in the crisis of Castile the region's prior commercial development ensured that the penetration of foreign capital was never as pronounced. The shift of the centre of gravity of the peninsula's economy from its north and centre to its south meant a movement to the area where native commercial traditions were at their weakest. The Genoese, in particular, came to dominate the whole zone. This position of dependency endured into the seventeenth and eighteenth centuries, even though there were shifts in the identity of the principal dominators, with the Dutch and then French replacing the Genoese.

# 7

# Decline in European History

This was formerly the case with the Assyrians who, having failed, passed under the Persians and all their subjects under the Macedonians, and the Macedonians under the Romans. And these events constantly occur in an alternating fashion according to chance of both time and tyche. Just as there is in an individual man, or in whatever animal, birth, progress toward the prime, the prime, afterward decay, and finally destruction and death, thus is it also in human affairs, politics and despotisms. These are to be seen in constant flux and change, in no way remaining constant, but coming into being, advancing, little by little decaying and changing into the opposite state, coming to an end and dying.

Melochites

The epigraph[1] serves as a reminder of continuities over the long term in speculation about decline and of Europe's position in the larger history of the whole civilization of the Afro-Eurasian area. It has, however, been decline in 'European' history on which I have concentrated, and so the bulk of this conclusion needs to be devoted to this. A number of particularities of this decline have emerged from the long narrative in which we have been involved.

Firstly, it has become apparent, that a distinction needs to be made between types of decline. That of 'empires' needs to be separated as a category from that of other types of political unit. Empires which have been referred to in the book include (brief references only in some cases) those of the early civilizations of Mesopotamia such as that of Akkad in Sumeria, and of Rome, Byzantium, Islam and Spain. These were all, primarily, territorial empires. I will argue that 'trading post' empires or 'thalassocracies' represent a different genus and I shall refer to them shortly. Their declines had various features in common. They were caused principally by what has been termed the problem of 'overreach' – an inability to retain control over the large areas which had been conquered. They were brought down or weakened both by external intrusion and by an internal dynamic consisting in increasing fiscal and other demands made upon their inhabitants, and by increasing interventionism as market systems deteriorated, which undermined the roots of their prosperity, resulting in agricultural and demographic atrophy. The common features in such a process have been well summarized in various studies by the American historical sociologist S. N. Eisenstadt and more recently by Paul Kennedy.[2] The aftermaths of such declines were long periods of demographic and economic weakness. It was not until the year 1000 that Europe recovered the population levels it had attained at the height of Roman expansion in AD 200. The Near East, the 'victim' of a succession of territorial empires, the Assyrian, the Achaemenid, the Hellenistic, the Roman, the Sassanid, the Byzantine, the Islamic and then the Ottoman, finally had the life squeezed out of it, its population stagnating at a near constant level of between 20 and 25 million between the years AD 200 and AD 1750, while that of Europe multiplied from a low point of 26 million in AD 600 to reach 80 million in 1300 and 140 million in 1750. This was the greatest and longest-lasting decline in the history of the Afro-Eurasian area, one whose consequences are still evident.

However, it is the argument of this book that such declines were not typical of 'Europe'. To be precise, the principal idiosyncrasy of European history has been the failure of empire and the existence of a pluralist political system. Spain's Habsburg period and attempt at European and, to some extent, global dominance was a consequence of two accidents, a dynastic one and the discoveries. These accidents nearly caused European history to be stopped in its tracks, but ultimately they did not succeed in eliminating, but merely distorted, that linear dialectic of geographical diffusion of cultural and technical skills which underpinned the European experience – the triumph of this stronger alternative being seen in the Spanish failure to put down the Dutch rebellion. Spanish decline consequently, however, had some of the characteristics of declines in empires – prolonged demographic and agricultural atrophy, dependency, sharp social divisions – though not all of them: it was to be moderated by Spain's sharing in 'European' traditions, which I shall be discussing below.

One particularity of declines in European history can thus be registered. The types of political units experiencing decline have not primarily been empires but smaller groupings. Indeed the 'pluralism' of European history is such that declines can be observed at the level of the village or small town, as well as at those of the city-state, nation-state or region. To provide a full characterization of the subject, something has first to be said about the general conditions for the existence of such a distinctive history of decline.

These general conditions were the same as those which historians have argued lay behind the unique dynamism of European society. That combination between Christianity (which provided universal and agreed social norms without the restrictions of empire), geographical situation (which provided shelter from nomadic invasion), exceptionally fertile agriculture and a competitive, and varied state system, which saved Europe from disintegration after the Black Death and provided a basis for continuous economic and social progress,[3] while it ensured that decline should be a widely experienced phenomenon (since a dynamic, progressive system implies losers as well as winners) at the same time determined that it should be experienced on the local level only and need not be as severe as that of empires. Those forces for social cohesion which underpinned success facilitated too the adjustment to decline; and evidently there also existed the possiblity of adapting to, and profiting from, the growth being experienced elsewhere. Decline in Europe consequently has on the one hand been more general than in any other previous society, but on the other, as it has purely been the reverse side of a dynamic system, has never had to be hopeless.

Byzantium's experience serves, we have seen, to make this point. Its easterly situation, on the threshold between Europe and the Near East, with their varying political traditions, and its unique historical experience of bridging the periods of Antiquity and the Middle Ages, resulted in its experiencing both types of decline, a form of the 'imperial' variant in the seventh and eleventh centuries, and the European pattern, relative rather than absolute, from the eleventh century.

In order, however, to arrive at this 'model' of decline in European history, we have clearly simplified things: I shall summarize the omissions. Europe did not advance purely on the basis of that process of technical and commercial diffusion from the Near East meeting with an internal dynamic consequent upon exceptionally favourable agricultural systems and communications, as outlined in the Introduction and

chapter 2. This may have been the fundamental motor, the most powerful dialectic, but its course was repeatedly interrupted by other agencies,
and it is only in the last two or three hundred years, since the period of
Mercantilism, that the process has been lifted to the front of political
priorities. This interaction of the economic with other primarily political
events has affected decline, as it of course affected progress, in a number
of ways. Firstly, since for most of European history there has been
warfare, political disturbance and dominance by states whose priorities
were not primarily materialistic, economic development has tended to
be 'interstitial' and concentrated in isolated areas. This has had the
consequence that concentrations of economic power have ended up in
being disproportionate to the general state of economic development.
Venice, Genoa, Florence, Milan, Amsterdam, Seville, Lisbon, Antwerp,
Bruges, Amsterdam and London were, following Constantinople, far
larger than would have been the case under fully free market conditions.
A contrast exists here with the more spontaneous pattern of commercial
development via city-states under the Greeks and the Phoenicians. The
result of such a pattern was, though, on the one hand inertia, with trade
and industry committed to certain channels and a resulting inflexibility
and slowness to adapt, and on the other, structural problems of a severe
kind when decline set in, with difficulty in adapting to changing economic
circumstances. Clearly during the last two hundred years, with a greater
degree of security, more universal subscription to economic values and
a greater extent of technological diffusion consequent upon industrialization, such extreme concentration of economic life has been less
marked.

Politics, in conjunction with the character of technology, also played
a determining role in the location of the principal economic centres up
to the nineteenth century. This tended to be in coastal areas. The technological grounds for this were the lower costs of sea over land transport.
As important, however, were the defence advantages arising from such
locations. Whereas trade on land could be brought to a standstill by
a hostile regime, trade by sea managed generally to elude attempts at its
control. A further factor reinforcing the lead of coastal areas was the
advantages which their situations gave them firstly in the introduction
of techniques from, and trading with, the more advanced Near East and,
later, on the Atlantic seaboard, for exploiting the sea routes to the east
and the resources of the New World. The force of these series of factors
is illustrated by the experiences of Venice and then Amsterdam: attention was drawn in chapter 3 to the parallels in the situation of these two
cities at key stages in European history, hemmed in by military pressure
and yet able to survive, and uniquely privileged in their contacts with

the most dynamic existing commercial centres. These factors, though, influence decline as they do success. They curtailed abruptly the economic aspirations of a range of internal centres, such as the towns of southern Germany in the sixteenth and seventeenth centuries, and they had the consequence that Europe's economic development did not take a course that at various times seemed likely: a gradual diffusion overland from the Mediterranean sources via southern Germany or France. Instead there was a relatively sudden metamorphosis, with a veritable collapse of the Mediterranean sector, which experienced long-term decline, and an abrupt expansion of the Atlantic powers.

Particularities of European decline consequent upon this pattern include this curtailment in growth and marginalization of many 'continental' commercial centres, abrupt decline for the great Mediterranean commercial centres and an unequally 'unnatural' extent of predominance of the succeeding Atlantic powers, which in turn occasioned structural problems of a severe kind as finally industrialization led to a more widespread growth process. Britain has been a principal sufferer here.

Just as the character of success has evidently (despite the great continuities just emphasized) changed over time consequent upon progress in techniques and changes in attitudes, so different forms of success have meant different forms of decline. A widening in the extent of trading activity, as broader social groups became involved, commercial centres extended their activities to manufacturing, and populations (and thus demand, and labour supply) grew, clearly caused scale to grow, the number of active commercial and industrial centres to increase, and competition to become fiercer. Styles of colonization changed, and already in the fourteenth century, as we saw, the Genoese and Venetians invented in the east Mediterranean the plantation economy later to be exported first to the Atlantic islands and then to the New World. Declines would consequently involve larger numbers of people, and larger geographical spaces, as trading-post and then territorial empires (as we saw in discussing Portugal and Spain) became involved. However, a more fundamental shift occurred with the triumph of the Dutch over the Spanish territorial empire. This triumph resulted in the most important of transitions. From this point it no longer remains accurate to talk of commercial states as merely 'interstitial'. 'Interstitiality' was now combined with political power. With the age of mercantilism, this became general. All European states saw that political success depended on combining economic and political power. Again the change has implications for decline: economic decline, as it implied political decline for any state, became a matter of greater concern, and more destabilizing internationally. The perils were all the greater insofar, as I have just argued, the economic dominances exercised by maritime states, followed up by the acquisition of large empires, were not natural ones. This magnifying of the issue which concerns us was reinforced by industrialization, which resulted in the mobilization of all members of society within functioning market systems. Decline would now represent a threat to whole populations. The outlook would have been worse, of course, had not the same widening of economic growth also increased the range of opportunities available. Even less than previously did declines have to be abrupt, though the problems posed for countries highly committed to certain trading patterns, and accustomed to maintaining high political profiles, are not, on the other hand, to be underestimated.

If these have been the defining characteristics of European decline, what have been its principal causes? For these we must return again to our discussion of Michael Mann's work in chapter 2. His examination of the experiences of the Afro-Eurasian zone over the very long term, from the birth of civilization, showed that a principal continuity in the history of the area has been a gradual westward and northward shift of the techniques and cultures of the first civilizations to areas in which they could be exploited in more favourable conditions from the point of view of factor supply (land, labour and raw materials). This process has been interrupted frequently and reversed occasionally, but it has clearly persisted. In the sixteenth century it jumped over the Atlantic and a new frontier was found, but its principles were the same. The Baltic zone earlier, it is the argument of Braudel, served the same purposes for the European economy which later were to be fulfilled by the Atlantic and America. Such a process implies, it is clear, repeated spatial shifts in the loci of industry and commerce: decline was built into such a dialectic, the decadence of the Aegean zone being followed by that of Italy and the Mediterranean as a whole, that of Spain being followed by those of Holland and Britain.

Political factors on various occasions distorted this process, slowing it down or accelerating it. The fall of the Roman empire and the barbarian invasions caused a relative revival of the east Mediterranean. The Mongol expansion likewise gave a new lease of life to the east Mediterranean in the thirteenth century. The expansion of Islam also slowed down the process of diffusion, isolating Europe from contact with the advanced civilizations, channelling what contact there was down the Italian peninsula. The Spanish Reconquista, and the reclaiming of the Tyrrhenian sea by Genoa, Pisa and Aragon had the reverse effect, widening the process of diffusion but, in doing so, bringing decline to areas like Amalfi, which had benefited from the status quo. The Ottoman expansion too, by excluding Europe from the east Mediterranean, served as a catalyst to the growth of oceanic trade. Habsburg ambitions likewise, as we have seen, first served to promote the Atlantic, then contributed to a Mediterranean revival before, with their frustration, bringing Spain and other parts of the empire down with them, thus contributing emphatically to the success of north-western Europe. Between them, Ottoman expansion and the Habsburg empire caused the extent of polarization between south and north, and east and west to be far greater than it would otherwise have been. These disruptions, however, one should emphasize, were not the motor of the process: they merely distorted, delayed or accentuated the trends occasioned by that powerful dialectic described in the previous paragraph.

Contributory to the process, it has often appeared, has been the conservatism and inflexibility of the established trading or manufacturing centres. Byzantium was gradually outclassed by Venice, Venice in turn by the Dutch, English and French, the Dutch by the English and then the English by the Americans, Japanese and continental competitors. 'Perhaps Venice's easily-acquired riches', Braudel speculates, 'imprisoned the city within a set of strategies determined by ancient custom', and generalizing from the Venetian failure he writes: 'leadership of a world-economy is an experience of power which may one day blind the victor to the march of history.'[4]

There are the clearest of parallels in the processes by which one state failed and another superseded it. The first step in the success of a rising maritime state generally lay in the making of inroads in the provision of shipping services for trade. It was here that the Venetians first made their mark in the trade with Constantinople, and it was their strengths in this area which enabled them to gain trading concessions from the Byzantines in the eleventh century. Similarly it was in shipping that Venetian and Genoese weaknesses became apparent from the sixteenth century, the Dutch, English, Ragusans, Portuguese and Basques taking their place. Naval power, as is well known, lay behind the English successes against both the Dutch and the French. Shipbuilding was the most labour- and capital-intensive of trading activities: it can be argued that it was the sector in which the competitive advantages, in terms of favourable factor supply situation, accruing to the areas to which the market economy was diffusing weighed most. We have also noted other continuities and repetitions: a growing inertia among commercial leaders in established entrepôts, an inability of manufacturers in such centres to adapt to competition, textile production, in particular, shifting from one place to another. Textiles, again, were a sector in which the factor supply situation was influential. Braudel and Mann, we noted in chapters 1 and

2, comment respectively on these cyclical patterns in decline and on the problem of 'institutionalization', and resulting inflexibility, in established centres.[5]

Clearly there were ways in which even a centre doomed to become less important because of the geographical shifts referred to could react in order to limit damage and to respond to the new distribution of economic forces. As just argued, one particularity of European decline was that it was not general but was always the reverse side of the coin to successes elsewhere, so that opportunities for a constructive response always existed. In one case, that of Portugal, we have argued that adjustments were never made as the opportunities of its frontier position were such that crisis was never serious enough. Stasis, rather than decline, is probably a more accurate way of defining its situation. More generally it can be seen that the opportunities to respond were not often fully exploited. Rather than innovating, or taking advantage of one comparative advantage which the older trading centre generally had, a high level of skills and an advantage in luxury or skill-intensive manufacturing because of this, the tendency was generally for the elites in such centres to use social and political coercion to conserve their privileges, forming themselves into territorial states and providing themselves thereby with populations and agricultural resources sufficient to guarantee a relative continuity in their ways of life. This is what Braudel meant, we noted, by the concept of a 'defection of the bourgeoisie' in the Mediterranean.[6] It has been emphasized in particular in the case of the Italian declines in chapter 5 but a shift of this kind from creative, wealth-creating entrepreneurial behaviour to an inward-looking, battening on local human and material resources can be said to be the usual response to decline. There were, however, cases of advantage being taken from the possibilities which opened from economic diffusion for new commercial and industrial specializations. The development of an important printing industry in Venice, diversification into a range of luxury manufacturing activities in Flanders following the decline of Antwerp, and the Dutch early eighteenth-century specialization in processing colonial products and their redistribution round Europe, leaving France and England to play the leading role in actual colonial development, are some examples of such responses. The Low Countries, with their many centuries' experience of industrial cycles are the best place for the analysis of varying responses to such crises.[7]

Finally we have come into contact with more than one type of decline within Europe, and some comment is necessary on this. There are the declines of former major industrial and commercial centres like Amalfi, Venice, Milan, Genoa, Florence, Barcelona and, between the fifteenth and eighteenth centuries, Antwerp and Amsterdam; these have rarely been total, some autonomy being retained, even if at the expense of local populations. Then there are those more abrupt declines, for example in Sicily, south Italy, Castile and Andalusia, which have been followed by dependency and an evident incapacity to respond in any positive way to economic opportunities elsewhere. These are all areas whose temporary prominence in commercial life was more the result of political developments than prior commercial and industrial specialization. Commercial growth was rapid in such centres, but it was a growth commanded from outside, and that fact, and the traditional character of the regimes which ruled these areas, resulted in both dependency and a near-complete lack of those sorts of commercial values which, for example by influencing tariff policies, might have contributed to moderating decline. Like Spain, southern Italy can be categorized as a victim of empire, and Anderson notes the strength of feudalism in the area which caused Frederick II to use it as his base for the creation of a unified monarchy in Italy.[8] The conservatism and exploitive relationship to local populations which characterized the old entrepôts were not attractive, but the elite which managed to conserve itself retained some autonomy, some capital and control over certain trading and industrial networks, which could serve their areas later when possibilities for industrialization emerged.

# Notes

## Introduction

1 The two-volume work was first published in French in 1949. I shall use the English translation of the second edition, published in London in 1972.
2 I. Wallerstein, *The Modern World-System: Capitalist Agriculture and the Origins of the European World-Economy in the Sixteenth Century* (3 vols, New York, 1974–88); F. Braudel, *Civilization and Capitalism: 15th–18th Century* (3 vols, London, 1981–4); J. Israel, *Dutch Primacy in World Trade, 1585–1740* (Oxford, 1989); M. Mann, *The Sources of Social Power*, vol. I, *A History of Power from the Beginning to AD 1760* (Cambridge, 1986).

## Chapter 1    Braudel's Mediterranean

1 If this is taken to start in *c.*3000 BC, with the development of the first civilizations, and if the ending of the Mediterranean's dominance is attributed to the seventeenth century.
2 European history in this book is held to have its origin in the seventh century, when the expansion of Islam brought the period of late Antiquity to an end and, in truncating the Mediterranean, created a structure within which a distinct European development took place.

3 Braudel *Mediterranean*, I, 241.

4 Ibid., 238.

5 Ibid., 239–41.

6 Ibid., 243–4.

7 Ibid., 241–2.

8 Ibid., 245–6.

9 Ibid., 402–3.

10 Ibid. 584–91.

11 Ibid., 594–9.

12 Ibid., 602–6. In the first edition of his work, on the basis of faulty data suggesting a collapse in Sicilian grain production, Braudel had posited for an earlier and more sudden turning-point in the sea's fortunes in the 1590s.

13 Ibid., 138–45. A graphic insight into how fundamental this timber problem was is provided by the restrictions imposed by Christian powers on the export of oars to the east Mediterranean for use by Turkish galleys.

14 Ibid., 606.

15 H. A. Miskimin, *The Economy of Later Renaissance Europe, 1460–1600*, (Cambridge, 1977), pp. 133–6.

16 *Braudel, Mediterranean*, I, 606–9.

17 Ibid., 609–12.

18 Ibid., 612–15.

19 Ibid., 615–21.

20 Ibid., 621–9.

21 Ibid., 629–42.

22 Ibid., 591 and see pp. 322–3 on 'Urban cycle and decline'.

23 Ibid., 146–8.

24 Ibid., 434–8 (section on 'General and local trends').

25 Ibid., II, 704–5: he cites Roupnel on the treatment of beggars in France: 'In the sixteenth century, a beggar would be fed and cared for before he was expelled. At the beginning of the seventeenth century, he would have his head shaven. Later he was more likely to be whipped . . .'

26 Ibid., 704, 725–34. He cites Drout on the metamorphosis in lawyers' expectations: 'These men of law, who a century previously had overthrown an old social order, had already by 1587, become a conservative body.'

27 Ibid., 734–56. Quotations on pp. 755–6.

28 Ibid., 826–35; the quotation is on p. 835. Braudel makes a claim for the influence of the Baroque, the culture of the declining Mediterranean civilization, being possibly greater than that of the Renaissance.

29 Ibid., I, 120–33, 389.

30 Ibid., II, 755–6.

31 Ibid., 901. *The Mediterranean* is divided into three parts: geographical, 'The Role of the Environment'; economic and social, 'Collective Destinies and General Trends'; and political, 'Events, Politics and People'. The order reflects his ranking of the relative importance of different causal factors. Events are categorized at one point as 'the ephemera of history' and

as passing 'across its stage like fireflies, hardly glimpsed before they settle back into darkness and as often as not into oblivion'.

32 French economist of the early twentieth century who exercised a great influence on the *Annales* school of historians with his views on economic cycles.

33 Braudel, *Mediterranean*, II, 892–900.

## Chapter 2  'World-Economy' and 'World Time'

1 I. Wallerstein, *The Modern World-System* (3 vols, New York, 1974–88), I, 3–11.
2 Ibid., 348.
3 Wallerstein's distinction between dependent unit and 'the whole' is similar to Marx's between 'structures' and events: on this as well as on the specific use of history referred to at this point see J. Tosh, The *Pursuit of History* (London, 1984).
4 Wallerstein, *Modern World-System*, I, 15–18.
5 See for example P. Baran, *The Political Economy of Growth* (London, 1957) and A. G. Frank, *Capitalism and Underdevelopment in Latin America: Historical Studies of Chile and Brazil* (London, 1969).
6 Wallerstein, *Modern World-System*, I, 38, 100–3, 301.
7 Ibid., 98, 356.
8 Ibid., 16, 355–6.
9 Ibid., 92, 95, 121–2, 185.
10 F. Braudel, *Civilization and Capitalism* (London, 1984), I, 23–6; III, 17–20.
11 Ibid., III, 7–10.
12 Ibid., 8.
13 Ibid., 24.
14 Ibid., 26–7.
15 Ibid., 27–32.
16 Ibid., 32–4.
17 Ibid., 35–8.
18 Ibid., 18.
19 J. Israel, *Dutch Primacy in World Trade, 1585–1740* (Oxford, 1989).
20 Ibid., pp. 1–4.
21 Ibid., pp. 4–7.
22 Ibid., pp. 7–11, 257–8.
23 Michael Mann, *The Sources of Social Power*, vol. I, *A History of Power from the Beginning to* AD *1760* (Cambridge, 1986).
24 Ibid., 30.
25 Ibid., 31.
26 Ibid., 93, 189.
27 Ibid., 81–2.
28 Ibid., 148–55.

29 Ibid., ch. 6 especially. Mann writes of the 'stimulus given by the Near East to a steadily widening geographical area and to the diverse power network there'.
30 Ibid., 190.
31 Ibid., 190–228.
32 Ibid., 164, 190.
33 Ibid., 190.
34 Ibid., ch. 9.
35 Ibid., 295: 'failure does not appear to have been inevitable.'
36 Ibid., 408.
37 Ibid., ch. 12.
38 Ibid., 15.

## Chapter 3   The 'Rise' of Europe

1 F. Braudel, *Civilization and Capitalism* (London, 1984), III, 97. On Flemish history J. A. Van Houtte, *An Economic History of the Low Countries, 800–1800* (London, 1977). A 'decline' study on the area is H. Van der Wee (ed.), *The Rise and Decline of Urban Industries in Italy and in the Low Countries (Late Middle Ages to Early Modern Times)* (Leuven, 1988).
2 This section on Venice is drawn from the following sources: G. Luzzatto, *An Economic History of Italy from the Fall of the Roman Empire to the Beginnings of the Sixteenth Century* (London, 1961) pp. 17–20, 31–5, 47–53; R. S. Lopez, *The Commercial Revolution of the Middle Ages, 950–1350* (Cambridge, 1976), pp. 63–6 and 'The Trade of Medieval Europe: The South', in M. M. Postan and E. E. Miller (eds), *The Cambridge Economic History of Europe* (Cambridge, 1987), II, 307–26; W. H. McNeill, *Venice: The Hinge of Europe, 1081–1797* (Chicago, 1974), chs 1–2; Braudel, *Civilization and Capitalism*, III, 106–37. For the notion of interstitiality see M. Mann, *Sources of Power* (Cambridge, 1986), I, 15–19.
3 F. Braudel, *The Mediterranean* (London, 1972), I, 72–5.
4 This section is drawn from Luzzatto, *Economic History of Italy*, pp. 26–8, 55–61; Lopez, *Commercial Revolution*, pp. 106–13 and 'The Trade of Medieval Europe', pp. 363–70. For the population levels N. J. G. Pounds, *An Economic History of Medieval Europe* (2nd edn, London, 1994), p. 258, though Lopez ('Trade of Medieval Europe', p. 343) gives the far higher figure of 200,000 for Milan and Venice in the fourteenth century.
5 Cited by Lopez, *Commercial Revolution*, p. 108.
6 On Genoa: Lopez, 'Trade of Medieval Europe', pp. 328–30, 344–55, and *Commercial Revolution*, pp. 106–8; G. V. Scammell, *The World Encompassed: The First European Maritime Empires, c. 800–1650* (London, 1981), pp. 155–83; Braudel, *Civilization and Capitalism*, III, 157–69; J. Heers, *Gênes au XVe siècle* (Paris, 1971), pp. 21–37, 233–58; O. R. Constable, 'Genoa and Spain in the Twelfth and Thirteenth Centuries: Notarial

Evidence for a Shift in Patterns of Trade', *Journal of European Economic History* 19 (1990), 635–56; Luzzatto, *Economic History of Italy*, pp. 53–5, 71–6.

7 D. Herlihy, 'Population, Plague and Social Change in Rural Pistoia, 1201–1430', *Economic History Review* 18 (1965), 225–44.

8 On the dynamism, then loss of momentum, of the Middle Ages see H. R, Trevor Roper, *The Rise of Christian Europe* (London, 1965).

9 Luzzatto, *Economic History of Italy*, pp. 86–91, 137–67; Lopez, 'Trade of Medieval Europe', pp. 348–52, 380–401 and *Commercial Revolution*, pp. 109–12.

10 Lopez, *Commercial Revolution*, pp. 102, 108, and 'Trade of Medieval Europe', pp. 399–400; A. Mazzaoui, 'The Cotton Industry in Northern Italy in the Later Middle Ages: 1150–1450', *Journal of Economic History* 32 (1972), 262–86.

11 H. A. Miskimin, *The Economy of Early Renaissance Europe, 1300–1460* (Cambridge, 1975), pp. 14–72, 116–63; Heers, *Gênes*, pp. 258–336 (translations from Heers by the author).

12 Scammell, *World Encompassed*, pp. 120–2; McNeill, V*enice*, ch. 2; Luzzatto, *Economic History of Italy*, pp. 137–54.

13 H. A. Miskimin, *The Economy of Later Renaissance Europe, 1400–1600* (Cambridge, 1977), pp. 20, 76, 142, 146, 165, 171; Heers, *Gênes*, pp. 291–336; C. Verlinden, 'From the Mediterranean to the Atlantic: Aspects of an Economic Shift (12th–18th Century), *Journal of European Economic History* 1 (1972), 625–46.

14 On Portugal's expansion: R. Davis, *The Rise of the Atlantic Economies* (London, 1973), pp. 1–14; C. Boxer, *The Portuguese Seaborne Empire, 1415–1825* (Pelican edn, London, 1969), chs 1–4; I. Wallerstein, *The Modern World-System* (New York, 1974–88), I, ch. 1; Miskimin, L*ater Renaissance Europe*, pp. 124–31.

15 On Spanish expansion: Davis, A*tlantic Economies*, ch. 3; J. H. Parry, *The Spanish Seaborne Empire* (Pelican edn, London, 1973), part I; Miskimin, *Later Renaissance Europe*, pp. 131–6.

16 On the European framework for Portuguese expansion and Antwerp's history: Davis, *Atlantic Economies*, ch. 2; Miskimin, *Early Renaissance Europe*, pp. 143–4 and *Later Renaissance Europe*, pp. 120–2, 126–8; Wallerstein, *World-System*, pp. 173–6; S. T. Bindoff, 'The Greatness of Antwerp', in *New Cambridge Modern History* (Cambridge, 1958), II, 48; Braudel, *Civilization and Capitalism*, III, 138–57; Van Houtte, *An Economic History of the Low Countries*; H. Van der Wee, *The Growth of the Antwerp Market and the European Economy (14th–16th Centuries)* (The Hague, 1963), II.

17 Citations from D. Sella, *Crisis and Continuity: The Economy of Spanish Lombardy in the Seventeenth Century* (Cambridge, Mass., 1979), p. 1, and 'Crisis and Transformation in the Venetian Trade', in B. Pullan (ed.), *Crisis and Change in the Venetian Economy* (London, 1968), p. 88; see

also Braudel, *Civilization and Capitalism*, III, 164–9; Miskimin, *Later Renaissance Europe*, pp. 165–7, and J. Israel, *European Jewry in the Age of Mercantilism* (Oxford, 1985).

18 Wallerstein, *Modern World System*, I, ch. 4, esp. pp. 187, 196.
19 J. Israel, *Dutch Primacy in Europe* (Oxford, 1989), pp. 1–11.
20 Braudel, *Civilization and Capitalism*, III, 207–8.
21 Israel, *Dutch Primacy*, ch. 1; Davis, *Atlantic Economies*, pp. 179–80.
22 Wallerstein, *Modern World-System*, I, 196, and see above, p. 29, for Israel's similar verdict.
23 Israel, *Dutch Primacy*, pp. 16–17, 40, 69–73; J. W. Smit, 'The Netherlands Revolution', in R. Forster and J. P. Greene (eds), *Preconditions of Revolution in Early Modern Europe* (Baltimore, 1970), pp. 19–53.
24 J. de Vries, *The Economy of Europe in an Age of Crisis* (Cambridge, 1976), pp. 70–3, 92–4, 211–13, 227–30.
25 On the Dutch penetration of the Iberian East and West Indian trades see Israel, *Dutch Primacy*, pp. 67–73, 156–87.

# Chapter 4   Byzantium: Declines in the Transition from Antiquity to the Middle Ages

1 If Emperor Constantine's making Constantinople capital of the eastern empire in AD 330 is taken as the foundation point, as it is, for example, by C. Diehl in *Byzantium: Greatness and Decline* (New Brunswick, 1957), p. 5.
2 *Hamlyn Historical Atlas* (London, 1981), p. 41.
3 P. Anderson, *Passages from Antiquity to Feudalism* (London, 1974), p. 284.
4 Diehl, *Byzantium*, pp. 5–12.
5 Diehl, *Byzantium*, pp. 13–22.
6 Anderson, *Passages from Antiquity*, p. 267. The two following paragraphs draw on pp. 265–72.
7 Ibid., pp. 272–7.
8 Ibid., pp. 277–9.
9 Ibid., pp. 281–3.
10 Ibid., pp. 283–4.
11 G. Ostrogorsky, 'Byzantine Cities in the Early Middle Ages', *Dumbarton Oak Papers* 13 (1959), 47–66; S. Vryonis, *The Decline of Mediaeval Hellenism in Asia Minor and the Process of Islamization from the 11th through the 15th Century* (Los Angeles, 1971).
12 M. F. Hendy, 'Byzantium, 1081–1204: An Economic Reappraisal', *Transactions of the Royal Historical Society* 20 (1970), 31–41.
13 S. D. Goitein, 'A Letter from Seleuceia (Cilicia) dated 21 July 1137', *Speculum* 39 (1964), cited by Hendy, 'Byzantium, 1081–1204', p. 48.
14 Hendy, 'Byzantium', pp. 41–52.

15 Views summarized by M. Angold, *The Byzantine Empire, 1025–1204* (2nd edn, London, 1997), p. 15. The classic interpretation is that of G. Ostrogorsky, *History of the Byzantine State* (2nd edn, Oxford, 1968). Full references to the authors mentioned in the historiographical summary between pp. 77–80 are included in note 19.

16 Angold, *Byzantine Empire*, pp. 15–16.

17 Ibid., pp. 16–18.

18 Ibid., pp. 19–23.

19 Ibid., pp. 173–80 for the section on the twelfth century. A. P. Kazhdan, *Derevna i gorod v Vizanti IX–XVV.* (Moscow, 1960); P. Lemerle, 'Byzance au tournant de son destin', in *Cinq Etudes sur le XIe siecle byzantin* (Paris, 1977), pp. 249–312; R. J. Lilie, *Byzantium and the Crusader States, 1096–1204* (Oxford, 1993); D. Nicol, *Byzantium and Venice: a study in diplomatic and cultural relations* (Cambridge, 1988); P. Magdalino, 'Aspects of twelfth-century *Kaiserkritik*, *Speculum* 58 (1983), 326–46.

20 M. F. Hendy, 'Byzantium 1081–1204: The Economy Revisited Twenty Years On' in his *The Economy, Fiscal Adminstration and Coinage of Byzantium* (London, 1989), III.

21 Ibid., pp. 3–9.

22 Ibid., pp. 9, 12–19.

23 Ibid., pp. 19–21.

24 Cited by Angold, The *Byzantine Empire*, p. 327.

25 Hendy, 'The Economy Revisited', pp. 41–8.

26 A. Kazhdan and A. Cutler 'Continuity and Discontinuity in Byzantine History', *Byzantion* 52 (1982), 429–30.

27 Ibid., pp. 441–7.

28 Ibid., pp. 447–8.

29 Ibid., pp. 454–63.

30 S. Runciman, 'Byzantine Trade and Industry', in M. M. Postan and E. E. Miller (eds), *The Cambridge Economic History of Europe*, II, *Trade and Industry in the Middle Ages* (Cambridge, 1987), 137–45.

31 A. Toynbee, *A Study of History*, (2 vols, abridged D. C. Somervell, London, 1960), I, 307–26.

32 Kazhdan and Cutler, 'Continuity and Discontinuity', pp. 464–78.

33 D. Abulafia, 'Asia, Africa and the Trade of Medieval Europe' in Postan and Miller (eds), *Cambridge Economic History of Europe*, II (2nd edn, Cambridge, 1987), 402–73.

34 Abulafia, 'Asia, Africa and the Trade of Medieval Europe', parts 1 and 2.

35 Hendy, 'Byzantium', p. 40.

36 F. Braudel, *The Mediterranean* (London, 1972), I, 593.

37 Anderson, *Passages from Antiquity*, p. 279.

38 Diehl, *Byzantium*, pp. 190–3.

39 F. C. Lane, *Venice: A Maritime Republic* (Baltimore, 1973), pp. 37–43.

40 Braudel, *Mediterranean*, I, 149.

41 F. Braudel, *Civilization and Capitalism* (London, 1984), III, 119.

42 Diehl, *Byzantium*, pp. 193–6.

43 See below, p. 148.
44 A. E. Laiou-Thomakadis, 'The Byzantine Economy in the Mediterranean Trade System: Thirteenth–Fifteenth Centuries', *Dumbarton Oaks Papers*, 34/5 (1980–1), 177–222.
45 A. Kazhdan, 'The Italian and Late Byzantine City', *Dumbarton Oaks Papers* 49 (1995), 1–22.
46 A. E. Laiou-Thomakadis, 'Italy and the Italians in the Political Geography of the Byzantines (14th Century)', *Dumbarton Oaks Papers* 49 (1995), 73–98.

## Chapter 5 Italian Declines

1 R. S. Lopez, 'The Trade of Medieval Europe', in M. M. Postan and E. E. Miller (eds), *The Cambridge Economic History of Europe* (Cambridge, 1987), II, 360, 379–85. See also R. S. Lopez and H. A. Miskimin, 'The Economic Depression of the Renaissance', *Economic History Review* 14 (1962), 408–26, the discussion between C. M. Cipolla, Lopez and Miskimin, 'Economic Depression of the Renaissance', *Economic History Review* 16 (1964), 519–29, and for a general discussion of the historiography of Italian decline see F. Krantz and P. M. Hohenberg (eds), *Failed Transitions to Modern Industrial Society: Renaissance Italy and Seventeenth Century Holland* (Montreal, 1975), especially pp. 16–18. Carlo Cipolla's 'Commentary' in this volume (pp. 9–10) provides the epigraph to this chapter.
2 'In economic terms, a low platform may serve for the launching of economic growth' (R. S. Lopez, *The Commercial Revolution*, Cambridge, 1976, p. 18); Lopez, 'The Trade of Medieval Europe', p. 377 for the quotation.
3 Lopez, 'The Trade of Medieval Europe', pp. 384, 391–2, 399.
4 R. S. Lopez, 'Hard Times and Investment in Culture', in A. Molho (ed.), *Social and Economic Foundations of the Renaissance* (New York, 1953), pp. 60–1.
5 See above pp. 47–50, 57–8.
6 D. Abulafia, 'Southern Italy, Sicily and Sardinia in the Medieval Mediterranean Economy', in his *Commerce and Conquest in the Mediterranean, 1100–1500* (London, 1993), pp. 8–17.
7 Lopez, 'The Trade of Medieval Europe', pp. 328–9.
8 C. McEvedy and R. Jones, *World Population History* (Harmondsworth, 1978), pp. 133–56, 209–40.
9 D. Abulafia, 'Asia, Africa and the Trade of Medieval Europe', in Postan and Miller (eds), *Cambridge Economic History of Europe*, II, 426, 432; F. Braudel, *The Mediterranean* (London, 1972), I, 116–17 (on north–south links at this point of the Mediterranean).
10 Abulafia, 'Southern Italy', pp. 14–16.
11 Lopez, 'The Trade of Medieval Europe', pp. 345–6.
12 F. Braudel, *Civilization and Capitalism*, III, 106–11.
13 Abulafia, 'Southern Italy', pp. 8–17.

14 D. Abulafia, *The Two Italies: Economic Relations between the Norman Kingdom of Sicily and the Northern Communes* (Cambridge, 1977); H. Bresc, *Un monde méditerranéen. Économie et société en Sicile, 1300–1450* (2 vols, Rome, 1986).

15 M. Aymard, 'Commerce et consommation des draps de Sicile et en Italie meridionale (XVe–XVIIIe siècles)', in M. Spallanzanie (ed.), *Produzione, commercio e consumo dei panni di lana (nei secoli XII–XVIII),* Istituto Internazionale di Storia Economica 'D. Datini', Prato (Florence, 1976), p. 133; Braudel, *Mediterranean,* I, 155, 579.

16 D. Abulafia, 'Southern Italy and the Florentine Economy, 1265–1370', *Economic History Review* 34 (1981), 377–88.

17 Braudel, *Mediterranean,* I, 579.

18 Aymard 'Commerce et consommation', pp. 127–39.

19 I. Wallerstein, *The Modern World-System* (3 vols, New York, 1974–88), I, 121.

20 S. R. Epstein *An Island for Itself: Economic Development and Social Change in Late Medieval Sicily* (Cambridge, 1992); *idem,* 'Cities, Regions and the Late Medieval Crisis: Sicily and Tuscany Compared', *Past and Present* 130 (1991), 32–6.

21 Epstein, 'Cities, regions and crisis', pp. 32–6.

22 Ibid., 31–3.

23 See above p. 50.

24 Aymard, 'Commerce et consommation', pp. 138–9.

25 H. A. Miskimin, *The Economy of Later Renaissance Europe, 1460–1600* (Cambridge, 1977), p. 74.

26 J. Heers, *Gênes au XVe siècle* (Paris, 1971), pp. 238–41.·

27 Epstein, *Island for Itself,* p. 275.

28 W. Kula, *An Economic Theory of the Feudal System* (London, 1976), pp. 86–93.

29 McEvedy and Jones, *World Population History,* p. 18.

30 Epstein, *Island for Itself,* pp. 406–7.

31 Braudel, *Mediterranean,* II, 849–54.

32 See above pp. 7–9.

33 S. Berner, 'Commentary' in Krantz and Hohenberg, *Failed Transitions,* p. 21.

34 Epstein, *Island for Itself,* pp. 405–12.

35 'However brilliant it might appear, with its great merchants, its fleet of large ships, its banks, its long-distance exchanges, the international trade of the sixteenth century sharpened the contrasts between the two economies, the two societies which it brought together' (Aymard, 'Commerce et consommation', p. 139).

36 Miskimin, *Later Renaissance Europe,* pp. 74–5.

37 C. Wilson and G. Parker (eds), *An Introduction to the Sources of European Economic History* (London, 1977), pp. 2–3.

38 P. Chorley, *Oil, Silk and Enlightenment: Economic Problems in 18th Century Naples* (Naples, 1965), *passim.*

39  G. V. Scammell, *The World Encompassed* (London, 1981), pp. 132–7; W. H. McNeill, *Venice: The Hinge of Europe* (Chicago, 1974), p. 131.

40  Scammell, *World Encompassed*, pp. 139–44; McNeill, *Venice*, ch. 4; P. Earle, 'The Commercial Development of Ancona, 1479–1551', *Economic History Review* 22 (1969), 28–44; J. Israel, *European Jewry in the Age of Mercantilism* (Oxford, 1985); D. Sella, 'Crisis and Transformation in Venetian Trade', in B. Pullan (ed.), *Crisis and Change in the Venetian Economy* (London, 1968), pp. 90–3.

41  J. Israel, *Dutch Primacy in World Trade* (Oxford, 1989), pp. 53–62, 96–101.

42  Scammell, *World Encompassed*, p. 142; F. C. Lane, 'Venetian Shipping during the Commercial Revolution', in Pullan, *Crisis in the Venetian Economy*, pp. 21–46; quotation on p. 44.

43  D. Sella, 'The Rise and Fall of the Venetian Woollen Industry' and C. M. Cipolla, 'The Economic Decline of Italy', in Pullan, *Crisis in the Venetian Economy*, pp. 106–46; R. T. Rapp, 'The Unmaking of the Mediterranean Trade Hegemony: International Trade Rivalry and the Commercial Revolution', *Journal of Economic History* 35 (1975), 499–525 and *Industry and Economic Decline in Seventeenth Century Venice* (Cambridge, Mass., 1976).

44  S. Ciriacono, 'Mass Consumption Goods and Luxury: The Deindustrialization of the Republic of Venice from the 16th to the 18th century', in H. Van der Wee (ed.), *The Rise and Decline of Urban Industries in Italy and in the Low Countries (Late Middle Ages to Early Modern Times)* (Leuven, 1988); P. Musgrave, *Land and Economy in Baroque Italy: Valpolicella, 1630–1797* (Leicester, 1992), pp. 8–9.

45  Pullan, *Crisis in the Venetian Economy*, Introduction, pp. 16–20.

46  Braudel, *Mediterranean*, I, 599.

47  S. J. Woolf, 'Venice and the Terrafirma: Problems of the Change from Commercial to Landed Activities', in Pullan, *Crisis in the Venetian Economy*, pp. 175–203; J. de Vries, *The Economy of Europe in an Age of Crisis* (Cambridge, 1976), pp. 53–5; McNeill, *Venice*.

48  Musgrave, *Land and Economy*, pp. 38–48, 64–75, 104–9, 182–4.

49  McNeill, *Venice*, pp. 226–7 and ch. 6.

50  D. Sella, *Crisis and Continuity: The Economy of Spanish Lombardy in the Seventeenth Century* (Cambridge, Mass., 1979), p. 24.

51  Braudel, *Mediterranean*, I, 72–5; Sella, *Crisis and Continuity*, p. 2.

52  Braudel, *Mediterranean*, I, 204–6.

53  Ibid., 72–4.

54  Sella, *Continuity and Change*, pp. 16–23.

55  Ibid., pp. 3–4.

56  Sella, 'Venetian Woollen Industry', p. 111.

57  Mazzaoui, 'The Cotton Industry in Northern Italy in the Later Middle Ages, 1150–1450', *Journal of Economic History* 32 (1972), 268–9; Sella, *Crisis and Continuity*, p. 10.

58  R. S. Lopez, 'Economic Depression of the Renaissance?' *Economic History Review* 16 (1964), 524 n. 4.

59 J. Hale, *The Civilization of Europe in the Renaissance* (London, 1994), pp. 94–142; Sella, *Crisis and Continuity*, pp. 42–6.

60 Ibid., pp. 28–36.

61 H. Kellenbenz, 'The Fustian Industry of the Ulm Region in the 15th and Early 16th Centuries', in N. B. Harte and K. G. Ponting (eds), *Cloth and Clothing in Medieval Europe: Essays in Memory of Professor E. M. Carus-Wilson* (London, 1983); Sella, *Crisis and Continuity*, pp. 22–3, 40–2, 57–8, 111–12.

62 Sella, *Crisis and Continuity*, pp. 1–2, 41–2

63 Ibid., pp. 61–71; Cipolla, 'Economic Decline of Italy', pp. 127–32.

64 Sella, *Crisis and Continuity*, pp. 86–9; J. de Vries, *European Urbanization, 1500–1800* (London, 1984), pp. 284–5.

65 Sella, *Crisis and Continuity*, ch. 4, and also pp. 90–7 for various explanations, pp. 97–147 for his interpretation.

66 Pullan, 'Introduction' in his *Crisis in the Venetian Economy*, p. 2.

67 P. Coles, 'The Crisis of Renaissance Society: Genoa, 1488–1507', *Past and Present* 11 (1957), 41.

68 Braudel, *Civilization and Capitalism*, III, 164–9.

69 Ibid., III, 170–3; B. R. Mitchell, *European Historical Statistics, 1750–1975* (London, 1980), pp. 87–8.

70 Scammell, *The World Encompassed*, pp. 201–20; Berner, 'Commentary', pp. 21–2.

## Chapter 6    Iberian Declines

1 These are H. Kamen's arguments in his 'The Decline of Spain: An Historical Myth?' *Past and Present* 81 (1978), 24–50.

2 A. MacKay, *Spain in the Middle Ages: From Frontier to Empire, 1000–1500* (London, 1977), p. 8.

3 S. P. Bensch, *Barcelona and its Rulers, 1096–1291* (Cambridge, 1995), ch. 3.

4 J. Vicens Vives, *Manual de Historia Económica de España* (6th edn, Barcelona, 1972), pp. 101–6; O. R. Constable, 'Genoa and Spain in the Twelfth and Thirteenth Centuries: Notarial Evidence for a Shift in Patterns of Trade', *Journal of European Economic History* 19 (1990), 635–56; H. A. Miskimin, T*he Economy of Later Renaissance Europe, 1460–1600* (Cambridge, 1977), pp. 635–56.

5 Constable, 'Genoa and Spain', p. 653.

6 Abulafia 'Southern Italy, Sicily and Sardinia, in the Medieval Mediterranean Economy', in his *Commerce and Conquest in the Mediterranean, 1100–1500* (London, 1993), p. 17 and see above p. 101.

7 O. R. Constable, *Trade and Traders in Muslim Spain: The Commercial Realignment of the Iberian Peninsula, 900–1500* (Cambridge, 1994), pp. 240–8.

8 See Abulafia, 'Southern Italy, Sicily and Sardinia' for comparisons in the degree of Genoese subordination of different areas.

9 F. Braudel, *The Mediterranean* (London, 1972), I, 606–8.

10 D. A. Herlihy makes a good case for a pre-1300, Malthusian check in population growth in 'Population, Plague and Social Change in Rural Pistoia, 1201–1430', *Economic History Review* 18 (1965), 225–44, and see I. Wallerstein, *The Modern World-System* (3 vols, New York, 1974–88), I, 38–9 for the general check in the Christian progress against Islam, from the Holy Land to Granada.

11 J. Heers, *Gênes au XVe siècle* (Paris, 1971), p. 321.

12 J. H. Elliott, *Imperial Spain, 1469–1716* (London, 1963), ch. 4.

13 'Hitherto isolated and insignificant, Portugal was more profoundly influenced by empire than states with other economic interests and political ambitions' (G. V. Scammell, *The World Encompassed*, London, 1981, p. 276).

14 A good overview is provided in the chapter on Portugal by F. Mauro and G. Parker in C. Wilson and G. Parker (eds), *An Introduction to the Sources of European Economic History* (London, 1977), pp. 63–80. Otherwise the three first phases are described in C. Boxer, *The Portuguese Seaborne Empire, 1415–1825* (Pelican edn, London, 1973).

15 A. C. Boyajian, *Portuguese Trade in Asia under the Habsburgs, 1580–1640* (Baltimore, 1993), pp. 46–8, 242.

16 Boxer, *Seaborne Empire*, p. 381.

17 C. Verlinden, 'La colonie italienne de Lisbonne et le developpement de l'économie métropolitaine et coloniale portugaise' and V. Rau, 'A Family of Italian Merchants in Portugal in the 15th Century: The Lomellini', in *Studi in onore di A. Sapori* (Milan, 1957), I, 615–28, 717–26; Scammell, *World Encompassed*, p. 181.

18 Wallerstein, *Modern World-System*, I, 43 n. 96; Heers, *Gênes*, pp. 321–37, p. 329.

19 Wallerstein, *Modern World-System*, I, 48–52; Braudel, *Civilization and Capitalism*, III, 138–43.

20 Boyajian, *Portuguese Trade*, pp. 31, 81–2; J. Israel, *European Jewry in the Age of Mercantilism* (Oxford, 1985), pp. 7, 24–5, 58–9.

21 Scammell, *World Encompassed*, pp. 246–8; Miskimin *Later Renaissance*, pp. 134–5; Boxer, *Seaborne Empire*, pp. 85–107; Wilson and Parker, *Sources of Economic History*, p. 70; C. A. Hanson, *Economy and Society in Baroque Portugal, 1688–1703* (Minneapolis, 1981), p. 216; F. Mauro, *Le Portugal et l'Atlantique, 1570–1670* (Paris, 1960), p. 510.

22 Boxer, *Seaborne Empire*, pp. 108–29; Israel, *Dutch Primacy in World Trade, 1585–1740* (Oxford, 1989), pp. 156–70, and *European Jewry*, p. 106.

23 Israel, *Dutch Primacy*, pp. 236–44.

24 Quoted in R. Davis, 'English Foreign Trade, 1660–1700' in W. E. Minchinton (ed.), *The Growth of English Overseas Trade in the 17th and 18th Centuries* (London, 1969), p. 81.

25 Mauro, *Le Portugal*, pp. 108, 510, 512–13.

26 J. de Vries, *European Urbanization 1500–1800* (London, 1984), p. 278.

27 Israel, *European Jewry*.

28 Wallerstein, *Modern World-System*, II, 185–7.

29 V. M. Godinho, 'Portugal and her Empire, 1680–1720', in J. S. Bromley (ed.), *The New Cambridge Modern History* (Cambridge, 1970), VI, 520–4.

30 Boxer, *Seaborne Empire*, pp. 152–79; Wallerstein, *Modern World-System*, III, 215.

31 H. E. S. Fisher, 'Anglo-Portuguese Trade, 1700–1774' in W. E. Minchinton (ed.), *The Growth of English Overseas Trade*, pp. 99–120; 'Lisbon, its English Merchant Community and the Mediterranean in the Eighteenth Century', in P. L. Cottrell and D. H. Aldcroft (eds), *Shipping, Trade and Commerce* (Leicester, 1981), pp. 23–44; 'Lisbon as a Port Town in the Eighteenth Century', in his edited *The British Seaman and Other Maritime Themes* (Exeter Maritime Studies, 1988), pp. 25–9; *The Portugal Trade: A Study of Anglo-Portuguese Commerce, 1700–1770* (London, 1971).

32 Wallerstein, *Modern World-System*, III, 214–15, 238–9, 249–50; J. Jobson de Andrade Arruda, 'Colonies as Mercantile Investments: The Luso-Brazilian Empire, 1500–1808', in J. D. Tracy (ed.), *The Political Economy of Merchant Empires: Sea Power and World Trade, 1350–1750* (Cambridge, 1992), p. 410.

33 D. Birmingham, *A Concise History of Portugal* (Cambridge, 1993), chs 4–6.

34 Godinho, 'Portugal and her Empire', pp. 536–40.

35 Boxer, *Seaborne Empire*, chs 2, 3, 5, 7; G. B. Souza, *The Survival of Empire: Portuguese Trade and Society in China and the South China Seas, 1630–1754* (Cambridge, 1986).

36 Mauro, *Le Portugal*, p. 512.

37 Boxer, *Seaborne Empire*, pp. 52, 56, 213–18.

38 Scammell, *World Encompassed*, pp. 292–4.

39 Israel, *Dutch Primacy*, pp. 60–73; Scammell, *World Encompassed*, pp. 297–8; Miskimin, *Later Renaissance*, p. 131; Boxer, *Seaborne Empire*, ch. 5.

40 Boxer, *Seaborne Empire*, pp. 116–21.

41 Israel, *Dutch Primacy*, pp. 24, 71; J. de Vries, *The Economy of Europe in an Age of Crisis* (Cambridge, 1976), p. 134.

42 Scammell, *World Encompassed*, pp. 247–8; Boxer, *Seaborne Empire*, pp. 87–95, 114–26.

43 N. Steensgard, 'The Growth and Composition of the Long-Distance Trade of England and the Dutch Republic before 1750', in J. D. Tracy (ed.), *The Rise of Merchant Empires: Long Distance Trade in the Early Modern World* (Cambridge, 1990), p. 152: 'The Portuguese bilateral trade with Asia was taken over by the more sophisticated organization of the companies. The Brazil sugar planters were beaten by the West Indians when the slave plantation was perfected as an economic machine.'

44 Godinho, 'Portugal and her Empire', pp. 537–40.

45 Israel, *European Jewry*, pp. 58–60.

46 Boyajian, *Portuguese Trade*, p. 243; L. M. E. Shaw, 'The Inquisition and the Portuguese Economy', *Journal of European Economic History* 18 (1989), 415–31.
47 Israel, *Dutch Primacy*, pp. 164–70, 236–40, *European Jewry*, pp. 106–13, 256–8.
48 Godinho, 'Portugal and her Empire', p. 539.
49 Vilar, *Histoire de l'Espagne* (14th edn, Paris, 1988), p. 24.
50 MacKay, *From Frontier to Empire,* p. xiv; Vicens Vives, *Historia Económica,* pp. 143–53.
51 Mackay, *From Frontier to Empire,* pp. 38, 70–8.
52 Vicens Vives, *Historia Económica,* pp. 230–6.
53 Mackay, *From Frontier to Empire,* pp. 58–70.
54 Ibid., p. 49.
55 Ibid., pp. 95–6.
56 Ibid., pp. 127–8; Vicens Vives, *Historia Económica,* pp. 251–2, 300–2; P. Vilar, *La Catalogne dans l'Espagne moderne: recherches sur les fondements économiques des structures nationales* (3 vols, Paris, 1962), I, 461–521.
57 See above, p. 9.
58 Vicens Vives, *Historia Económica,* pp. 241–6; MacKay, *From Frontier to Empire*, pp. 121–7.
59 Mackay, *From Frontier to Empire*, pp. 130–1.
60 Vicens Vives, *Historia Económica,* pp. 252–4.
61 Ibid., p. 252; MacKay, *From Frontier to Empire*, pp. 171–3.
62 Vicens Vives, *Historia Económica,* p. 277.
63 Ibid., pp. 228–30; MacKay, *From Frontier to Empire*, pp. 184–6.
64 Vicens Vives, *Historia Económica,* pp. 250–1.
65 MacKay, *From Frontier to Empire,* p. 1.
66 In the introduction to I. A. A. Thompson and B. Yun Casalilla's *The Castilian Crisis of the Seventeenth Century: New Perspectives on the Economic and Social History of Seventeenth-Century Spain* (Cambridge, 1994), p. 2.
67 Vicens Vives, *Historia Económica,* pp. 301–3.
68 A. Castillo, 'Population et richesse en Castille durant la seconde moitié du XVIe siècle', *Annales: Économies, Sociétés, Civilisations* 20 (1965), pp. 719–33; J. E. Gelabert, 'Urbanisation and deurbanisation in Castile, 1500–1800', in Thompson and Yun Casalilla, *The Castilian Crisis,* pp. 184–5; D. Ringrose, 'The Impact of a New Capital City: Madrid, Toledo and New Castile', *Journal of Economic History* (1973), 765; J. Nadal, *La población española (siglos XVI a XX)* (3rd edn, Barcelona, 1975), pp. 34–5; B. Bennassar, *Valladolid au siècle d'or* (Paris, 1967), pp. 161–208.
69 P. Vilar, 'The Age of Don Quixote', in P. Earle (ed.), *Essays in European Economic History* (Oxford, 1974), p. 101. The second epigraph to ch. 6 is quoted from this volume.
70 V. Pérez Moreda, 'The Plague in Castile at the End of the Sixteenth Century and its Consequences', in Thompson and Yun Casalilla, *The*

*Castilian Crisis*, pp. 32–59; Nadal, *Población española*, pp. 39–41; Bennassar, *Valladolid*.

71 Vicens Vives, *Historia Económica*, pp. 265–7, 303–5, 384–5; Nadal, *Población española*, pp. 48–59.

72 Vicens Vives, *Historia Económica*, pp. 305–7, 383–5; Nadal, *Población española*, pp. 60–80; J. H. Parry, *The Spanish Seaborne Empire* (Pelican edn, London, 1973), pp. 231–3; Vilar, *La Catalogne*, I, 619–20.

73 J. Casey, 'Spain: A Failed Transition', in P. Clark (ed.), *The European Crisis of the 1590s: Essays in Comparative History* (London, 1985), pp. 209–11.

74 Gelabert, 'Urbanisation and deurbanisation', p. 182; de Vries, *European Urbanization*, pp. 330–1.

75 Tables drawn from de Vries, *European Urbanization*, pp. 277–8. J. H. Elliott emphasizes that the demographic crisis is above all Castilian in his 'The Decline of Spain', *Past and Present* 20 (1961), reprinted in C. Cipolla (ed.), *Economic Decline of Empires*, London, 1970), pp. 196–214.

76 G. Anes, 'The agrarian "depression" in Castile in the seventeenth century', in Thompson and Yun Casalilla, *The Castilian Crisis*, pp. 60–71; B. Bennassar, 'Consommation, investissements, mouvements de capitaux en Castille aux XVIe et XVIIe siècles', in *Conjoncture économique, structures sociales: hommage à Ernest Labrousse* (Paris, 1974), pp. 142–4; J. Casey, 'Spain: A Failed Transition', pp. 211–16.

77 Vicens Vives, *Historia Económica*, pp. 313–16; Bennassar, 'Consommation, investissements', pp. 147–8: 'even better-off peasants fill their houses with expensive furniture, fine linen and tapestries.'

78 J. Torras, 'L'economia castellana al segle XVI. Un esquema', *Recerques* 16 (1985), 159–69.

79 E. Llopis Agelan, 'Castilian Agriculture in the Seventeenth Century: Depression, or "Readjustment and Adaptation"?' in Thompson and Casalilla, *The Castilian Crisis*, pp. 87–94; Vilar, 'Age of Don Quixote', p. 106; Torras, 'L'economia castellana', p. 169.

80 Llopis Agelan, 'Castilian Agriculture in the Seventeenth Century', pp. 77–87, 94–5.

81 L. M. Bilbao and E. Fernández de Pinedo, 'Wool Exports, Transhumance and Land Use in Castile in the Sixteenth, Seventeenth and Eighteenth Centuries', ibid., pp. 102–3, 107.

82 A. García-Baquero González, 'Andalusia and the Crisis of the Indies Trade, 1610–1720', in Thompson and Casalilla, *The Castilian Crisis*, pp. 124–35.

83 Vilar, *La Catalogne*, I, 599–602.

84 Cited by Elliott, 'Decline of Spain', p. 186.

85 J. K. J. Thomson, 'Proto-industrialization in Spain', in S. C. Ogilvie and M. Cerman (eds), *European Proto-industrialization* (Cambridge, 1996), pp. 85–101; Casey, 'Spain: A Failed Transition', pp. 216–18.

86 Braudel, *Civilization and Capitalism*, III, 143–51.

87 Vilar, *La Catalogne*, I, 543–4, 549 (for quotation), 563–5, 588–92.

88 A. Calabria, *The Cost of Empire: The Finances of the Kingdom of Naples in the Time of Spanish Rule* (Cambridge, 1991), pp. 1–6.

89 Vicens Vives, *Historia económica*, pp. 295–6, 419; P. and H. Chaunu, 'The Atlantic Economy and the World Economy', in Earle (ed.), *Essays in European Economic History*, pp. 119–20.

90 J. Israel, 'Spanish Wool Exports and the European Economy, 1610–1640', *Economic History Review* 33 (1980), pp. 193–211.

91 M.-T. Pérez Picazo and G. Lemeunier, 'La sericultura murciana. Producción, difusión y coyuntura, siglos XVI–XX', *Revista de Historia Económica* 5 (1987), 553–78.

92 J. I. Fortea-Pérez, *Córdoba en el siglo XVII: las bases demográficas y económicas de una expansión urbana* (Salamanca, 1979: résumé of thesis), pp. 48–9 and 'The Textile Industry in the Economy of Cordoba at the End of the Seventeenth and the Start of the Eighteenth Centuries: A Frustrated Recovery', in Thompson and Yun Casalilla, *The Castilian Crisis*, p. 139; García-Baquero, 'Andalusia and the Crisis of the Indies Trade', p. 129.

93 Vilar, *La Catalogne*, I, 544–52; J. K. J. Thomson, *A Distinctive Industrialization: Cotton in Barelona, 1728–1832* (Cambridge, 1992), pp. 34–6.

94 Scammell, *World Encompassed*, pp. 177–83; Vilar, *La Catalogne*, I, 550–2; J. Edwards, ' "Development" and "Underdevelopment" in the Western Mediterranean: The Case of Cordoba and its Region in the Late Fifteenth and Early Sixteenth Centuries', *Mediterranean Historical Review* 2 (1987), 3–45.

95 García-Baquero, 'Andalusia', pp. 116–18.

96 Bilbao and Fernández de Pinedo, 'Wool Exports', p. 106.

97 Calabria, *Cost of Empire*, pp. 22–3.

98 Fortea-Pérez, 'The Cordoban Textile Industry', p. 139.

99 García-Baquero, 'Andalusia and the Indies Trade', pp. 130–5.

100 R. Davis, *The Rise of the Atlantic Economies* (London, 1973), pp. 52–5, 157–60; Vicens Vives, *Historia Económica*, pp. 352–74, 395.

101 J. Casey, *The Kingdom of Valencia in the Seventeenth Century* (Cambridge, 1979), pp. 80–2.

102 D. O. Flynn, 'Fiscal Crisis and the Decline of Spain (Castile)', *Journal of Economic History* 42 (1982), 132–3; Braudel, *Mediterranean*, I, 532–4.

103 P. Vilar, *Or et monnaie dans l'histoire* (Paris, 1974), pp. 177–206.

104 Casey, 'Spain: A Failed Transition', pp. 219–20; Flynn, 'Fiscal crisis', pp. 145–6; Braudel, *Mediterranean*, I, 533–5; Elliott, 'Decline of Spain', pp. 192–5.

105 Casey, 'Spain', p. 220.

106 Elliott, 'Decline of Spain', p. 187.

107 Braudel, *Civilization and Capitalism*, III, 164–9.

108 Bennassar, 'Consommation, investissement', p. 146; Wallerstein, *World-System*, I, 30.

109 A. Marcos Martín, 'Medina del Campo: An Historical Account of its Decline', in Thompson and Yun Casalilla, *The Castilian Crisis*, p. 229.

110 C. R. Phillips, 'Time and Duration: A Model for the Economy of Early Modern Spain', *American Historical Review* (1987), 531–62.

111 Casey, 'Spain', p. 224.

112 G. Parker, 'David or Goliath? Philip II and his World in the 1580's'; in R. L. Kagan and G. Parker (eds), *Spain, Europe and the Atlantic World: Essays in Honour of John H. Elliott* (Cambridge, 1995), pp. 245–66.
113 Wallerstein, *Modern World-System*, I, 191; II, 158.
114 Kamen, 'Decline of Spain', pp. 43–4.

## Chapter 7  Decline in European History

1 Cited by S. Vryonis, *The Decline of Mediaeval Hellenism in Asia Miner* (Berkeley and Los Angeles, 1971), p. 410.
2 See entry 'Empires' in *The International Encyclopedia of the Social Sciences*, (New York, 1968), V, 41–9 and his 'The Causes of Disintegration and Fall of Empires: Sociological and Historical Analyses', *Diogenes* 34 (1961), 82–107; Paul Kennedy, *The Rise and Fall of the Great Powers: Economic Change and Military Conflict from 1500 to 2000* (London, 1989).
3 See the emphasis placed on this characteristic of European history by E. L. Jones, *The European Miracle*, (Cambridge, 1981), chs 3–7, P. Anderson, *Passages from Antiquity* (London, 1974) parts II and III, and M. Mann, *Sources of Social Power* (Cambridge, 1986), I, ch. 12.
4 F. Braudel, *Civilization and Capitalism*, III, 128, 132.
5 See above pp. 13–14, 33–4.
6 F. Braudel, *The Mediterranean* (London 1972), II, part 2, section IV, i.
7 W. H. McNeill, *Venice: The Hinge of Europe* (Chicago, 1974), ch. 5; H. Van der Wee, 'Structural Changes and Specialization in the Industry of the Southern Netherlands, 1100–1500', *Economic History Review* 28 (1975), 203–21; Braudel, *Civilization and Capitalism*, III, 153; D. Ormrod, 'English Re-exports and the Dutch Staple Market in the 18th Century' in D. C. Coleman and P. Mathias (eds), *Enterprise and History: Essays in Honour of Charles Wilson* (Cambridge, 1984), pp. 89–115.
8 Anderson, *Passages*, p. 167.

# Index